Inside: Rethinking Scotland's Prisons examines the foundations of Scotland's troubled prison system, with a significance for prisons everywhere. Some 'first principles' questions are asked.

What is the prison system's historical context? What is the organisational perspective of the system? And on what philosophical understanding of punishment is it based?

When so much public money and a vast administrative bureaucracy services the prison system, why isn't it working?

Writing with the first-hand insights of a working governor who has extensive practical experience, Andrew Coyle argues that the root of our prisons' instability should be traced not to the prisoners – but to the system in which they are held.

Society's habit of sending those who break its laws into exile behind high prison walls has led those who work within these walls to feel that there are no other organisations quite like prisons. Sentencers, professionals, commentators and the public should learn what prisoners and prison staff already know – that prison is primarily a punishment, and is inherently negative.

But this is not a pessimistic picture. Clarity of purpose can often open up possibilities and opportunities for change.

History, philosophy, politics, and organisational behaviour – an extensive agenda. This timely and important book is essential reading for all who have an interest in the future of imprisonment in Scotland and beyond.

Andrew Coyle has worked in the Scottish Prison Service since he joined as an assistant governor in 1973. He has served in Edinburgh Prison, Polmont Borstal and in Prison Service Headquarters. His first governor's post was at Greenock Prison. He was governor of Peterhead Prison from 1988 to 1990, and is now governor of central Scotland's custom-built, long-term prison at Shotts.

In 1984 he was awarded a Winston Churchill Fellowship which he used to travel through North America studying its various prison systems. In 1986 he gained a doctorate from the University of Edinburgh for his thesis on the organisation of the Scottish Prison Service.

He regularly writes articles and papers, and between 1986 and 1989 he was chairman of the Prison Governor's Committee and made numerous public appearances to speak on behalf of his colleagues.

Scottish Child is an independent, co-operatively run organisation which aims to increase awareness of the importance of children and childhood in society. It is involved in publishing, event organisation and other activities, working with a wide range of groups and individuals to encourage discussion of, and action on, social, cultural and political issues. It publishes the bi-monthly magazine *Scottish Child*.

INSIDE

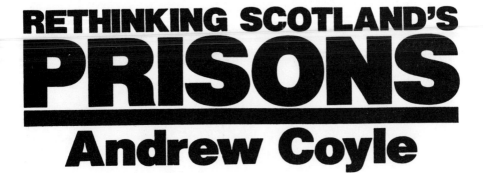

RETHINKING SCOTLAND'S PRISONS

Andrew Coyle

© Andrew Coyle and Scottish Child 1991
All rights reserved

First published in 1991 by
Scottish Child
40 Shandwick Place
Edinburgh EH2 4RT

British Library Cataloguing in Publication Data
Coyle, Andrew
  Inside: Rethinking Scotland's Prisons
  1. Scotland. Prisons
  1. Title
  365.9411
  ISBN 1 873392 01 X

Typeset by Outline, Torphichen Street, Edinburgh
Printed and bound in Great Britain by
Billing & Sons, Worcester

To my father,
whom I love and respect

Contents

Preface

It takes a particular sort of person to earn his livelihood by locking up fellow human beings. Working in the prison system for many years undoubtedly leaves its mark on a person. One survives by recognising the abnormality of what one does, by being a bit uncomfortable about it, by questioning the justification for imprisonment, by seeking to understand why such a system has to exist.

I share the sentiments of a famous former prisoner, Vaclav Havel, in one of his 'Letters to Olga':

> It's interesting, though, that I never feel sorry for myself, as one might expect, but only for the other prisoners and altogether, for the fact that prisons must exist and that they are as they are, and that mankind has not so far invented a better way of coming to terms with certain things.

In our society, when someone admits to having been 'Inside' everyone understands what is meant. That is my starting point.

This book attempts to take imprisonment back to its beginnings, to strip it to its most essential features. It recognises that there can be nothing positive about the act of locking someone up. However, any gathering of human beings, even when they are keeper and kept, must have a soul of some form or other. The negative act of imprisonment can have positive consequences and this book tries to suggest how the positive may be uncovered.

I have always had one foot in the camp of the academics and the other in that of the practitioners. Many friends and colleagues from both worlds have helped mature my thinking; from the University of Edinburgh, such as Derick McClintock, Peter Young, David Garland and Jackie Tombs; from the world of the prison service, such as Roger Houchin, Allan Webster, John Irvine and Peter McKinlay. To them, and to many others, I owe grateful thanks.

The final format of this book has been greatly improved by the consistent support and advice of my editors at Scottish Child: Rosemary Milne, Colin Chalmers and, most of all, Derek Rodger.

My last word of thanks is the most important: to Joyce, Paula, Mairi, Alan and Gemma, who have encouraged me for so many years.

Andrew Coyle
January 1991

Author's Note: Prisoners and prison staff are referred to throughout this book as 'he'. This reflects the reality that some 97% of prisoners, and a similar proportion of staff in Scottish prisons, are male.

Introduction

> I suspect that one of the reasons why the problems of the
> prisons, for example, continue undiminished in spite of the
> awesome number of written words expended on them is that very
> few people write from first-hand experience, apart from
> occasional forays into the institutions in search of data of a
> particular kind. (Brody, 1983)

The prison is an emotive institution and writing about the organisation of a prison system from first-hand experience does present certain difficulties. Those who live or work within this system are not necessarily any more free from prejudice of one form or another than are those who have no first-hand knowledge of its organisation.

The basis of imprisonment is that one group of human beings deprives another group of human beings of liberty. The preconceptions which many of us have about prison and imprisonment go in some respects to the root of relationships among members of society and many of the assumptions or beliefs held about penal systems cannot easily be supported by hard data or evidence.

The practitioner who strays into the world of the academic is likely very quickly to have to attempt to balance on a delicate tightrope. As an academic one may have to accept the strong likelihood that one's findings will be unacceptable to policy makers as a basis for action. As a practitioner one is a participant in the bureaucratic power structure and may have to abdicate the privilege of a distanced exploration of policy possibilities.

> He who innovates is not heard; he who is heard does not
> innovate. (Merton, 1957)

Administrators in any large organisation are quite likely to be suspicious of research, if for no other reason than that it may well challenge, or at least question, the status quo. This is particularly the case in the closed world of prison administration where there may be fear of embarrassment at a possible disclosure of administrative deficiency. In the course of his research at Bristol Prison, Emery (1970) makes reference to the initial difficulty which he faced:

> Cooperation between social scientists and prison officials is plagued from the beginning by the common assumption that the former are, as a profession, antagonistic to prison officials and what they stand for.

This was not a problem which I faced, having already established my credentials in the prison world. The difficulty of which I had to be aware was that of separating the practical assumptions on which so much of my daily work as a prison official was based from the need to maintain an intellectual rigour in my research.

The development of the prison systems in the United Kingdom has often been portrayed as an evolutionary process; a logical development which began with the introduction in the nineteenth century of the physical separation of prisoners and the use which was made of that separation; which then proceeded through the reformative impetus, first with younger prisoners and later with adults, which spanned the first half of the twentieth century. The more recent history has covered the period of retrenchment which succeeded the *Report of the Inquiry into Prison Escapes and Security* (Mountbatten Report, 1966).

The developmental school of thought, popular among practitioners, views the present period of follow-up to the recommendations made by the Committee of Inquiry into the United Kingdom Prison Services (May Report, 1979) as the opportunity for another step forward, possibly towards the establishment of stronger links between the prison and the community at large. However, this evolutionary perspective, which assumes a rational and continuously developing philosophical foundation for the way in which imprisonment is used in our society, is not borne out by a study of the last 150 years of penal history.

Instead, depending on the degree of one's optimism, this development can be described at its most fundamental level as consisting of a series of unrelated changes which have been brought about principally as a result of external pressures; or at its highest level it can be seen as a cyclical movement which gives the appearance of continuous development but which in reality involves a regular regurgitation of broadly similar principles.

Two sets of actors have been ever present in the penal system: prisoners and staff. Prisoners have been little changed by their experiences over the last 150 years. They have always been well aware that they have been sent to prison as punishment; that the experience to which they have been subjected has been essentially a negative one and that their best hope has been to minimise its harmful effects. The phrase 'serving time' underlines the reality that the main objective of the prisoner is to complete his sentence.

One might argue that prison staff have been hardly affected by the passage of time either. Generally speaking little attention has been paid to the position of staff as an integral part of each successive change in the system. In return, staff have been equally dismissive of the system. Historically, the stance held by staff has been both realistic and consistent. Officers have seen their duty as being to carry out the legal requirement to deprive prisoners of their liberty, and have considered everything else as additional. As a result they have been regarded as reactionary, not least by their own management, as the latter gained in influence. Since the pivotal role of the prison officer tended to be ignored both by his employer and by other interested agencies, the support of his peers became increasingly significant. This led to the growth and increased influence of his trade union, the Prison Officers' Association (POA).

Two of the most quoted texts dealing with prisons as systems are Clemmer's *The Prison Community* (1958) and Sykes' *The Society of Captives* (1971). These books have become classics of their kind but it has been pointed out that the most striking feature of both of them is that the prison officer emerges merely as 'a cipher', 'a cog in the disciplinary machine'. This absence of comment on staff is not peculiar to these two authors, rather they are typical of the genre. Despite an increasing amount of research into correctional processes over the last twenty-five years or so, little has been written about the prison officer.

This is an unfortunate gap on two counts. Firstly, no assessment of a prison system can be complete without some account of the role of staff. Secondly, on operational grounds no prison system can hope to develop without the cooperation of the prison officer.

The prison service as presently constituted is an arm of the civil service. As such one of the major functions of management is to interpret the various pressures on behalf of political masters and to respond in an appropriate manner. One of the most enduring and influential pressure groups in prison matters is the POA and as a result it is reasonable to suggest that the policy of prison management is sometimes dictated as a response to staff influence. A recent and important example of management response to this form of staff pressure was the establishment of the May Committee of Inquiry into the United Kingdom Prison Services in 1978. Given this important feature of penal organisational policy one should bear in mind that the POA and its sister association, the Scottish POA, with which I am particularly concerned, are first and foremost trade unions. Their primary and proper objective, like any other trade union, is to pursue the best interests of their members. These may often, but will not always, equate with the best interests of the prison service or of the prisoners.

Prison staff cannot of course be studied in isolation. On the contrary, it is impossible to discuss satisfactorily the recruitment, roles and work of staff without paying due attention to the organisation within which they are employed and without attempting an analysis of more general aspects of penal policy and administration. To concentrate on staff to the exclusion of other features of the system would be to go to the opposite extreme of the pendulum which in the earlier literature concentrated on prisoners. It is necessary rather to examine the prison system as an organisation, containing both captors and captives who interact with each other.

In succeeding chapters I try to go beyond the interaction which takes place in any individual prison to describe that which takes place within the organisation as a whole and to show how the principal actors in this context are not prisoners and staff but prison staff and central administrators. An important outcome of this approach should be the conclusion that the concerns of management and of personnel are complementary rather than contradictory.

This is not to tread an entirely new path. Since the mid 1970s there has been a small but significant number of researchers in this area. Much of the work has been fragmented. It is surprising, for example, how many pieces begin with the assertion that there has been little or no work done previously in this field. It would appear that this is not a new phenomenon in prison research:

One of the main deficiencies of correctional research is that so
many projects are conducted as though no research had been
done before, as though their researcher were ignorant of previous
research. The only contribution of much correctional research,
therefore, is to confirm earlier research findings. (Schnur, 1958)

Having made that point, one is bound to agree with Dobash (1979) that
there is 'an absolute paucity of systematic research' into Scotland's
penal system despite the fact that by nature of its size and organisation
the Scottish prison system lends itself to such investigation.

The absence of precedent presents a problem in the present context
in that prior knowledge on the part of the reader of the historical
development of the Scottish prison system cannot be assumed, nor can
assumptions be made about the level of understanding of the principles
which have led to the extended use of imprisonment as the ultimate
sanction of the criminal court.

In these circumstances it is necessary to outline the historical
context of imprisonment in Scotland. This history is presented with an
emphasis on the organisational perspective which is relevant to the
argument. The comprehensive history of imprisonment in Scotland
remains to be written. The organisational history of the Scottish prison
system provides a basis for understanding how the penal sanction of
imprisonment has been exercised in Scotland. In order to appreciate
this properly one has to be aware of the philosophical basis for
punishment in general and for imprisonment in particular. Once an
acceptable definition of the purpose of imprisonment has been reached
one can proceed to examine the context within which imprisonment
should be imposed in the future and what objectives might be set
for it.

This is an extensive agenda to set for a single volume and could lay
it open to the criticism of attempting to meet the needs of too diverse
a readership. Nevertheless, the various strands are so interwoven that
it is impossible to separate them completely; each has a relationship
with the other.

In general terms the Scottish prison system has evolved along similar
lines to other western prison systems. It has, however, had several
unique features and influences, some of which have not been the
subject of previous research. I argue that there have been three main
phases of development; the first two of which were sequential, the
third less obviously so and more the result of bureaucratic processes.

The first phase covers the years between 1835 and 1877. During this period the prison system in Scotland was taken progressively under central control. Particular attention is paid to the career of William Brebner in Glasgow in the first half of the nineteenth century. Brebner, whose career has hitherto been neglected by penal historians, arguably deserves to be described as the founding father of the Scottish prison system. He established a separate system of confinement in Glasgow several years before the Eastern Penitentiary in Philadelphia was built, placed specific importance on what would be called today the 'through care' of prisoners and developed a programme of training which was used for staff throughout the country.

The second historical phase of development covers the tenure of office of the Prison Commission for Scotland between 1877 and 1929. During this period the traditions of the earlier phase were consolidated and although many processes ran parallel with those introduced in England they were not identical. The Scottish Prison Commissioners retained their close links with other elements in the criminal justice process in Scotland and resisted English attempts to influence, for example, the development of Peterhead Convict Prison.

Another example of the parallel but separate development in Scotland is to be found in the *Report from the Departmental Committee on Scottish Prisons* (1900). This report came five years after the (English) *Report from the Departmental Committee on Prisons* (1895). The latter, known as the Gladstone Report after its chairman, is well known to penal historians, many of whom would describe it as a watershed in penal development. The former report, produced by a committee of inquiry chaired by the Earl of Elgin and Kincardine, was of far greater influence in Scotland but has not previously been the subject of research. The Elgin Report is central to an understanding of Scottish prison administration at the turn of the century in a way that the Gladstone Report is not. The Elgin Committee tackled the main problem facing the Scottish prison system, which was an increasing prisoner population as a result of the high number of convictions for petty offences, most of them related to drunkenness.

The third phase in the development of the Scottish Prison Service, which began in 1929 and continues today, arguably represents a new direction rather than a continuation of the first two phases. For the first time in the history of the Scottish prison system, a considered and successful move was made to transfer the system out of its precise location within the criminal justice process to a location on the periphery of that process firmly within the mainstream of the civil service. The government, and more exactly the administrative civil service, took over direct responsibility for the running of the prison system and in so doing moved it outside the direct boundary of the criminal justice process.

The main justification for this change was a desire by management to ensure that prison staff were seen to be primarily civil servants rather than a 'law and order' occupation. It is symptomatic of the anonymous but far-reaching power wielded by Scottish Office officials without discerning political scrutiny that this alteration could be implemented in Scotland without any significant political or public debate. A similar change in England, delayed by the Second World War, eventually took place in 1963 in the face of powerful opposition both in parliament and the press. This structural change has been responsible for many of the difficulties presently facing the prison service.

The concepts and theories which underlie the arguments presented in this work are contained in chapter seven. By describing the place of the prison system within the sociology of organisations, it is argued that it is legitimate to undertake a comparative study of the prison system as a bureaucratic organisation. The traditional types of bureaucratic organisation are reviewed, paying particular attention to the concepts of authority and control.

By definition, an organisation can have only one primary goal. In the case of the prison system, the objective which the criminal justice process requires of it is that it should contain prisoners in conditions of necessary security, that it should deprive them of their liberty for a set period.

However, one feature of bureaucratic organisations is that those who work within them are unlikely to be satisfied with a single objective. Secondary goals are likely to emerge. This is quite acceptable as long as the secondary goals are not confused with the primary goal. This is particularly important in situations where the former are not obviously compatible with the latter.

In general terms the distinction between primary and secondary goals was recognised in the Scottish prison system until the demise of the Prison Commission for Scotland in 1929. Until that point the prison system had been clearly identified as part of the criminal justice process and the tightly knit Scottish legal profession, which had a close involvement with the prison system, did not allow it to lose sight of the primary purpose, secure custody.

Scotland had a well-developed tradition of expansion of the secondary goals of imprisonment but never at the expense of the primary goal. This distinction was not so well-maintained in England and after 1929 became somewhat blurred in Scotland. The secondary goal which was given greatest prominence was that of rehabilitation.

The increasing emphasis on this element of imprisonment coincided with the introduction to prisons of what can be described as proto-professional staff, most of whom saw their primary goal as rehabilitation of prisoners. This confusion of goals is not peculiar to the prison system. Many organisations find themselves with stated goals which are different from their real goals. One danger of this dichotomy of objectives is that maintenance of the organisation becomes an end in itself.

The confusion of goals is more of a problem for outside observers and for management. Junior staff, in our case prison officers, tend to retain sight of the primary goal; they know full well that their primary responsibility is secure custody. Because of their closed working conditions and traditionally restricted social environment prison staff have a strong identity. This has contributed to the emergence of staff as an organisation within the organisation and one of the main pressure groups within the system. Management, as part of the mainstream civil service, has responded to this pressure in a traditionally bureaucratic manner, occasionally by confrontation but normally by a series of accommodations which have meant that staff have in practice been a major influence on how the prison system has developed.

The conclusion to be drawn from this examination of the prison service as a bureaucratic organisation is that the difficulties which it faces at present are largely structural rather than due to any shortage of resources. It is necessary that the service should regain its proper place within the criminal justice process and should reinstate the penal model of imprisonment. Such a model will be humanitarian for its own sake and not cloaked in any rehabilitative jargon. It will allow staff to play a central role and will turn away from the spectre of executive justice which has always hung over the rehabilitative model of imprisonment.

In chapter nine the focus is further sharpened to concentrate on the place of the prison officer in the Scottish Prison Service. Staff influence in the Scottish Prison Service has been exercised principally through the vehicle of trade union activity in the Scottish Prison Officers' Association. This began in an attempt at combined union activity between police and prison staff. The fact that management was able to disrupt this combination was to prove a significant factor in the demolition of the argument of prison staff for parity of status with the police. The main power in the SPOA, unlike the Prison Officers' Association in England and Wales, has remained at the national rather than the local level and this has enabled the union to push for a more participative form of management.

The prisoner and the prison officer have always recognised that prison is essentially a negative experience, but that recognition is only a beginning. To say that rehabilitation, understood as change imposed on an individual from external sources, is wrong in principle and in practice is only to clear the decks for a more positive statement. Progress from the rehabilitative ideal to the justice model of imprisonment was merely an honest admission that criteria of justice are as relevant for those who operate the prison system as for those who are detained within it. Chapter nine sets out a positive agenda for our prison system in which one can integrate the need for secure custody and good order with a recognition that the prisoner retains certain rights and that if he is treated in a responsible manner he in turn is more likely to act responsibly, both during his time in prison and after release.

One last point of clarification is required concerning the scope of the arguments presented. They are not concerned at the local level with the prison as an institution, nor with prisoners within a prison, nor even with staff within a prison. They concentrate instead on the prison system as an example of one among several large bureaucratic organisations. In common with many other organisations the prison system has several unique features, not least of which is the particular role which has been played by staff in its development. At the same time it has to be recognised that the prison system has several fundamental features which are similar to those in other large bureaucracies. Some at least of the weaknesses of the prison system are consequences of failings in its organisational structure.

In presenting these arguments only passing reference is made to the discussion which is taking place in many quarters today as to the role of punishment as a tool of social control or an expression of power within society. This discussion frequently focuses on the use of imprisonment in particular. It has been described by David Garland (1982) as the 'development from penology to the social analysis of penality'. This discussion addresses issues of considerable importance which are much wider than the line of argument pursued in the present volume. They have been presented comprehensively elsewhere (Foucault, 1977; Scull, 1977; Ignatieff, 1978; Cohen, 1983 and 1985) and are not directly related to the present argument.

This is not to say that there are no points of contact. It is not sufficient to concentrate on technique and administration. Political and other external influences are highly relevant to a proper understanding of how the prison system has developed. Furthermore, prison history has not been a matter of continuing development and evolution with each successive phase being an improvement on the previous. There can be little argument with Michel Foucault's proposition that the justification of the right to punish has shifted from the vengeance of the sovereign to the defence of society and that the key elements in this change have been a shift from punishment of the body to that of the mind, the development of a state apparatus of punishment, the classification of 'delinquents' by an increasing body of professionals and their segregation in special institutions, the most dominant expression of which is the prison.

Stanley Cohen (1983) has suggested that there are three principal models of change in the prison system, each based on a particular ideological position. The first presents a conventional picture of all change as a record of progress and sees the main obstacle to advancement being lack of proper resources; what is needed is 'more of the same'.

He describes the second model as the 'we blew it' version. This regards the earlier reformative thrust as a disastrous failure and considers that rather than attempt to improve prisoners the system should aim to limit damage.

The third model, the 'it's all a con' perspective, has three further sub-divisions. The first of these in fact sees the prison system as a success. Its hidden but real agenda has been the domination of class interests for the sake of a capitalist economy and in this respect the aim of the prison system has been achieved (Ignatieff, 1978). The second sub-division is a starker presentation of the same argument: the prison system is a control mechanism which is used to ensure the survival of the capitalist ruling classes and its use as directly linked to a specific mode of production (Rusche and Kirchheimer, 1939). The final version refers to the complex relationship between power and knowledge. The offender becomes the 'delinquent'; he is separated from the rest of his class and is encouraged to be docile through a system of 'dressage' (Foucault, 1975).

The prison system is not capable of simple analysis. Cohen makes a powerful point when he argues the need for a 'looser' model of correctional change, not based on any one ideology, for each of them contains an element of truth but none has the prerogative. The approach to analysis of the prison system adopted in the following pages allows for such a model and is a conscious attempt to produce a synthesis of the theoretical and the practical. That such a synthesis is needed cannot be denied. The issues require to be addressed at a theoretical level but they do not remain there. Any lingering doubt about this was dispelled with the television pictures which flashed around the world from Strangeways Prison in early 1990, just as they had done from Peterhead Prison in autumn 1987. The words which Winston Churchill addressed to parliament when he was Home Secretary ring just as true today as they did in 1910:

> The mood and temper of the public with regard to the treatment
> of criminals is one of the most unfailing tests of the civilisation
> of any country.

1 'The Thieves' Hole'
Local Prisons before 1835

In his commentary on *The Social Life in Scotland in the Eighteenth Century* (1899) Henry Graham paints a desolate picture of conditions in Scottish prisons.

> The receptacle for prisoners in a village was a 'thieves' hole', a little hut with damp earthen floor, with hardly a glimmer of light from the tiny opening, through which the snow drifted and the wind swirled in mad career through the room, and out again, under and above the ill-fitting doors - through a hole in which the wife of the constable, intent on other avocations, thrust the food for the inmates. A small country town had for its residence for prisoners a vile thatched room, perhaps fourteen feet long, dark, filthy, and fireless, and in winter perishingly cold, where for months untried prisoners waited till the circuit court opened to hear their case; while for security they were sometimes loaded with chains and fastened to an iron bar or bedstead. In county towns, however, the tedium of long waiting and long seclusion was relieved by rough revelry. In places like Stirling and Perth convicts indulged in olden times in their rude carouses, the money allotted for the food of criminals and debtors being often applied to buy drink; and felons with sympathetic friends got from the jailers, at thrice their normal price, refreshments of ale and whisky, and had merry meetings in which their warders joined heartily at the prisoners' cost.

In fairness, Graham does point out that 'prisoners were few, the terms of imprisonment were short, and if the gaols were miserable hovels they were never crowded'.

In fact, using severity of sentence passed by the courts rather than

the state of prisons as a yardstick, Scotland had at that time a comparatively liberal penal tradition on three main counts: levels of capital
punishment, of transportation and of imprisonment. In respect of each
of these A.G. Shaw (1966) has noted:

> The only bright spot in Great Britain seems to have been
> Scotland.

An examination of records for the last thirty years of the eighteenth
century shows that between 1773 and 1793 the average number of
executions for the whole of Scotland in any one year was six. In
Edinburgh the average was three every two years and indeed between
1773 and 1776 there were no executions in the capital city. Over a
twenty year period at the end of the eighteenth century 134 Scots were
sentenced to death and only 97 of these were actually executed. This
was in stark contrast to the situation in England. During the same
period in London and the County of Middlesex, which together had a
population about half the size of that in Scotland, 1,910 criminals were
sentenced to death and 890 were executed. The pattern continued into
the nineteenth century. In 1832, records show that only six criminals
were sentenced to death in Scottish courts.

Transportation was not introduced into the Scottish penal system
until 1776. During the following ninety years the Scottish rate of transportation per head of the population was never much more than a
quarter that in England. In both countries the vast majority of those
transported were convicted of theft although those sent from Scotland
tended to be more serious offenders.

While imprisonment was competent as a punishment for most
crimes it was used comparatively rarely. This fact was confirmed by
Advocate Henry Home Drummond in his evidence to the 1826 Select
Committee of the House of Commons on Scottish Prisons:

> The instances of imprisonment as a punishment for other
> offences than theft and assault, are not numerous; and the long
> periods of imprisonment that take place in England are unknown
> in Scotland, where the period very rarely exceeds a year.

There were several reasons for this pattern of punishment. In the first
place it does appear that there was comparatively little serious crime
in Scotland throughout the eighteenth and early part of the nineteenth
centuries. Henry Graham reports that house-breaking and robbery

were extremely rare, although immorality was rife, 'especially among the peasantry'. Most crime came about as a result of frequent drunken brawling. In his annual report for 1837 the newly appointed Inspector of Prisons for Scotland drew attention to this fact.

> On my enquiring of Mr. Henderson, the Procurator Fiscal for Caithness – a county abounding in assaults – on this point, his expressive reply was, 'Sir, I never knew a sober assault.'

The conclusion drawn by the Inspector of Prisons, even after such a short acquaintance with Scotland, was unequivocal.

> Of all the immediate causes of crime and offences in Scotland drunkenness is by far the most potent.

If there was less serious crime, it is also true that sentences handed down by the courts were milder. Even when there was a conviction for a capital crime judges were slow to pass sentence of death. An important feature of the Scottish system was the discretionary power which it conferred on judges to pass alternative or modified sentences according to the age or condition of the criminal or to take account of other mitigating circumstances. This was in stark contrast to the situation in England where most crimes carried statutory punishments, whatever the circumstances in which they had been committed.

A further factor was the continued availability of corporal punishment in one form or another. A common official in most communities was the locksman, so called because he was entitled as part of his wages to a handful or lock of grain from every sack that came to market. As well as being the jailer for petty offenders this individual was responsible for public flogging which was a common punishment for theft. Minor offenders might well find themselves fastened by the neck to the kirk walls by means of iron collars or 'jougs', from which term presumably comes the modern slang 'to be in jug' for imprisonment. Graham graphically describes one of the more immediate forms of punishment:

> Great public satisfaction was felt when a well-known offender sat upon a cuck-stool, with neck and hand in the pillory, having his ears nailed to the same . . . On such occasions the crowd was great and deeply interested.

We might well imagine that it was.

Despite the relatively small number of criminals sentenced to imprisonment in Scotland during the period up to the early part of the nineteenth century, all commentators agree with the conclusion reached by the 1826 Select Committee.

> The result of this inquiry has, in the opinion of your Committee,
> been to show, that with a few exceptions, the state of those
> Prisons is very defective in point of security, accommodation
> and management, while the funds from which such prisons ought
> to be improved are, in most instances, inadequate to that
> purpose.

Examples of the poor state of the prisons abound. This was further reflected in the poor quality of the staff who were placed in charge of these establishments, the majority of them on a part-time basis. At one point it was reported that Linlithgow jail was in the charge of a blind man. The jailer at Alloa combined his duties with that of chimney sweep and, reported the Inspector of Prisons, 'judging from his appearance, I should presume that he carries on an extensive business'. The opinion which the Inspector formed of the staff in most of Scotland's prisons in the 1830s was similar to his description of the officer in charge of Dumbarton prison.

> The keeper is probably a well-meaning man, but he is not at all
> qualified for the government of prisoners.

Management of some of the county prisons was particularly poor. In many of these prisons there was no separation of prisoners. In Perth, for example, local people were affronted by the constant round of idleness and corruption. As late as 1838 the keepers of Stirling prison were discovered bringing 'spirituous liquors' into the prison. In the following year the government Inspector of Prisons found it necessary to draw the result of his inspection of Glasgow Gaol to the attention of the Lord Provost of the city:

> It seems to me to be proved, that garnish is frequently exacted,
> and that prisoners are often ill-treated who refuse to pay it; that
> many prisoners are subjected to various kinds of tyranny on the
> part of their associates, and particularly that prisoners about to
> give King's evidence are ill-treated; that there is much
> quarrelling, fighting, swearing, obscene language, and gambling;

that prisoners often pawn their clothes and steal from one another; that drinking among the prisoners is sometimes carried to intoxication; and that robberies are planned to be executed after liberation; that some of the servants of the gaol have assisted in conveying articles to the pawn shop; that officers generally are very ignorant of the proceedings that are going on; and are not vigilant in the detection and punishment of offences; and lastly, that some of the officers occasionally set a bad example themselves.

Mr. McCall, Governor of the Gaol, did not take this criticism lying down, although his letter of explanation to the city fathers has a plaintive tone to it. He recognised the value of confining prisoners in separate cells and, had he been given the facility to do so, he confidently states 'without any vanity on my part', he would have governed the prison in as positive a manner as any other man. This defence was to be used by many governors over the following 150 years: if only proper and sufficient resources were provided . . . Identified failures were the result not of weak management but of inappropriate funding. Neither did the Town Council take kindly to this new form of interference by central government, responding tartly that,

Under the present governor, the committee are assured the gaol has been better regulated than it was under any of his predecessors.

Which leaves the observer wondering what on earth the prison had been like before.

The first major piece of legislation affecting prisons in Scotland had been passed in 1597. Until that date every barony, lordship and burgh in Scotland had its own prison for committing local offenders. That year saw the introduction of a statute entitled 'Prison Houses suld be bigged within all Burrowes' which placed on burghs sole liability for the construction and maintenance of prisons. This statute further obliged burghs to accept into their prisons all offenders lawfully presented to them by the king's officers, sheriffs, stewards, baillies or whoever. Prisoners were to be maintained at their own expense. At that time burghs enjoyed significant privileges in terms of both land and trade and the burden then imposed on them by the monarchy in respect of prisons was of little inconvenience. At that time too, imprisonment was hardly known in Scotland as a direct punishment for crime.

By the beginning of the eighteenth century burghs had lost much of their wealth. In 1819 a further statute was passed which enabled but did not oblige counties to give aid to burghs to improve, enlarge or build their gaols. Needless to say, there was little enthusiasm on the part of counties to make use of this new power. The result was a large number of small, run-down and badly managed prisons and lock-ups which were used inconsistently and intermittently by the courts.

Before 1835 there is hardly any justification for referring to a *prison system* in Scotland. Almost every prison was run under an independent process financed by the relevant local authority. What is important to recognise in relation to developments which were to come later was that there did exist a clearly understood *system of imprisonment*.

The majority of crimes which were committed related in some way to misuse of alcohol, either in the case of assaults because the perpetrator, the victim or both were drunk at the time, or in the case of thefts because the perpetrator needed the means to purchase alcohol or the victim presented the opportunity for easy pickings while under the influence. The authorities saw little benefit in imprisoning this type of offender at considerable public expense. Punishments were usually much more immediate and often corporal. In the case of more serious offences the prevalence of common law and the consequent absence of statutory punishments allowed the judiciary to exercise a significant degree of discretion in punishing criminals.

Within this social and legal context prisons were by and large places where criminals were to be held while awaiting trial or until such times as an outstanding debt was paid. After trial they were used to hold the prisoner until sentence was carried out, be that execution, transportation or banishment. Rarely were they used as places of punishment in themselves. Since they were primarily transit camps providing a service of simple containment little attention was paid to their management or to a need for the development of any form of prison regime. The majority of these prisons were little more than legalised cells existing to serve the courts.

One of the unforeseen consequences of the establishment of a *prison system* in Scotland after 1835, particularly within a structure which retained the close link between the prison and the criminal justice process, was that the whole context of imprisonment changed. Sentences of direct imprisonment became more common. That in turn led to an acceptance of the need to develop regimes in prisons. In due course it was suggested that these regimes could have a reforming influence on individuals, thus affecting future rates of recidivism. Once this hope was voiced abroad the notion of imprisonment as being something more than punishment became fashionable. The judiciary was convinced by these arguments and rates of direct imprisonment increased.

One of the arguments advanced in this book will be that Scotland has never been completely at ease with the concept of the prison as a total institution capable of imposing rehabilitation on offenders. At best this notion has been modified by a recognition that external factors are at least as important in deciding whether a prisoner is likely to commit further crime. Of greater importance is the fact that Scottish prisons have never broken the umbilical cord which connects them to the criminal justice process which they serve. This link brought prisons into being and without it they would have no justification for continued existence.

It will be shown in later chapters that an internal appreciation of the fundamental importance of the continuing relationship between the prison system and the rest of the criminal justice process, has allowed the Scottish service to develop an alternative philosophy of imprisonment to replace the commonly understood, and now discredited, version of rehabilitation more quickly than has been possible elsewhere.

2 William Brebner
Founding Father of the Scottish Prison System

In any analysis of the Scottish penal system, particularly one which takes account of both the method of treating prisoners and the role of staff, a primary position should be awarded to William Brebner. In an almost single-handed manner Brebner established a system of separation of prisoners in the Glasgow Bridewell, or 'house of correction', several years before a similar system was introduced into the Philadelphia Penitentiary in North America and subsequently achieved prominence in what became known as the 'Philadelphia System' of imprisonment. He extended his influence beyond the prison boundary with the establishment of a House of Refuge for released prisoners and a rudimentary form of after-care. With regard to staff, he addressed himself to rates of pay, hours of attendance and annual leave and also found himself administering in Glasgow Bridewell what was in effect the training school for Scottish prison staff. At one point a few years before his death, Brebner was simultaneously Governor of the two Glasgow prisons and of the General Prison at Perth as well as being Superintendent of the Lanarkshire Prisons.

Brebner's obituary in the *Glasgow Herald* of 10 January 1845 described his achievements as follows:

> Mr. Brebner, as Governor of the Glasgow Bridewell,
> commenced his system of prison discipline and amelioration
> long before there were any Acts of Parliament to encourage and
> help him. For a lengthened period of years, the Bridewell here
> has been regarded as the model prison of the kingdom, and
> scarcely a work of reform has been commenced in any of the
> jails of Scotland in which his advice has not been asked, and

taken, and in Ireland, also, the benefits of his aid have been readily acknowledged. Among the philanthropists of the United States of America his name is as well known as amongst the people in our own city, and it is admitted that, in that country, the system of which he is the originator has been found the most successful in reclaiming the depraved. But more than this, the details of his plans have been requested by the Institute of France and more than once formed the subject of the approving comment and discussion of the members. And all this while, Mr. Brebner, as a private citizen, moved so noiselessly and unobtrusively out and in amongst us, that, but for the recital of his good deeds, which came from others, not himself, we might have been unaware that such a man formed a member of our community.

William Brebner was born in 1783 in Huntly, Aberdeenshire. It is somehow appropriate that such a key figure in penal history should have come from the north-east of Scotland, whence have come so many subsequent members of the Scottish Prison Service. He worked for a short period as a shipping clerk in Aberdeen before securing the post of Clerk and Assistant to George Andrew, first Governor of the Glasgow Bridewell. In 1792 the Bridewell had been established in temporary accommodation in College Street, Glasgow, and in 1798 moved to a permanent site in Duke Street. When Andrew died some ten years after the Bridewell opened in Duke Street, Brebner succeeded him as Governor, a post which he held until his death in 1845.

The original Bridewell in Duke Street contained 115 cells. By this time the notion of imprisonment as a punishment in itself was gaining acceptability. Indeed, it would have been that very concept which had led to the construction of the Bridewell. A further wing containing 150 cells was opened in December 1824. This additional accommodation gave Brebner the opportunity to put into practice his theories concerning the separation of prisoners. A contemporary press cutting described the state of the Bridewell in 1799:

From want of sufficient accommodation to meet the swelling population, it not unfrequently happened that as many as six, eight and ten individuals were chained together in the same cell – eight feet by seven – ill ventilated and horribly arranged. The old and the young were mixed together – the hardened and the most pliable.

In contrast a Select Committee of the House of Commons on Scottish Prisons was able to report that in 1826 in the Glasgow Bridewell:

> The prisoners are kept separate, and at constant work from six o'clock morning till eight at night.

Much has been written about the respective merits of the so-called separate and silent systems of imprisonment which were introduced into prisons in the first half of the nineteenth century. The former was based on the principle of keeping prisoners separate from each other at all times, locating them in separate cells where they were given a fixed amount of work to do each day. In its most extreme forms prisoners who gathered in chapel for religious services were placed in boxes which were enclosed on three sides, opening in such a way that prisoners could see only the chaplain. When at exercise in open yards prisoners were required to wear hoods over their heads so that they could not see their comrades at exercise with them. The silent system in contrast allowed prisoners to gather together daily at work. However, a rule of silence was strictly enforced with severe punishment for those found breaking it.

In the United States of America these different systems of imprisonment were first practised respectively in the Philadelphia Penitentiary in Pennsylvania and in Auburn Jail in New York. In time the two models of imprisonment came to be known internationally as the Philadelphia and the Auburn systems. In 1835 the British government appointed five Inspectors of Prisons. The Inspector for the Home District (of England), William Crawford, was sent to America to learn something of the new American systems. On his return he reported:

> The Eastern Penitentiary is, in fact, with some trifling difference in its arrangements, but a counterpart of the Bridewell at Glasgow, a prison which was in operation five years before the erection of the prison at Philadelphia.

Under the new regime prisoners in the Bridewell began work in their cells at six o'clock in the morning and, with only short breaks, continued at this until eight in the evening, when their hammocks were passed in to them and they were expected to go to sleep. The work provided varied from monotonous oakum picking to sophisticated print cutting, depending both on the capability of the prisoner and the contracts which could be won locally. Prisoners were allotted enough work to keep them occupied for about eleven hours each day, which was comparable with the average then worked by labourers in surrounding factories. This routine continued unfailingly day after day.

There was virtually no contact between prisoners. They were, however, visited at regular intervals by the governor and the chaplain. It was argued that this arrangement ensured that prisoners did not suffer mentally and that their physical health was better in the Bridewell than when they were at large. The industrial production of the prisoners not only paid for their own maintenance in the Bridewell but also covered most of the salaries of the staff 'whose superintendence they have rendered necessary by their own acts'.

Frederic Hill, the newly appointed Inspector of Prisons for Scotland, was well aware that Brebner had developed his particular system of prison discipline in an original manner and not from the experience of others. In his annual report for 1845 he commented:

> Before the establishment in America of those prisons which have attracted so much attention, this unassuming but excellent man, remarkable alike for the clearness of his intellect and his untiring benevolence, had organised and successfully conducted the system of which, in many respects, theirs was but a repetition.

In 1839 a General Board of Directors of Prisons in Scotland was established with the primary responsibility of overseeing the construction of a General Prison in Perth. When considering in their annual report for 1840 what type of regime should be introduced at this new prison they had no hesitation in turning to Brebner's example for inspiration.

> The Bridewell of Glasgow, however, has acquired a reputation, not in Scotland alone, but throughout Europe, for its discipline and management, and the beneficial effects produced in its prisoners. For a course of years, antecedent even to the establishment of the celebrated Eastern Penitentiary of Philadelphia, the name of which has been, by continental writers, conferred on the system, the managers of the Glasgow Bridewell have pursued the course which the later experience of other countries, and the opinions of the highest authorities, as well as the confirmed judgement and experience of its own managers, pronounces to be the best. To us, in particular, this gratifying circumstance affords both authority and encouragement, as it

tends to show that the system that we find more strongly
recommended by reason and authority, and the experience of
other countries, is also to be found well adapted to the
disposition, habits, and circumstances of prisoners in Scotland.

The basic flaw in the separate system, as indeed in the silent system,
as they were both later developed in the United States and in England
was that they presumed the possibility of reformation in the individual
within the vacuum of a total institution. In this fundamental aspect the
system developed by Brebner was distinct from the later separate
system.

He was in no doubt that the process of reformation in any individual
could only be commenced rather than completed within an institution.
It is tempting to suggest that not only was his penal philosophy in
advance of that of the Gladstone Committee of 1895 but that it was also
in advance of the May Committee of 1978. Brebner was in no doubt as
to the primary purpose of the prison system. It was to be the servant of
the court in carrying out the legal decision to deprive a citizen of his
liberty for a fixed period in punishment for a wrong done.

In 1822 it was decided to extend the Bridewell in Glasgow to enable
it to serve the County of Lanark as well as the city so that, according
to the Council Minutes of February 1822, 'More efficient means could
be exercised for the punishment and amelioration of the delinquents'.
Brebner by that date had been Governor of the Bridewell for several
years and would have had some influence in formulating the dual
objectives of 'punishment and amelioration'. Brebner did not view
imprisonment as reformative in itself but he did consider it to be his
duty to use the period of imprisonment as positively as possible within
the circumstances and certainly to ensure that there was no deterioration during the period of imprisonment. He achieved this first by
exercising a basic humanity and kindness towards the prisoners and,
according to contemporary reports, by encouraging his staff to do
likewise. He then employed each prisoner on relatively productive
labour. Finally he introduced a system of basic education by teachers
who were members of staff.

Brebner went further than mere separation of prisoners. He introduced a simple classification by sex and age. The original part of the
Bridewell was allocated to female prisoners (at that time over one in
three prisoners in Scotland were female) and a female staff was
appointed. The first annual report of the Inspector of Prisons for
Scotland noted that 'This is, I believe, the only prison in Scotland

where females are attended exclusively by female officers'. By 1841 when Glasgow Gaol and the Bridewell were united into one prison under Brebner's charge, he included among his female staff three teachers, a porter, six warders and a gate keeper.

Juvenile offenders, as they were then known, who in the mid nineteenth century were sometimes of tender years, were subjected to a different regime by Brebner. He considered that the form of separation which he required of adults was unsuitable for juveniles. Every effort was made to teach the youngsters a trade and 'to train them in tolerably good habits'. In his annual report for 1836 the Inspector noted that Brebner

> says he has no difficulty in securing situations for prisoners on their leaving the Bridewell, provided he can express a favourable opinion of their conduct, and the improvement that has taken place in them; which he is almost always able conscientiously to do, provided the prisoners be tolerably young when they enter, and provided they remain a sufficient length of time in the first instance.

Despite attempting to use custody in this positive manner Brebner had no doubt that, in so far as reformation of the individual was possible, it would be achieved within the wider community rather than in prison. Not long after the extension to the Bridewell was completed Brebner was appealing in the city for a new institution to be constructed so that juveniles could be taken out of the Bridewell completely. Mr Miller, Superintendent of Police in the city, who was later to succeed Brebner as Governor on the latter's death, supported the proposal and a subsequent public appeal raised the sum of £10,000. In February 1838 the Glasgow House of Refuge for Boys opened its doors. In their first annual report the Directors of the new institution made clear their debt:

> Mr. Brebner, Governor of the Glasgow Bridewell (whose name the Directors cannot mention without recording their sense of his ability and benevolence), declared his conviction, founded on experience, that penal confinement for so short a period as that to which young criminals are usually sentenced, however valuable as the commencement of a remedial process, was by itself, as a means of reformation, nearly useless. He had made it known to the public, that the youth upon whom it appeared to have produced the best effects, not only found no opening to earn their bread by honest industry, but were watched on the day of

their liberation by the profligate and the criminal, and drawn
back, alike by the absence of every virtuous, and the presence of
every vicious influence, to the course they had resolved to
abandon.

From its opening the House of Refuge was used by Glasgow magistrates as a form of diversion to avoid sending juveniles to prison.
Within a very short time there were 200 boys in residence and it
became an integral part of the city's provision for young delinquents
to such an extent that in 1841 it was given support from the rates. In
1840 a House of Refuge for females was opened and it too was given
benefit from rate support.

Brebner was not so successful in his efforts to establish a House of
Refuge for liberated adult offenders. At one point he was so concerned
at the lack of provision for poor and destitute in the city that he opened
the door of the prison to voluntary prisoners. In 1839 he had three such
prisoners. Two years later the Inspector of Prisons noted that there
were '40 persons in the prison of Glasgow who had voluntarily
subjected themselves to all the rigours of imprisonment'. Some of
these had been in the prison for over a year, subject to all the
requirements of prison discipline, accommodated in ordinary cells and
working for over ten hours each day. The General Board of Directors
of Prisons could not let this pass. They instructed the County Board of
Lanark to discontinue the practice since . . .

> . . . was liable to serious objection, as tending unduly to affect
> the state of public opinion with respect to imprisonment as a
> punishment, to interfere with the proper disicipline of the Prison,
> and to increase without the authority of the law, the expense of
> its management.

The penal philosophy which Brebner had evolved and had put into
practice with the enthusiastic support of the local managers was
extensively adopted by those who were appointed by central government to introduce consistent standards into Scottish prisons. Almost
every one of the early annual reports of the Inspector of Prisons
contains fulsome praise both of the Glasgow Bridewell and of Brebner,
to such an extent that other governors and keepers must have been
heartily sick of having him held up as an example to them. The first
such report in 1836 set the tone which was to be frequently repeated.

> Of Mr. Brebner's qualifications for the office he holds it is

scarcely necessary for me to speak. The remarks I have already
made show that I think very highly of him, and in expressing
this opinion I am but confirming, as far as in me lies, the
judgement of the public at large, which has rightly assigned to
him much of the merit belonging to the Glasgow Bridewell.

That the Inspector of Prisons felt it appropriate to make such eulogistic
comment on William Brebner and his prison management was doubt-
less a reflection on the state of other prisons in the country and their
poor management. It is also worth noting the extent to which Frederic
Hill, who had been appointed by the government, felt able to make
public criticism both of individual governors and of the County Boards
which were responsible for oversight of local prisons. This was a
feature of annual reporting which disappeared once the prisons were
taken under central control.

In drawing attention to the abominable conditions in other prisons
and the lack of qualifications among staff, Hill frequently recommended that Brebner should be asked to supply one of the officers he
had trained in Glasgow to govern other prisons. Almost all County
Boards responded positively to this recommendation. In 1835 Governors trained by Brebner were appointed in Ayr and Lanark, in 1838 in
Dumfries, in 1839 in Dundee, and in 1840 in Dumbarton, Hamilton,
Cupar, Inverness and Kirkcudbright. In 1841 the Inspector noted:

In procuring good keepers and matrons, Mr. Brebner, the
Governor of the Prison of Glasgow, has again afforded great
assistance, both by giving up well-trained officers of his own and
by training new officers. Mr. Brebner's services indeed have
now been extended, in one way or another, to almost every
County in Scotland.

The high standard of Brebner's staff did not come about by accident.
He was clearly as much interested in the welfare of his officers as in
that of the prisoners. By 1838 he had set up a comfortable room for
staff and engaged a teacher to come in the evenings to teach officers,
who attended on a voluntary basis when their day's work was completed. Although attendance was optional we are told that most staff
attended.

Brebner then turned his attention to the hours which his staff
worked. Although they were not atypical of the period at fourteen or
fifteen hours daily he considered this too heavy a burden to allow them

necessary time to relax. Within a few years he had obtained the approval of the County Board to reduce their hours of attendance to twelve a day spread over six days a week. He also arranged for them to have one week's paid holiday each year.

In 1841 the first Governor of the new General Prison at Perth sought information from governors around the country as to levels of pay. He found that in Glasgow warders were paid 18s. a week. Free accommodation, coals, light and washing were reckoned to be worth another 3s. or 4s. Brebner told his new colleague that he would like to raise the salary of his best officers to 25s. a week. The pay of the Glasgow warders was slightly above average for the country. At that time by comparison policemen in the city were paid between 20s. and 30s. each week. In 1838 Brebner's own salary was £300 per year and by 1843 it had been increased to £525, a substantial sum at the time.

With the move towards the centralisation of the prison systems in Scotland Brebner's knowledge and experience was in great demand. Although Glasgow Town Council had not taken kindly to the criticism of the management of Glasgow Gaol made in 1839 by the Inspector of Prisons, they did ask Brebner to make periodic visits and to advise the governor. In 1840 the two establishments were united as Glasgow Prison under the command of Brebner. The former gaol at Glasgow Green becoming known as the South Prison and the bridewell in Duke Street as the North Prison. In line with the Inspector's recommendation the Prison Board for the County appointed Brebner to be Superintendent of all the Lanarkshire Prisons.

Before the new General Prison opened at Perth in the spring of 1842 the General Board of Directors of Prisons had tried to entice Brebner to accept the post of governor but he had steadfastly refused, being unwilling to leave his life's work in Glasgow. In July of that same year the newly appointed Governor was dismissed because of financial irregularities and Brebner agreed to take on the post on a temporary basis, refusing the renewed entreaties that he should do so in a permanent capacity.

William Brebner remained Governor of the Glasgow Prison until his death on 6 January 1845, which appropriately enough occurred while he was on official business. He had caught a morning train to Edinburgh to attend a meeting of the General Prisons Board. Immediately after entering the offices of the Board he suffered a massive heart attack and died instantly. The man who owed most to Brebner in a professional capacity, Frederic Hill, the first Inspector of Prisons, described the circumstances of Brebner's death in his autobiography (1893).

> My esteemed friend Mr. Brebner, Governor of the Glasgow Bridewell, of whom I have already spoken, may be said to have lost his life in the advocacy of industrial prison work. He overtaxed his strength in preparing his voluminous evidence on this subject for the Prison Board, taking scarcely any rest for some nights previous to their meeting. Just as his evidence was to be given he was stricken with apoplexy, and died in my arms. Mr. Brebner was so highly esteemed that the Town Council of Glasgow voted him a public funeral. He was followed to the grave by crowds of all classes, and the police in attendance recognised many who had formerly been in Mr. Brebner's charge as prisoners.

Notwithstanding the broadly similar penal statutes which apply through the whole of the United Kingdom, the Scottish prison service has over the years retained a distinctive approach in several important matters. William Brebner personified many of these. He came from the north east of the country, which has been a fertile recruiting ground for the service. He had no military background, a feature which distinguished many Scottish penal practitioners from their colleagues south of the border. Most importantly, despite all the effort which he expended on introducing and developing the separate system of imprisonment, he retained a pragmatic understanding of the limited possibility of reform within the prison setting. Courts are concerned with justice; a court sentences an individual to imprisonment as punishment for an offence committed. Once the individual had been admitted to prison Brebner considered that it was his task as governor to ensure that the man or woman, while undergoing the punishment of imprisonment, did not deteriorate physically or mentally and that he was presented with the opportunity of using the period of imprisonment to learn a work skill, to undertake education or to make use of any other resource which was available. Brebner also began the tradition, which has been continued by successive generations of prison governors, of maintaining an interest in his former charges through an involvement in the wider community.

In his report for 1845 the Inspector of Prisons recounted the following anecdote:

The keeper of one of the prisons, who had not been under Mr. Brebner's care, or in any way indebted to him for his appointment, declared to me on one occasion that he never returned home from a visit to the prison of Glasgow without being benefitted by his interview with Mr. Brebner, either, as he said, by learning some new fact which he could apply to the improvement of his own prison, or by being warmed by the conversation of such a man to a more earnest and higher sense of his duties.

Brebner was undoubtedly a product of his own era and, within his context, can take his place among the major Scottish Victorian philanthropists. The eulogies which were accorded him sound exaggerated to our ears but it should be remembered that, as is often the case in Scotland, most of them came after his death. Until the advent of his champion, Frederic Hill, he had ploughed an isolated furrow. There can be little doubt that there was great need in Glasgow in the first half of the nineteenth century for the work which he did. At the time there was no Poor Law provision in Scotland, each parish being responsible for care of its own indigent members. Brebner recognised the need for more comprehensive provision, arguing energetically for what were then known as 'houses of refuge' for juveniles, women and men.

His professional career began in the period when Scottish prisons were entirely under the control of the local authorities and it ended five years into the period when the General Board had taken over direction of all prisons in the country, which were administered directly by County Boards. The members of the General Board and the majority of the County Boards had no experience of prison administration. Neither had Frederic Hill, the first Inspector of Prisons. For practical advice they all turned to Brebner and many of the developments in prisons in the first half of the nineteenth century, some of which lasted for a considerable time, can be traced directly to him. The contribution made by William Brebner to the development of the Scottish prison service has gone largely unrecorded until now. It would scarcely be an exaggeration to describe him as its founding father.

3 The Growth of Central Control
Prison Management between 1835 and 1877

The general state of prisons in Scotland prior to 1835 was no worse than that in England and Wales. Indeed, given the relatively higher rate of imprisonment south of the border, conditions there were often much worse. But varying degrees of concern about this state of affairs had been expressed over a continuous period of fifty years or more by a succession of individuals.

John Howard was in Scotland on three separate occasions between 1779 and 1783 and visited prisons from Jedburgh to Inverness. He found little to praise, describing the prisons as 'dirty and offensive' (Howard, 1784). Nonetheless he did comment favourably on the low level of imprisonment in the country, which he suggested was 'partly owing to the shame and disgrace annexed to imprisonment'.

In 1812 James Neild retraced Howard's path and found the situation little changed (Neild, 1812). A few years later Joseph Gurney and his sister, Elizabeth Fry, toured prisons in Scotland and the north of England (Gurney, 1819). They were particularly critical of the burgh gaols which 'expose those who are confined in them to a very dreadful degree of suffering'. Reference has already been made to the critical findings of the House of Commons Select Committee on Scottish Prisons in 1826.

The Prisons Act, 1835
The first sign of government response to these growing expressions of concern was the Gaol Act of 1823. The most significant piece of legislation, however, was the Prisons Act of 1835. The provisions of

this act involved a recognition that no longer could central government leave the oversight of prisons entirely in the hands of the various local authorities.

The Secretary of State was empowered to appoint up to five individuals to visit and inspect every gaol, bridewell, house of correction, penitentiary, prison or other place of confinement of prisoners in Great Britain and to examine any person holding office in such an establishment, to inspect all books and papers relating thereto and to inquire into all relevant matters. The inspectors were to make separate reports in writing, all of which were to be presented to Parliament.

The first such Inspector to be appointed with responsibility for Scotland was Frederic Hill, brother to Rowland of 'penny black' stamp fame. In his autobiography (1893) Hill was honest enough to admit that he had long cherished a desire to obtain some sort of post in government administration. His opportunity came with the passing of the 1835 Act, and with the support of several 'influential' friends he applied to Lord John Russell, Home Secretary, for one of the newly announced posts. He recounts his response when the news came through:

> I was sitting reading in Matthew's Chambers in Chancery Lane,
> and such was my delight that I skipped about the room for joy,
> and, tradition says, jumped over a chair!

Hill's delight arose from the fact that at last he had obtained a government appointment rather than from any particular desire to work in the field of prison reform, about which he knew nothing before taking up post. However, at the age of thirty-two years he threw himself wholeheartedly into his new work and by November 1835 was in Edinburgh ready to begin his first tour of inspection. The Home Secretary had warned Hill that the Scottish prisons were in a bad state and this assessment was soon confirmed. After his first round of inspections Hill was confident enough to list the major problems:

> The following appear to me to be the principal evils at present
> existing in the Prisons of Scotland:
> 1. Want of the means of Separation of Prisoner from Prisoner,
>   and of the means of preventing Intercourse from without.
> 2. Want of Employment, and of a Provision for instructing
>   the Prisoner in a Trade, or other means of earning an honest
>   Livelihood, on leaving Prison.

3. Want of Mental, Moral and Religious Instruction.
4. Insecurity of the Prisons.
5. Want of Arrangements for securing that the Condition of Prisoners shall in no respect be better than that of honest Labourers.
6. Great Expense of many of the Prisons, especially the smaller ones.
7. Frequent Incompetency of the Keepers of the Prisons, and want of Female Officers.
8. Want of the means of Inspection.
9. Want of Cleanliness and Ventilation.
10. The excessive quantity of Time which the Prisoners pass in bed.
11. Want of an adequate Motive in the separate Burghs and Counties for taking the effectual Measures for preventing the recurrence of Crime, and for promoting the Reform of the Offender.
12. Paralyzing effect on the Administration of Criminal Justice, arising from the bad state of the Prisons.
13. Injustice of the present System, which often entails considerable Expenses on a small Burgh or County, in the Punishment of Offenders not residing within it, and for whose Crimes it is not justly accountable.
(*Annual Report, 1836*)

The extensive nature of this list demonstrates how quickly Hill had come to terms with his field of responsibility. He achieved this, as have so many others who have taken on positions of responsibility in the supervision or administration of prisons, by identifying those who were both influential and knowledgeable and by making full use of their advice. From the outset he did not hesitate to acknowledge his debt to William Brebner at Glasgow Bridewell. The list detailed above shows that at this early stage Hill was already committed to the separate system of imprisonment rather than the silent system.

During his initial year in office Hill travelled the length and breadth of the country, inspecting most of the 170 prisons of various descriptions. He divided them into five groups. The first was of seventy block houses, most of which consisted of only one room. The second class included about eighty burgh gaols, most of them holding no more than two or three prisoners. The third group consisted of twelve county prisons. The fourth class was made up of the larger prisons, eight in number, and included two at Aberdeen, a gaol and a bridewell at

Edinburgh, the Glasgow Gaol, the prisons at Paisley and Jedburgh and the new prison at Dundee. The final class contained only one establishment, the Glasgow Bridewell, which, as described in the previous chapter, Hill found to be 'the largest and much the best prison in Scotland'. The greatest total number of prisoners in Scotland at this time was about 2,400 and the average about 1,800.

On his appointment Lord John Russell, the Home Secretary, had warned Hill that he would find the prisons in Scotland in a bad state. The new inspector soon confirmed this assessment:

> the picture that gradually unfolded itself before my eyes was far
> worse than anything I had anticipated. (Hill, 1893)

Hill found that in most cases prisoners were not separated from each other, nor from access to the outside world. There was little work, employment, instruction or religious intervention. Prisoners spent much of their day in idleness, passing time with fellow prisoners. Security was lax and there was little in the way of cleanliness or ventilation. There was no incentive in either the burghs or the counties to make any attempt at encouraging criminals to live more law abiding lives. Moreover, small burghs and counties were often saddled with the responsibility of caring for prisoners who neither lived nor had committed crimes within their jurisdiction.

The Prison Act, 1839

Although Hill came to the inspectorate with no previous experience of prisons, he soon set out his own views as to how the prison system should develop:

> The entire management of the Prisons in Scotland (including the
> appointment of the officers) and the control of the Prison Fund,
> to be placed in the hands of Government; a detailed account
> being presented to Parliament showing how the money has been
> applied, the average number of prisoners in each Prison, the
> value of their productive labour, the clear average cost of each
> prisoner, and a balance for or against every Prison.
> (*Annual Report, 1837*)

Hill argued specifically for a uniform system of prison management to be applied across the country; for the construction of a few main prisons which could be used on a national basis; for the separation of prisoners; for female prisoners to be placed under the supervision of female staff; for all prisoners to be required to work; for instruction in some form of trade or skill which would allow them to find work on being released from prison; for provision to be made for 'mental, moral and religious education'; for the provision of a refuge to which juvenile offenders could go on release; for the establishment of a separate asylum to take lunatics out of prison; for burghs to be relieved of their historical responsibility for the maintenance of prisons and for this cost to be met from a general fund.

The arguments presented by the inspector were in tune with the evangelical and utilitarian concepts of the age (Forsythe, 1981). Unremittingly Hill pressed the point that there was little hope of improvement while the general management of prisons remained in local hands and the basic principles of prison discipline as understood by penal reformers of the time were not applied. The government of the day recognised the strength of the argument and accepted that the previous permissive legislation was insufficient to provide essential financial relief for the hard-pressed burghs. By 1837 the Lord Advocate acknowledged in parliament that the local prisons were 'a disgrace to Scotland, and could not be allowed to continue'.

The outcome of this pressure was the enactment in 1839 of *An Act to improve Prisons and Prison Discipline in Scotland.* The central provision of this statute was that

> it is expedient, with a view to the Adoption of Efficient
> Means for the Punishment and Repression of Crime and
> Reformation of Criminals, that Provision should be made for the
> Erection and Maintenance of more secure and convenient
> Prisons, and for the better Management thereof, and the
> Establishment of a well-regulated System of Prison Discipline
> therein, by the Appointment of a Board of Directors of Prisons
> acting on a uniform System, and invested with Power to erect
> and maintain proper Prisons, and regulate the Discipline and
> Management of all Prisons in Scotland, and for raising the
> necessary Funds by means of a general Assessment on Property
> within the several Counties and Burghs in manner hereinafter
> provided.

Thus, at one fell swoop, the disparate structure of local prisons was abolished to be replaced by a centrally appointed General Board of Directors of Prisons. In laying down the composition of the General

Board of Directors the Act took account of the fundamental link between prisons and the rest of the criminal justice process. This connection was an important feature of the Scottish penal system to a degree which was not the case in England. The General Board of Directors was to consist of the Lord Justice General, the Lord Justice Clerk, the Lord Advocate, the Solicitor General, the Dean of the Faculty of Advocates, all *ex officio,* and fourteen other persons to be appointed under royal warrant, five of whom were to be Sheriff Deputies. The only salaried member of the Board was to be the Secretary. With one exception, which will be described later, all prisons were to be under the management of County Boards. These latter, consisting of members appointed by the county commissioners and the burgh magistrates, were to have responsibility for the daily superintendence and maintenance of all prisons within the county under direction of the General Board.

The statute was quite precise about the authority to be vested in the General Board of Directors. It was to 'possess and exercise the full Power of Administration and Management of all Prisons in Scotland'. This was to be carried out either directly or where appropriate through the new County Boards. It was to authorise the building, use and closure of prisons. The General Board was entitled to suspend or dismiss staff employed by the County Boards.

This new era in the management of Scottish prisons was summarised in the power given to the General Board

> of regulating the Confinement, Treatment and Diet of all Civil
> and Criminal Prisoners, and of separating and setting them to
> work, and taking all due Means to train them in good and
> industrious Habits.

This well-regulated system of prison discipline, mirroring that which was already established in the Glasgow Bridewell and broadly similar to that which the Inspectors of Prisons in England had found in the Gloucester Penitentiary, betrayed the undoubted influence of Frederic Hill in drafting the legislation, a fact which he acknowledged both in his autobiography and in his annual report for 1840. His influence was further extended when he was appointed a member of the General Board.

The Act received Royal Assent in August 1839 and the new Board of Directors held its first meeting in September 1839. Viscount Melville was appointed chairman and the Hon. John Murray, Advocate, was appointed secretary at an annual salary of £700. These two men, together with Hill, were to be instrumental in establishing the Scottish system of prison discipline during the course of the mid nineteenth century.

The new statute came into force on 1 July 1840. In its first annual report the Board was able to record

> that so completely had all previous arrangements been made, and so well disposed were all parties concerned to give effect to the new system, that the management of the whole prisons in Scotland passed from the former authorities to the County Boards established under the Act, without the concurrence of any difficulty of the slightest importance. Considering that there were about 170 prisons in Scotland, great and small, and that almost every prison had its own separate managers, we think that while this circumstance is highly creditable, both to the former authorities, and to those who have succeeded them, it may at the same time be held as a testimony of the state of public feeling being strongly in favour of the system now established.

The Board of Directors immediately addressed itself to the matter of drawing up a set of general rules which were to be applied to every prison in the country. Largely under the influence of Hill an introductory set of rules was drawn up for approval of the Secretary of State by July 1840 and came into force in all prisons 'in so far as the present state of the buildings would permit' on 1 November 1840. The new rules required that:

> all building work was to be carried out under public contract following proper tendering procedures;

> every prison was to have a sufficient number of properly qualified officers, female staff were to look after female prisoners and no prisoner was to be placed in any position of authority;

> no appointment was to be made on any ground other than superior qualifications;

> except in special circumstances approved by the General Board no one over 40 years of age was to be appointed to any office; preference was to be given to those between the ages of 25 and 35;

> officers were at all times to conduct themselves towards

prisoners with kindness and good temper, yet with firmness and self-respect;

every prison was to be kept properly warmed, ventilated, lighted and perfectly clean;

female prisoners were to be kept quite apart from male prisoners; every prisoner was to have daily exercise in the open air;

each prisoner was to be visited daily by the governor or matron and weekly by the surgeon and the chaplain; prisoners who did not belong to the Church of Scotland could be visited by their own clergyman;

spirituous liquors, smoking, card playing, profane and abusive language, whistling and singing were prohibited;

proper registers and a governor's journal were to be kept;

cheap, wholesome and sufficient diet was to be provided without charge to prisoners;

every prisoner was to be visited in his cell by a member of staff at least ten times each day;

prisoners were to rise no later than six in the morning and to go to bed no earlier than nine in the evening;

all convicted prisoners, if certified fit, were to be supplied with enough useful and productive labour to keep them occupied for ten hours each day. The profits from any additional work were to be credited to prisoners and paid to them on liberation;

prisoners were to be required to wash regularly and were to be supplied with clean clothes;

prisoners sentenced to three months or more imprisonment who were illiterate were to be taught to read and write;

convicted prisoners were not to receive visits except in special circumstances;

under good management there should be little need for punishment; if offences were committed the punishment should as near as possible relate to the offence; there was to be no corporal punishment.

The Prison Act of 1839 heralded the end of the era of idiosyncratic local prison management and ushered in the age of the disciplined tradition of the penitentiary which Howard had been advocating for

some fifty years and which had been operating in the Glasgow
Bridewell for thirty years. The tradition of what would later be described as 'dressage' had arrived.

The General Prison at Perth 1838-1860

As well as pressing in his earliest reports for the administration of
Scottish prisons to be centralised, Hill had advocated that 'a few
Penitentiaries' should be provided for general use. He specifically
recommended that Fort George in the north and the former military
depot at Perth should both be converted into penitentiaries, capable of
holding respectively 150 and 500 prisoners, and that Glasgow Bridewell should be further enlarged for use as the main prison in the
country.

According to the terms in which it was first introduced, probably
drafted by Hill, the 1839 Bill envisaged all Scottish prisons being
under the direct management of the General Board without any local
tier of management. It further proposed that there would be four main
prisons in Scotland: Glasgow Bridewell to hold prisoners from the
west; the new prison at Perth to hold those from the east; Aberdeen to
take prisoners from the north-east and Fort George to deal with the
north.

Hill felt at liberty to describe these proposals in his fifth annual
report and made clear his regret that the Bill had been amended. The
Inspector's comments could not have upset the Secretary of State, or
if they did he was prepared to ignore them. He sent 200 copies of the
report to the new General Board with a request that they be circulated.
Despite the influence of the Inspector, the Board took an early opportunity to demonstrate its independence:

> considering that there are some observations in the concluding
> part of the Report in which they do not wish to appear as
> concurring, and which might be implied by their distributing it,
> they therefore decline to do so, and direct that this be reported to
> the Secretary of State. (*Minute Books of the General Board of
> Directors, 1839–1860*)

Although several of Hill's original proposals were amended or considered too radical for immediate introduction, the argument that the
former Napoleonic prison at Perth should be renovated and brought
into use as a general prison was accepted.

In the latter years of the eighteenth and early part of the nineteenth centuries thousands of French prisoners were interned in Great Britain and accommodation had urgently to be provided for them. In 1806 the first prison was built to house them at Dartmoor. A wooden prison was constructed in 1810 at Valleyfield near Penicuik, some nine miles south of Edinburgh, and within a year or so about 5,000 prisoners of war were detained there. In 1811 work began on a more permanent prison at the South Inch of Perth between the main Edinburgh Road and the banks of the River Tay. The impressive stone structure was completed in record time and part of it was ready for accommodation by August 1812. Between then and its closure in July 1814 it held up to 7,000 prisoners. One can imagine that this unexpected increase in population had a traumatic effect on the lives of the douce burghers of Perth. An interesting description of this, including the daily markets which the prisoners were allowed to conduct within the walls of the prison, can be found in the *Historical Sketch of the Old Depot* written by William Sievwright in 1894. Extensive extracts from this work are included in Joy Cameron's book on Scottish prisons (1983).

After the prisoners of war departed many of the substantial buildings in the new prison were rented out to local merchants as granaries. However, George Penny, a local historian, had other thoughts on how the depot might be put to more suitable use:

> It is admirably adapted for granaries, but it might be far better
> occupied as a national bridewell – where convicted felons,
> instead of being sent out of the country at so great an expense,
> could be employed in labour to maintain themselves. In such a
> place as this, prisoners could be properly classified: the males
> kept apart from the females, and the old hardened offender
> separated from the young in crime. Here they might be
> employed, being men of respectable character in their midst,
> having charge, and imparting instruction. This would have a
> better effect than a hundred task-masters with the whip over
> them. Besides, supported by their labour, they might be
> instructed, and come out at the expiry of their term with a small
> sum to set them agoing again in the world, better men than when
> they went in. (Penny, 1836)

Penny must have caught the ear of Frederic Hill when the new Inspector of Prisons paid his first visit to Perth in 1836. In his first annual report the latter commented that the former military prison 'may be advantageously converted into a prison for criminals'. He repeated this recommendation in 1838. The suggestion was accepted by the government and one of the main provisions of the 1839 Act was the transfer of the lands and buildings of the depot to the new General Board of Directors which was in turn

> . . . authorized, as soon after the passing of this Act as they shall
> find convenient, to alter, enlarge, and complete the said
> Buildings at Perth, and maintain the same as General Prison for
> the Custody of Persons convicted of crime whose respective
> Sentences of Imprisonment shall be for a Period of not less than
> Six Months, which Prison shall be under the sole and immediate
> Superintendence and Management of the said General Board.

The Act went on to provide that all offenders sentenced to one year or more should in future be transferred to the new General Prison, while those sentenced to between six months and one year *could* be sent there.

The General Board took up office on 11 September 1839. In deciding which system of discipline was to be developed at the new General Prison the Directors had to choose between the separate and the silent systems of imprisonment. In their first annual report the Directors described the choice which faced them: whether to select the system which involved 'separating prisoners by day and by night in cells of sufficient dimensions for health, and properly warmed and ventilated, accompanied with labour and religious and moral instruction'; or to select the silent system, according to which 'the prisoners sleep in separate cells, which are generally of small dimensions, and are made to work in company in classes during the day, under a strict enforcement of silence, with a view to cut off all opportunities of intercourse'. The Directors doubted if the latter system was at all practicable and noted that there was no prospect of enforcing it without the strictest discipline and the greatest frequency and severity of punishment. Given the presence of Frederic Hill on the Board there was little doubt that the Directors would settle for the separate system, having been advised that it was already operating effectively in several prisons in the country.

The next task of the Board was to appoint a governor for the new prison. The Lord Advocate and the Inspector of Prisons were appointed as a sub-committee to consider and report as to who should be appointed and what salary he should be paid. Not surprisingly they attempted to recruit William Brebner but he refused to leave his work in Glasgow, presumably not merely on the grounds that his salary there was 500 guineas per year while the salary proposed for Perth was £400. The sub-committee eventually went south of the border to make a nomination and settled on an individual named Walter Ruding Deverell. The Board accepted this recommendation and, with the approval of the Home Secretary, Deverell took up his new post on 25 March 1841.

The new governor was given responsibility for appointing, fixing the salaries of and dismissing all staff, apart from the chaplain, matron, teachers and surgeon, in consultation with the General Board. Deverell made enquiries of the major local prisons and discovered that senior warders in Glasgow were paid 18s. a week together with allowances equivalent to 3s. or 4s.; those in Edinburgh received between 14s. and 16s. a week although more than half were pensioned soldiers. Similar salaries were paid in Dundee and Aberdeen, while in Perth County Prison the average was 14s. By comparison Glasgow police constables received between 13s. and 20s. a week while those in Perth were the lowest paid at 10/6d a week. According to Deverell, writing to the General Board in 1841, the latter 'are generally taken from the humblest class of Common labourers, who possess little indeed of the intelligence, manual skill, and moral energy demanded for Warders in the General Prison'.

Deverell expected to recruit a better class of staff to the General Prison and he was quite clear in his recommendation to the Board of Directors:

> I have thus ascertained the opinion of a number of individuals, who have peculiar means of acquiring a trustworthy knowledge of the character, qualifications, and wages of the classes in question; and those opinions I have found to concur with my previous conviction, – now additionally confirmed by the declaration of numerous applicants – that, such Officers as the great moral purpose of the General Prison require, cannot be induced to remain for less wages than 20s. a week. I find, in fact, that really respectable persons possessing the requisite physical, mental, and moral qualifications, with technical skill adequate to teach one or more of the mechanical arts, are not willing to undergo the constant seclusion, and rigid discipline of such establishments, (except as a temporary means to a more satisfactory end), unless they can reckon upon at least that amount of salary.

The General Board of Directors agreed that the wages of warders in the General Prison should vary between 16s. and 21s. a week, while the head warder was to be on a scale extending to 30s a week. The annual salary of Deverell was to be on a scale between £400 and £500. Salaries of the full-time chaplain, surgeon and matron were to be respectively £250, £150 and £100 yearly.

The only member of staff who had any previous experience of working in a prison was the matron, Mrs Catherine MacMillan, who came from a similar post in the North Prison of Glasgow. It was decided that the prison would require only six warders when it opened at first. The Board concurred with Deverell's request that his six new recruits required some form of training. It was agreed that they should go for a week to Aberdeen Prison, a week to Dundee Prison, and for a month to Glasgow to learn from Brebner. Deverell made the argument that this training would be indispensable for the new staff but he did not push for anything more than this.

> I consider the time I have mentioned quite sufficient to
> enable any intelligent and observant man, and of course no other
> would be selected, to make himself master of all the essential
> matters in the routine of Prison duties which throughout the
> whole year are merely repetitions of what is to be seen in one day.

The new General Prison was opened on 30 March 1842.

Within months a major management problem had to be faced. The members of the General Board were summoned to an emergency meeting on 15 July 1842 'to receive and consider Report by the Inspector of Prisons on his examination of the General Prison and of facts which have come to light relating to the conduct of the Governor'. Following this meeting Deverell, along with the Head Warder and the Clerk were dismissed. The Minute and Letter Books of the General Board of Directors provide little detail of what had gone wrong. The annual report of the Board published in 1843 comments that Deverell 'was deficient in [some of the qualifications] which are deemed to be essential' for the conduct and superintendence of a prison. The Inspector's report for 1842 makes a similar comment. The only indication that the failing may have been financial is contained in a letter from the General Board to Deverell, dated 3 August, which advised him that:

> The Finance Committee having considered your accounts for the
> quarter ended 25 June last have directed various explanations to

be obtained from you with regard to them and vouchers to be furnished.

This was an inauspicious start for the new prison and must have been a considerable embarrassment for the new Board of Directors. That it was not inclined to show the least clemency towards Deverell may be deduced from the letter which was sent to him by the Secretary on 27 September 1842.

> I observe from an advertisement that a sale of 'the whole furniture in the Governor's House' is to take place tomorrow forenoon. As the Board have not granted permission for the sale taking place *in the house* I have on their behalf to request that the furniture should be carried out of doors previous to the sale commencing and that the people attending it shall not be permitted to enter the House . . . I beg to know if you will remove the furniture as I propose. Should tomorrow be wet you may have the use of the old Guard Room in front of the Governor's House in which to conduct the sale.

Problems with the post of governor continued. It was again offered to and refused by Brebner although he agreed to fill the vacancy on a temporary basis. In October the Board appointed William Rankine, Manager of the Dalkeith and Leith Railways, but, having considered what the post involved, he declined to take it up. Finally, on 6 December 1842 Brebner was able to hand over to the new Governor, James Stuart, formerly Superintendent of Police in Edinburgh. The Board was more fortunate in this choice and Stuart was to remain Governor for a full twenty years until ill health forced his retiral on 9 December 1862. At the time of the appointment of the new Governor the Board wrote to advise him, the chaplain and the surgeon that they must co-operate for the good of the prison. They were, however, at pains to emphasise to the latter two members of staff and also to the matron that they were subordinate to the governor in matters relating to the management of the prison.

The Introductory Prison Rules of 1840 had laid down that prisoners should be given an amount of work each day which could reasonably be expected to keep them occupied for ten hours. The profit from any work in excess of this was to be placed to the prisoner's credit and paid to him on liberation. In 1843 the Directors decided that this money could, at the governor's discretion, be sent out by a prisoner to his family.

In that same year the magistrates and tradesmen of Perth complained to the Board that work done by the prisoners was likely to have an undue influence on the market for labour at Perth. This concern did not impress the Directors, who replied that they did not intend to place any limit on the work to be done at the General Prison. They did agree that goods so manufactured should not be sold below the market price nor should their sale be limited to the Perth area.

By 1845 there were 219 male and 109 female prisoners in the General Prison. At that time, in addition to the chaplain, surgeon, matron and teachers, the staff of warders in the male section of the prison included a head warder, a store warder, a shoemaker trades' warder and assistant, a weaver trades' warder and two assistants, a tailor trades' warder and assistant and a mechanics' trade warder; five discipline warders, three sub-warders and an exercising warder with assistant, a cookhouse warder, a waterhouse warder, a furnace warder, an out-of-door warder, an outer-gate warder, an inner-gate warder and an inside night-warder. The matron had under her a female staff consisting of a sub-matron, four discipline warders, a laundress, an exercising warder and a door warder.

The daily routine was well established. Staff came on duty at six o'clock. They immediately distributed tools to the prisoners who, once they had swept their cells and washed, set to work. Breakfast was distributed at 7.30am, immediately after which the warders took their break. Outside exercise began at 8.15am in the winter and 6.15am in the summer. The teachers, who taught prisoners in their cells, came on duty at 8.00am, working for eight hours on week days, for two hours on Saturdays and for five hours on Sundays. Dinner was served at 1.00pm and 'accomplished in 12 minutes'. One half of the warders finished duty at 6.00pm each evening. Supper was served to the prisoners at 7.00pm and at 8.30pm working tools were removed. At 8.45pm hammocks were slung, at 8.55pm lights were put out and cell doors checked. At 9.00pm the main staff went off duty. Only half of the staff were on duty on Sundays.

It was part of the responsibility of the chaplain to make contact with each prisoner's family, if he had one, and to make preparations for release. Through a network of parish ministers and other volunteers attempts were made to find work for prisoners and to keep contact with them after liberation. In 1846 the General Board reported that they had

much reason to be satisfied with the manner in which this important duty has been performed – the result being that of the

260 prisoners, viz, 195 males and 165 females who were liberated during the year, no fewer than 118, viz, 85 males and 33 females, have obtained employment, and are now, so far as can be ascertained, conducting themselves well.

One wing of the General Prison had been allocated to juvenile prisoners. Among the earliest arrivals in the General Prison had been three children under the age of twelve who were serving between eighteen months and two years and six between the ages of twelve and sixteen sentenced to two years or more in prison. Initially young prisoners spent a month in solitary confinement in the main prison before being transferred to the Juvenile Wing. This procedure gave rise to concern and there is evidence that the surgeon recommended that it should be waived in the case of particularly young prisoners. In November 1847 the General Board directed that juveniles should be allowed to exercise ten at a time with a view to relaxing the system of separate confinement. Despite this the strain of separate confinement took its toll of young prisoners and the Governor's journal contains several references to attempted, and in some cases successful, suicides. In January 1850 the first recorded escape from the General Prison took place from the juvenile wing although the two prisoners involved were recaptured almost immediately. Two warders were temporarily suspended as a result and the Governor was 'reprimanded and admonished' by the Chairman of the General Board.

In July 1853 a new wing was completed at the General Prison, giving it accommodation for a total of 670 prisoners. The Governor's report for December 1855 lists the prisoners as follows:

260 males and 283 females;
52 juveniles;
20 imbeciles and 8 epileptics;
32 male and 13 female lunatics.

The total staff at this time numbered 65. In July 1856 alterations were made in the arrangements for allocating different classes of prisoners. From that date all male convicts, some of whom had previously been held in the General Prison, were to be transferred on sentence direct to convict prisons in England. All female convicts sentenced in Scotland were to be held in the General Prison as were all females sentenced to more than nine months' imprisonment.

The effects on individual prisoners of strict separation, even when visited regularly by staff, continued to give cause for concern and within a few years there was evidence that it was being relaxed even for the adult prisoners. In his annual report for 1856 the Inspector reported a change in the regime of separate confinement which allowed prisoners to work together in groups of three for two hours a day and to exercise together for at least ninety minutes. During these times they were allowed to 'talk on proper subjects'.

Putting the prisoners to useful work had always been an important feature of the separate regime and in 1855 the Board of Directors appointed a superintendent of stores and manufactures in the General Prison. The man appointed 'had considerable experience as a salesman'. His wage was part salary and part commission of the profit from prison labour. The Board was as unlucky with this post as it had been with that of Governor initially and the following year the post holder was dismissed. In July 1859 the Board decided to appoint a steward who would perform the dual functions 'both of an ordinary House Steward and Superintendent of Manufactures'. The Governor of Dundee Prison was appointed to the post. In the same year a permanent Clerk of Works was appointed in the General Prison.

By the time the Board of Directors of the General Prison demitted office in December 1860 the regime was well established as a model for all other prisons in Scotland, and the Board itself had taken firm control of the oversight of the management of all local prisons. For some the new model was a barren system, devoid of humanity. For the majority of observers at the time it was

> an exemplar, a beacon, with its hierarchical pyramid of
> salaried meritorious staff, its board of directors, its clearly stated
> philosophy of prison discipline, its purpose-built architecture,
> its grim forbidding monologues of inurement, misery and
> redemption to the worlds outside and within, the one to be
> deterred, the other redeemed. (Forsythe, 1981)

The Local Prisons

Following his first tour of inspection of Scottish prisons in 1836 the new Inspector estimated that the average number held in Scotland's 170 prisons at any one time was about 1,800 prisoners, with a maximum of about 2,400. As one would expect, these prisoners were concentrated in the larger town gaols and bridewells. The majority of the smaller prisons held only a handful of prisoners. Many of the seventy or so lock-ups frequently lay empty while the eighty or so burgh gaols held an average of three or four prisoners at any one time. With one or two notable exceptions there was little in the way of discipline or organised regime in any prison. The circumstances which the newly appointed Inspector uncovered at Fortrose Gaol in 1837 were typical of the smaller establishments of the time:

> The Fortrose Prison is a wretched place, quite unfit for use. The authorities of the town have applied several times to have it condemned, but in vain, and prisoners still continue to be put into it, not only from Fortrose and Rosemarkie, but from part of the county also. The prison consists of a single room, formed out of part of the ruin of an old cathedral: it is damp, cold, dirty, and insecure; and moreover, it is infested with rats.

Conditions in Perth Gaol, with an average of thirty prisoners excluding debtors supervised by two members of staff, were representative of those prevailing in medium sized and larger establishments:

> The only interruption to the otherwise constant round of idleness and corrupt association, is a lesson given in each ward once a week by the chaplain, and the performance of public worship on the Sunday.

The 1839 Act of Parliament had given the newly formed Board of Directors of Prisons authority to regulate the discipline and management of all prisons in the country. Acting on their own account and also through the offices of the Inspector of Prisons, who was one of their number, the Directors were determined that a common structure and discipline should be introduced throughout the country. The main mechanism for this to happen was the set of Prison Rules introduced in 1840.

Then, as now, local authorities were none too keen to be dictated to by any form of central administration and in several instances the Board of Directors had to take a firm line. The minutes of one of their meetings in April 1841 recorded that:

> The General Board have received with much surprise the recent intimation from the County Board of Edinburgh that the County Board 'do not admit the power of the General Board to disallow the Resolution' of the County Board. The General Board are not aware that any doubt can be entertained in regard to their power to regulate and direct and control any matter respecting the

management, administration, and discipline of all the Gaols in Scotland. That power the General Board are resolved to assert, and, if necessary, to enforce.

The superior authority of the Board of Directors was, however grudgingly, accepted by the County Boards, although from time to time the Board still had to reinforce their statutory position, as in 1847 when writing to the Prison Board of Lanarkshire:

The General Board at all times feel the greatest reluctance to interfere with the local authorities in the management of the Prisons under their jurisdiction, but cases may occur wherein the duty imposed by law upon the General Board compels them to notice any deviations from the Rules prescribed either by Act of Parliament, or by the Regulations sanctioned by the Secretary of State, and to use their best endeavours to restore a proper system of management where it had formerly prevailed.

This last was a reference to problems at Glasgow Prison, recognised for so long as a model for all other prisons. The population of the prison had increased to a level at which it had become impossible to observe the letter of the statutory rules. For example, prisoners were being allowed to exercise in groups in corridors and to make contact with each other during these periods. An increasing number of prisoners were being used as pass men and women in various domestic duties about the prison.

The County Board initially responded in firm terms to the General Board, indicating that, although the letter of the Rules was being breached, the spirit of the Act was being honoured. That is an argument which has been used several times over the last 150 years when administrators have found it convenient or necessary to ignore individual statutory provisions.

In 1852 there were further problems at Glasgow Prison, this time to do with staff unrest. Following the death of William Brebner in 1845 Superintendent Miller, head of the city police force, was appointed to replace him. Three years later Miller returned to his former position and Captain John Mullen became Governor of the prison. In July 1851 several members of staff were dismissed by the Governor following publication of an open letter to members of the County Board complaining of irregularities in the management of the prison. The County Board appointed a sub-committee to investigate the allegations.

In August 1851 this group reported back. One complaint had been against the 'revolting' behaviour of a particular officer towards two named prisoners. The report found no evidence to confirm this accusation but expressed satisfaction that the Governor had dismissed the officer concerned. The charge that the Head Warder had been guilty of 'grossly offensive language and conduct' towards female staff was upheld and the committee noted with satisfaction that the officer concerned had resigned. The committee went on to record the fact that as a body the staff had not been working harmoniously and had concealed what had been going on from the Governor, largely out of fear of the Head Warder. The fact that they had done this had seriously impaired their 'moral influence on the prisoners'.

Only one of the officers who had helped draw up the letter to the County Board was reinstated. The others involved were aggrieved at this and took the matter up with the General Board, going on to make additional accusations against Governor Mullen. The matter was referred to the County Board which carried out further investigation. The outcome was a motion put to the County Board concluding that enough of the accusations had

> been sufficiently proved as to bring out a considerable amount of indiscretion and neglect on the part of Governor Mullen in his general management of the Establishment and that the affairs of the Establishment as recently conducted have been in such a state as to render some change absolutely necessary.

The motion was passed on the Chairman's casting vote. The evidence which had been gathered, together with notice of the motion was forwarded to the General Board in Edinburgh. The matter was referred to Home Secretary Walpole who recommended that the Governor should be strongly admonished as to his future behaviour and that a close watch should be kept on how he carried out his duties from then on. Mullen was duly summoned to the offices of the General Board for the warning.

Among the irregularities which had taken place was the fact that prisoners had carried out and been paid for private work for members of staff, including copying out a code of Scripture references as a personal service for the chaplain, for which the prisoner concerned had received a suit of clothes in payment. The Governor had taken food from the prison stores to feed his ponies, although it was recognised that he had paid for this; he had also used prisoners to look after his ponies and to refurbish a stable. Mullen was also called to task for providing his family with prison soap and for allowing them to use the prison horse and cab to go shopping in Glasgow. These latter may have been explained by the fact that he had eight children!

In his annual report for 1852 the Inspector of Prisons in referring to the situation at Glasgow Prison made it quite clear where his sympathies lay. Noting that there had been 'some unpleasant feeling between the Governor and some of his subordinates', he went on to make what could be taken as an implied criticism of the County Board:

> when a spirit once gains admission among the subordinates of a
> large prison, to damage those above them, it is not easily
> eradicated; and a Governor having at all times a very difficult
> task to perform, needs the liberal support of those above him,
> and ought not to be too scrupulously judged on trifles.

There are indications that the staff at Glasgow continued to be dissatisfied with the way the Governor managed the prison. However, he clearly had the support of his superiors from then on and when he died in 1854 the Minutes of the County Board eulogised his achievements as Governor.

It is apparent both from central reports and from the minute books of several County Boards that by the end of the 1850s the principle of central oversight of the general management of all prisons was well established. This is in contrast to the situation in England during the same period, and the fact that such a degree of central control existed at this time in Scotland should be borne in mind later when we come to discuss the implications of the Prison (Scotland) Act of 1877.

Prison Staff 1835-1860

Given the large number of small prisons scattered throughout Scotland in 1835 it was rare to come across staff who were employed other than in a part-time capacity or who at most included supervision of the local prison in other duties. In his autobiography (1893) Frederic Hill had this to say about the staff whom he met when he first took up the appointment of Inspector of Prisons:

> The appointment of the county prison keepers was in the hands
> of the Commissioners of Supply, as they were called. These
> were, for the most part, country gentlemen, who had no
> knowledge on the subject of prison discipline. The burgh prison

keepers were appointed by the burgh magistrates or 'bailies'. These bailies were unpaid officials, quite ignorant of prison matters, and were under no controlling authority. The result can be easily imagined. Most of the keepers had no idea of any duty beyond the safe custody of their prisoners, and some of them presented examples of drunkenness and profligacy as bad, perhaps, as could be found amongst the prisoners themselves.

The annual reports presented by the Inspector are replete with references to the poor quality of staff he encountered. His general assessment of the majority of gaolers and keepers was that they were not bad men, indeed in many cases they were well-meaning, but they simply had no knowledge of what they were meant to do other than to prevent prisoners from escaping and even that degree of knowledge could not safely be assumed. In several prisons keepers augmented their meagre salaries by selling food to prisoners. In others they stayed some distance from the prison and only visited when other duties, such as that of constable or town officer, permitted.

Displaying the pragmatic approach which was later to become virtually the hallmark of Scottish prison administration, Hill turned to the one establishment in the country which had a relatively well-trained staff. Time and again he recommended, both in his annual reports and in private correspondence to County Boards, that they should seek staff from Glasgow Bridewell. Hill was in no doubt that the key to the efficient management of a prison was the appointment of competent, properly trained staff. A significant proportion of his early annual reports is taken up with comment on the relative worth of individual governors and keepers. He consistently impressed on the local authorities that they should set a high standard for their prison staff:

A Keeper, for instance, may be a good kind of man, and perform the more evident of his duties with diligence and regularity, and yet be very unfit for his office. But how difficult it is to make this apparent to the persons whose enquiries have not led them to see how many qualifications ought to be united in the director of a Prison! (*Annual Report, 1837*)

With the establishment of the General Board of Directors he lost no time in ensuring that his views in this area were taken on board and that the opportunity presented by the 1839 Act to renew the appointments only of those staff who were efficient was taken up. In May 1840 Hill

Table of Scottish Prisons for Year to 30 June 1852

COUNTY	PRISON	NUMBER OF PRISONERS			GOV'NRS' SALARY	NUMBER OF WARDERS	
		Male	Female	Total	£	Male	Female
Aberdeen	Aberdeen	51	29	80	310	9	2
	Peterhead	3	2	5	20	-	-
	Huntly	-	-	-	13	-	-
	Fraserburgh	-	-	-	13	-	-
Argyll	Inverary	13	4	17	75	1	-
	Campbeltown	5	1	6	50	-	-
	Lochgilphead	1	-	1	25	-	-
	Tobermory	-	-	-	15	-	-
Ayr	Ayr	56	22	78	130	4	1
	Largs	-	-	-	31	-	-
	Cumnock	-	-	-	31	-	-
	Stewarton	-	-	-	31	-	-
	Saltcoats	1	-	1	31	-	-
	Irvine	-	-	-	15	-	-
	Kilmarnock	10	3	13	52	-	-
Banff	Banff	12	1	13	55	-	-
	Keith	-	-	-	9	-	-
	Cullen	-	-	-	9	-	-
Berwick	Greenlaw	12	2	14	90	-	-
	Duns	-	-	-	5	-	-
Bute	Rothesay	4	1	5	50	-	-
Caithness	Wick	6	1	7	46	-	1
Clackmannan	Alloa	11	5	16	70	1	-
Dumbarton	Dumbarton	18	4	22	80	1	-
	Helensburgh	-	-	-	7	-	-
	Kirkintilloch	-	-	-	-	-	-
Dumfries	Dumfries	38	11	49	100	3	-
Edinburgh	Edinburgh	296	314	610	500	22	9
	Court Buildings	5	3	8	41	-	-
	Musselburgh	4	1	5	39	-	-
Elgin	Elgin	7	3	10	45	1	1
	Forres	-	-	-	10	-	-
Fife	Cupar	38	14	52	100	3	2
	Dunfermline	12	5	17	66	1	-
Forfar	Arbroath	2	3	5	46	-	1
	Brechin	1	-	1	35	-	-
	Dundee	108	86	194	208	6	2
	Forfar	15	4	19	55	1	1
	Montrose	10	7	17	59	1	1

Haddington	Haddington	15	6	21	80	1	-
	Dunbar	-	-	-	12	-	-
	North Berwick	-	-	-	5	-	-
Inverness	Inverness	15	11	26	100	3	1
	Lochmaddy	2	-	2	40	-	-
	Portree	1	-	1	35	-	-
	Fort William	1	1	2	55	-	-
Kincardine	Stonehaven	9	2	11	50	-	-
Kinross	Kinross	2	1	3	30	-	-
Kirkudbright	Kirkcudbright	15	7	22	80	-	-
	Maxweltown	-	-	-	15	-	-
Lanark	Glasgow	368	283	651	400	39	13
	Lanark	16	4	20	75	1	1
	Hamilton	34	7	41	80	2	1
	Airdrie	12	10	22	75	1	-
Linlithgow	Linlithgow	12	8	20	52	1	-
Nairn	Nairn	1	-	1	45	-	-
Orkney	Kirkwall	1	1	2	35	-	-
Peebles	Peebles	10	1	11	53	-	-
Perth	Perth	57	36	93	125	5	1
	Dunblane	5	1	6	40	-	-
	Blairgowrie	-	-	-	5	-	-
Renfrew	Paisley	64	47	111	135	4	3
	Greenock	18	16	34	80	2	1
	Port Glasgow	-	-	-	18	-	-
	Pollockshaws	-	-	-	15	-	-
	Renfrew	-	-	-	10	-	-
Ross & Cromarty	Dingwall	6	2	8	65	1	-
	Tain	2	-	2	40	-	-
	Cromarty	1	-	1	31	-	-
	Stornaway	1	1	2	40	-	-
Roxburgh	Jedburgh	23	4	27	107	2	-
	Hawick	-	-	-	10	-	-
	Kelso	-	-	-	5	-	-
Selkirk	Selkirk	3	1	4	60	-	-
Stirling	Stirling	75	34	109	104	5	1
	Falkirk	2	-	2	30	-	-
Sutherland	Dornoch	2	-	2	56	-	-
Wigtown	Wigtown	4	2	6	45	-	-
	Stranraer	2	14	16	75	1	-
Zetland	Fort Charlotte	1	-	1	45	-	-
Perth	General Prison	423	8	431	500	38	3
TOTAL		**1942**	**1034**	**2976**			

wrote a lengthy letter to Lord Melville, Chairman of the Board of Directors of Prisons, at the latter's request describing in detail the qualifications which might be looked for in senior prison staff. He began by pointing out that no matter what was done in planning a prison, in providing funds and in drawing up regulations, the crucial factor in determining whether it was to be well run was the appointment of suitable staff. The Inspector pointed out that with the forthcoming need to re-appoint all staff in accordance with the 1839 Act there would be an opportunity to make a fresh start and he listed qualities which he considered necessary:

> The Governor of a large prison should be a person of strong native talent, and of great decision of character, yet of kind and affable manner; he should possess a great insight into human character, and into the various causes of crime, and the springs of action; and he should be influenced by a strong desire to promote the permanent welfare of the prisoners committed to his charge. He should be possessed of powers of command, and of holding others to responsibility; and in order to maintain these effectually, it is necessary that he should be able to determine what everyone under his authority can reasonably be expected to perform, and to judge of the manner in which every duty is discharged.

Hill recommended that no one over the age of forty should be appointed an officer and that the salary should be such as to attract people of above-average qualifications and character. He went on to describe what was to be expected of female officers, of chaplains and of surgeons. He concluded by recommending that the governor of the main prison in each district should superintend the smaller prisons. The Inspector drafted a letter which the General Board subsequently approved and which Lord Melville sent to all County Boards advising them of the importance of appointing efficient governors and keepers to each prison. Hill's principal recommendations were incorporated into the first set of Prison Rules approved by the Secretary of State in July 1840.

By the following year the Inspector was able to report that his recommendations were being implemented by many County Boards although he returned to the question of salaries and conditions of service:

I have again to express my regret that the duties of the
warders are so heavy, while at the same time their remuneration
is so low. The experienced Governor of the Prison of Glasgow
has given it as his opinion that the work of a warder is as
laborious, hour for hour, as that of an ordinary mechanic; and yet
in many prisons the warders are on duty fourteen or fifteen hours
per day, with a share of attendance on the Sunday in addition.
With such an amount of confinement, and with wages generally
all from fourteen shillings to eighteen shillings a week it cannot
be expected, except in particular cases, that persons of superior
character, and possessing the other qualifications required,
should offer themselves for the situation; or that those holding it
should be able to perform their duty with the cheerfulness and
alacrity which ought to distinguish a prison officer; or that they
should be able to find time for self improvement and the
gratification of the domestic affections. One of the warders of the
prison of Edinburgh stated that he seldom saw his children
except on Sunday; and that he was obliged to leave home before
they were awake in the morning, between five and six o'clock,
and that he did not get back till between nine and ten at night,
when they were going to bed.

A basic premise of the new regulations was that governors and keepers
should be employed in a full-time capacity and should not have other
duties. In 1845 the Board of Directors found it necessary to remind
County Boards that they should cease the practice of combining the
role of prison governor with that of messenger-at-arms, sheriff's
officer, burgh officer, police officer or constable.

Within a few years the Inspector was able to note that the new
officers being appointed 'more and more nearly' approached the
standards laid down by the General Board. He also noted the beginnings of a tradition which was to have great significance in later years:
that 'appointments have been made by promoting good subordinate
officers to be keepers of small prisons'. Hill was at pains to underline
that there was little point in carefully selecting senior prison staff
unless the warders also were 'of high moral character' since it was they
who dealt most directly with prisoners. In his annual report of 1844 he
was encouraged to note the good influence which subordinate staff
were exerting on prisoners:

In some prisons an unusual degree of good conduct is induced,
and the number of punishments kept low, by the personal

influence of the officers, and by their care in reasoning with prisoners before resorting to punishment.

In 1842 the chaplain at Edinburgh Prison had told the Inspector that staff frequently had more influence on prisoners than he could ever hope to have since

a word from them was more effective than one from the chaplain, because the prisoners felt that what was said could not proceed from the mere performance of a duty, but from a real interest in their welfare.

In his earlier reports Hill supported Brebner's contention that any reform which was achieved in prison was of little use if there was not continued support for the prisoner after liberation. In 1846 he was able to report substantial progress in this respect, noting that many prisons operated some form of supervision over prisoners for some time after they were released. This supervision was often undertaken by the governor himself or by the chaplain but in Perth County Prison in the mid 1840s another method, which was later to be developed widely in Scotland, was being employed. Young men from the neighbourhood came into the prison under the supervision of the chaplain and got to know prisoners who were shortly to be liberated. They did their best to find these men employment on release and kept contact with them in the community. Once a month this group of volunteers met with the governor, the chaplain and the sheriff substitute to discuss progress of the scheme.

In 1846 the County Board of Lanark approved the appointment of an officer at Glasgow Prison who was given the task of establishing contact with friends of prisoners who were about to be released 'in order to facilitate their safe return to society'. This officer maintained contact with prisoners after liberation. The Inspector of Prisons recommended that similar appointments should be made in all large prisons.

There were several other examples of ways in which the role of the warder was being developed beyond that of turnkey. Teacher-warders, for example, were appointed in several prisons in the 1840s. This in turn led to a need for a higher standard of warder and in 1847 the Inspector recommended a substantial increase in salaries in order to attract suitable recruits.

By 1847 the General Board of Directors and the Inspector had succeeded in enforcing uniform standards throughout Scotland to such an extent that a new set of Rules was drawn up and approved by the Secretary of State. These rules laid down requirements and standards for the appointment of a 'sufficient number of well-qualified officers' in each prison. The role of the governor was clearly defined, covering many items which remain extant today: the Governor's Order Book, the role of the deputy governor, the daily journal, security requirements and daily inspection.

By the late 1850s the organisation of prison staff was more or less complete and in 1858 the General Board of Directors was able to report that:

> The subordinate officers, with few exceptions, have conducted themselves with strict propriety, and they have been zealous in the discharge of their duties.

This was a significant improvement on the comments of the first Inspector that many staff were not able, efficient or trustworthy.

The Scottish System of Prison Discipline

Theories of imprisonment and of prison management over the last two centuries have been of continuing interest to students of public administration, of criminal and of social justice. While details of the arguments presented have been altered, and the emphasis has shifted as penal theories have developed and new justifications for imprisonment have been advanced, the fundamental assumption on which discussion is based remains significantly unaltered.

Imprisonment is an expression, in Britain today the ultimate expression, of the power which those who control society exercise over individuals within society. The act of imprisonment realises that power by controlling the detailed activities of the prisoner, by disciplining as far as is possible his every movement. Justification for this complete form of discipline has been advanced on several fronts: protection of the public, general and individual deterrence, retribution or reform. It is important to recognise that these theories come after the event and are used to justify the fact of imprisonment. The exercise of power and the need to discipline precedes them. This reality is central to an understanding of any prison system. It is a reality as important today as it has been in the past; a reality which is recognised by those who live and work in prison, whatever the style of their uniform. Prison riots are more likely to be against the use of power in prison than against material conditions. Major disturbances in the 1980s in Scottish prisons, which have taken place in modern, well-equipped prisons as well as in antiquated ones, have underlined this point.

Foucault (1977) has described the study of the metamorphosis of punitive methods in terms of the history of power relations. The move towards a legitimate exercise of power which would exert punishment in an accountable fashion, rather than exact vengeance, paved the way for an increased use of imprisonment in which punishment could at least be measured by the length of sentence imposed. It also allowed punishment to be used as a technique for the coercion of individuals. In common with other institutions a distinguishing feature of the prison was to be meticulous attention to detail in which the prisoner was to be reformed by subjection to discipline at every turn.

A key feature of the new discipline of imprisonment introduced in the latter part of the nineteenth century was the isolation of the prisoner from all but those influences which were to contribute to the disciplinary process. This isolation took two main forms: that which kept prisoners *separate* from each other at all times and that which allowed prisoners to work alongside others but demanded that they remain *silent* at all times.

The distinction between the two systems of management was first recognised in the United States where the operation of the silent system in New York was contrasted with that of the separate system in Pennsylvania. In the early part of the nineteenth century the debate was introduced to England. Those prison authorities which opted for the silent system were attracted by the ease with which it was possible to introduce it within existing buildings and without any significant increase in staff. The military precision which its operation required made it particularly popular to some. However, the application of the silent system required a degree of harshness in the administration of prison discipline which was unacceptable even in those times. It was impossible in practical terms to enforce complete silence and to preclude all forms of communication among large numbers of prisoners. Strength of argument at the time was on the side of those who promoted the separate system and the extensive prison building programme which took place during the first half of the nineteenth century contributed greatly to its spread.

Of the five Inspectors of Prisons appointed in 1835 two, Williams and Hawkins, who were respectively responsible for the north and east and the south and west of England, favoured the silent system and three, Crawford and Russell from the Home Counties and Hill from

Scotland, favoured the separate system. The degree to which the Inspectors were prepared to argue their opinions in public and in their annual reports would not be possible within modern bureaucracy but it did excite considerable public discussion on this 'most prominent topic'. Official debate of the time on the relative merits of the two systems is documented in McConville (1981).

Although official history has attributed the birth of the separate system of imprisonment to the Pennsylvania Penitentiary and subsequently in Britain to Pentonville Prison in 1842, reference has been made in chapter two to the earlier development of a broadly similar system in Glasgow Bridewell under William Brebner.

The Scottish system had several distinguishing characteristics. Brebner had little faith in the reformatory power of the prison unless it paid close attention to the environment from which the prisoner had come and to which he would return on release. This was achieved by communication with families, by education, by providing training in work which might be available to the prisoner on release and by making arrangements for support after liberation.

Under the influence of Brebner, Frederic Hill became a firm supporter of this amended form of the separate system. He encouraged its introduction into other Scottish prisons and ensured that it was adopted for the new General Prison at Perth in 1842. The system was described as 'separation without solitude'. Prisoners received 'at least ten visits daily' from chaplains, teachers and others and during this period there is frequent reference in official reports to the good done by staff who were prepared to talk to prisoners. Although prisoners were not allowed to speak to each other it should be noted that the screened boxes in chapel and the face masks used during exercise periods which were so common in England were experimented with only briefly in Scotland before being dismissed. One important feature of the Scottish system was the emphasis placed on productive rather than unproductive labour. Prisoners were given an allocation of this work estimated to occupy them for ten hours each day. Any work done in excess of this allocation resulted in payment which the prisoner could send to his family or else receive directly on liberation. Staff in the General Prison at Perth in 1845 included instructors in shoe-making, weaving, tailoring and mechanics.

This was not the separate system of imprisonment as it was understood in England. William Crawford and Joshua Jebb, who were by then English Convict Prison Commissioners, visited Perth General

Prison in 1844 and subsequently wrote to the General Board of Directors of Prisons to express their concern.

> In our inspection of this Prison we found much to commend in several of its departments. The discipline, however, appears to us to be strikingly defective in several important particulars. In the employments assigned to the prisoners, there is nothing which partakes of the character of hard-labour. The prisoners are allowed a portion of their earnings, which is either reserved for them until their discharge, or sent, at their request, to their relations. The deprivation of personal liberty is still farther alleviated by the prisoners being allowed to write to their friends, and receive visits from them once in three months, and to receive letters from them at all times. The arrangement of the windows admits of communication between prisoners in adjoining cells, and deprives the separation of its most severe character; and the general administration of the discipline is more characteristic of an institution having simply in view an object of benevolence, than of a prison, the design of which is to punish, as well as to reform. On these several points, we submit, that measures should be taken for rendering the discipline more stringent.
> (*Report to the General Board, 19 September 1844*)

The English commissioners had no authority in Scotland although they had visited Perth Prison at the invitation of the General Board of Prisons. The comments which they submitted after their 'inspection' clearly rankled with Frederic Hill. In his annual report for the following year he took pains to point out that twice as many people in proportion to the respective populations had been sentenced to transportation in the three preceding years in England as in Scotland. In Scotland there was no provision for Poor Law relief for able bodied persons.

Given these two differences Hill suggested that proof of the efficacy of the Scottish system of prison discipline was to be found in the fact that re-committal rates in Scotland were no higher than in England. He went on to provide a comprehensive critique of the Scottish version of the separate system of imprisonment.

> I believe, and I think the experience of Scotland alone has been sufficient to demonstrate the fact, that the separate system, if not made an iron rule, and resorted to in all cases without reference to the age and mental condition of the offender, can be applied

with perfect safety, and (for moderate periods of time) with great moral benefit; that is, provided the prisoners be placed under humane officers, and supplied with useful labour for their working hours, and with interesting and instructive books for their leisure time; for, without these, I should protest against the separate system.

Again, I believe the notion that the prisons in Scotland have, to a great extent, lost their penal character to be quite unfounded; on the contrary, I am of the opinion, notwithstanding all that has been done to improve the condition of the prisoners, that to the really criminal in habits the prisons were never so much dreaded as at this moment.

I attribute the mistake to the superficial view likely to be taken by anyone who walks through one of the present prisons in Scotland, and who does not take various matters into consideration which it is necessary to bear in mind. Such a visitor will see a number of people neatly dressed, clean, in small rooms certainly but sufficiently warm and tolerably well lighted, busily engaged at spinning, weaving, shoe-making, mat-making, knitting, sewing, picking old cords, and various other kinds of work; and in his round he will probably meet the chaplain and teacher, employed in exhortation and instruction. If he waits till dinner-time he will see the prisoners get a meal of plain but wholesome food; and if he should possibly stay till bed-time he may see them comfortably lodge for the night in their hammocks. And such a visitor may say to himself, on quitting the prison, 'Why, what is there penal in all this? These people are probably better fed, better clothed, and better lodged than they would be in their own houses, or than many an honest man is who never injured society! Such a system must act rather as a premium to crime than as a terror to evil-doers.'

But let the visitor reflect that, first, as respects the honest workman, the prisoner has entirely lost his freedom, and ceased to be his own master; that he is not only cut off from family and friends, but that, generally, he is deprived of companionship altogether; that he must neither whistle, sing, nor shout; that day after day, and month after month, except at the intervals of exercise, he is confined within the four walls of his little cell, Sundays and holidays affording no relief, the very changes of the season almost unknown to him, for all, at least, that he can partake of their charms – who let him think of this, and he will probably be of opinion that, although the prisoners were fed on turtle, instead of barley broth and slept on down, instead of straw, there would still be few applicants among the honest

working class for permission to occupy their places.
(*Annual Report of Inspector of Prisons for Scotland, 1845*)

This public declaration of the Scottish position underlines not only the difference from the strict version of the separate system but also provides a topical response to the principle of less-eligibility by addressing head on the relationship between the treatment of prisoners and the conditions of the honest working man.

This view was shared by the General Board of Directors and in November 1844 it wrote to the Home Secretary in response to the comments of the English Convict Prison Commissioners. It admitted that there was no hard labour in Perth General Prison but reminded the Home Secretary of the statutory requirement that prison labour should be 'useful'. It further reminded him that it was he who had approved the rule which permitted crediting earnings to prisoners and that this was done to encourage them to acquire habits of industry. The Board went on to point out that all contact between a prisoner and his friends had to be approved by the governor of the prison and that this was allowed with a view to encouraging domestic ties and social stability.

Whatever the logic of the Scottish argument it transpired, not for the last time, that English officials were more adept than their Scottish counterparts at influencing political masters. They were able to convince the Secretary of State that it was more important for prison labour to be penal and deterrent than that it should be productive. Hill had asked to be transferred to one of the English Inspectorates to be nearer his family in London. By this time he was the most influential of the inspectors and might have hoped to be given the Home District which covered London. Instead he was posted in 1848 to the Northern and Eastern District of England, quite probably because his more moderate expectations of what imprisonment might reasonably hope to achieve would not have been welcome in London.

Hill's immediate successor in Scotland was Captain Donatus O'Brien. Within a matter of months O'Brien was transferred south and was subsequently appointed a Director of Convict Prisons in England. The third Inspector of Prisons in Scotland was Captain John Kincaid. He was willing to advocate the standard discipline of the separate system. In 1850 he recommended to the General Board of Directors that the crank machine, a form of labour which was very tiring for the prisoner but which had no useful outcome, should be introduced as a system of penal labour. In the face of such pressure from the government, now supported by the Inspector of Prisons, the Directors accepted the inevitability of hard labour:

> The result of our enquiries was, that we came to be satisfied that
> Penal Labour, by means of Crank-machinery is to be viewed, as,
> on the whole, the most efficient and suitable description of Hard
> Labour in Prisons, and the one, therefore, which must chiefly be
> looked to for affording the means of giving due effect in
> Scotland to Sentences of Imprisonment accompanied with Hard
> Labour. (*Annual Report, 1853*)

In the interests of bringing Scotland into line with mainstream thinking on the separate system the Home Office had sent to Scotland the strictest of their Inspectors (McConville, 1981). At his insistence the General Board introduced in 1852 a provision whereby all convicted prisoners, male and female, during the first month of sentence were required to sleep on a wooden guard bed rather than in a normal bed or hammock. Kincaid spread this practice to prisons in the north of England when his responsibilities were extended there.

The changes introduced in this way, which some might argue were retrogressive and designed merely to bring the prison regime in Scotland into line with that in England, were adopted by the new administration after 1860. Thus was the standard style of the separate system introduced into Scottish prisons; a style of which Brebner would not have approved and which was to lead to reports of mental and other illness among prisoners.

The Managers of the General Prison: 1860–1877

The General Board of Directors of Prisons had been set up following the 1839 Prison Act with a two-fold remit. The first part had been to supervise local prisons, to ensure that they had a sound system of management and that there was a uniform, well-regulated pattern of discipline. The second part of its remit was to establish and maintain a General Prison for Scotland at Perth.

The Prisons (Scotland) Administration Act, 1860, abolished the General Board and on 31 December 1860 replaced it with four Managers of the General Prison. In a review of this arrangement the Prison Commissioners for Scotland commented when they took up office that the abolition of the General Board

> was not due to its inefficiency, but to its having brought to a
> virtual conclusion the purposes for which it was established.
> (*Annual Report, 1879*)

The process of centralisation of the management of prisons and the creation of a central administrative organisation was well under way. According to the 1860 Act oversight of the County Boards passed directly to the Secretary of State. In practice he delegated almost all of his powers to the four Managers of the General Prison. Three of the latter were appointed *ex officio*, the Sheriff Principal of the County of Perth, the Inspector of Prisons and the Crown Agent. The fourth was to be Stipendiary Manager and Secretary. Doctor John Hill Burton, Advocate, who had been Secretary to the General Board since 1854, was appointed to this post.

The professional background of the new Managers reinforced the close link between the burgeoning central prison administration and the rest of the criminal justice process which had been confirmed by the composition of the earlier General Board of Directors. This relationship extended to the County Boards, which were required to include the local sheriff among their number.

The General Prison at Perth was to hold three classes of prisoner: ordinary prisoners sentenced to nine months or more, or those sentenced to shorter periods on instruction of the Secretary of State; convicts under sentence of penal servitude or transportation; and criminal lunatics.

The first female convicts had been admitted to the General Prison in 1855 and arrangements were made in 1863 to hold a limited number of male convicts there instead of transferring them after sentence to English convict prisons. Very soon after their admission to the establishment the Managers became aware of the problems likely to occur in the management of prisoners who were serving comparatively long sentences. It was accepted that for these prisoners at least a variation on the usual restrictions of the separate system of imprisonment was necessary and some of them were allowed to work outside. Discontent among the prisoners serving long sentences continued and in the week between Christmas and New Year there was a series of incidents which culminated in the Sheriff-Substitute being called to the prison with a contingent of the local militia.

> Order was quickly restored, and an opportunity immediately
> afterwards taken by the Managers to suppress all manifestations
> of discontent and exact rigorous obedience to the regulations.
> (*Annual Report of the Managers, 1863*)

In their subsequent report on the incident to the Secretary of State the

Managers pointed out that it was a singular disadvantage to have only one prison, however large, designated for convicts, that is, those prisoners who under earlier legislation would have been eligible for transportation.

Convicts were eligible for remission of part of their sentences subject to good behaviour. In today's prison system it has been generally established that a prisoner's eligibility for remission subject to good behaviour is an entitlement rather than a privilege. Until comparatively recent times, however, it has often been argued that remission was no more than a privilege. In this respect it is worthy of note that the Managers of the General Prison held the view, according to their annual report for 1862, that remission was to be regarded as an entitlement and they were reluctant to recommend its forfeiture. The basis for the opinion adopted by the Managers in this respect is relevant to a modern discussion on the use of remission and parole. It was their view that

> the exercise of any material influence over the length of the
> sentences of criminals is not a function suitable to executive
> officers intrusted with their custody. (*Annual Report, 1864*)

In this respect the Managers of the General Prison were probably 120 years ahead of their time and, had their opinion been sustained by their successors, the prison system of the mid twentieth century might not have had to work its way through the minefield which developed because of the gulf between the length of sentence passed by the court and the actual time spent in prison by the person who had been sentenced.

The Act of 1860 had required that a set of rules for staff should be drawn up. This was duly done and for the first time warders were obliged to satisfy the various requirements necessary to obtain a civil service certificate in order to work in the General Prison. When this requirement was introduced the Managers took the opportunity to point out to the Secretary of State that the salaries of the staff at Perth were significantly lower than those of their counterparts in England. The Secretary of State recognised this discrepancy and the wages of the staff at Perth were duly increased, with the exception of that of the governor, which remained at the level at which it had been set when the prison was opened in 1842.

In 1867 the Managers issued a new set of rules for the General

Prison together with a set of detailed regulations. The latter included the following injunctions to staff:

> Prison officers have in their hands an unfortunate and degraded class of their fellow-creatures whose condition calls for peculiar treatment and special qualifications. It is ever the object of the Managers to support a broad line of distinction between this class and the Officers, as persons whose character and conduct entitle them to be intrusted with highly responsible duties. The Managers trust that the Officers themselves will cooperate in this effort by showing on all occasions a worthy self-respect. They will remember that they are dealing with persons who are feeble in mind as well as sinful, and if they should find that they have to encounter irritability, passion and unreasonableness, they will show their superiority by preserving a demeanour of quiet firmness. Nothing so completely insures an Officer's command over the criminal class as their finding it impossible to irritate him into any unworthy display of passion.

This statement includes an assumption, which would be contentious today, that staff as a body are better people than prisoners. This type of assertion foreshadowed the paternalism of what was later to become known as the rehabilitative model of imprisonment, founded on the belief that the keeper is by definition a better person than the above kept. However, what should not be ignored in the above quotation is the belief expressed by the Managers in the important influence which officers could have on prisoners. A recognition of this cardinal precept has been a continuing feature of the development of prison management in Scotland.

In many respects the seventeen years' tenure of office of the Managers of the General Prison was uneventful. It was significant in that it consolidated the central government supervision of Scottish prisons which had begun with the appointment of the first Inspector in 1835. This supervision, particularly in so far as it was delegated by the Home Secretary in London first to the General Board and subsequently to the Managers based in Edinburgh, was much more direct in nature than that exercised during the same period in England. It was also less remote in that local and national interests were well represented by a combination of members of the close-knit legal fraternity and what were delicately referred to in the annual report for 1879 as 'statesmen in retirement whose voice was likely to be influential with the political rulers of the day'.

There was no equivalent in England to the General Prison at Perth, which, it should be emphasised, was not a convict prison, although it did hold convicts during the first year of sentence, but a central prison holding prisoners from all over Scotland who had been sentenced to nine months' imprisonment or more. The General Prison was in many respects used as a model for all other prisons. Its rules and regulations were transferred almost verbatim for application in prisons which were administered by County Boards. It might well be argued that by the mid 1870s the only responsibility in prison matters which remained firmly with local authorities was that of raising the necessary finance. This was a responsibility which the authorities were happy to lose. So in Scotland the climate was ready for the changes which were to be introduced by the Prisons (Scotland) Act, 1877, an Act which sealed central government control of prisons.

4 The Consolidation of Central Control
The Prison Commission for Scotland: 1877-1929

> We suggest that the intellectual error made in 1876–7, and one
> often but less exclusively repeated in our day, was the
> assumption that, because the administration of prisons by the
> County and Borough Authorities had become inadmissible, the
> administration of all the prisons by a Department of the Central
> Government was necessarily the best, or more correctly, the only
> alternative. One of the lessons of Political Science is that the
> 'opposite of the wrong' is seldom, ever, found to be 'the right'.
> (Webbs, 1922)

The Prisons Act of 1877, which applied to England and Wales,
involved more significant organisational changes than the parallel
legislation in Scotland. South of the border the convict and local
systems were separate. Central oversight of the various local systems
was much less direct and it was foreseen that central control would lead
to a greater degree of anonymity than was likely in Scotland. The
legislation as far as Scotland was concerned was the logical conclusion
to the increasing centralisation of the Scottish system which had been
taking place progressively for almost forty years. In England, on the
other hand, the legislation was seen as introducing an alternative
system. Opposition to this new arrangement never quite died as can be
adduced from the above quotation.

J E Thomas (1972) has commented that this centralising legislation
was the result not of political ideology nor of philosophical dogma but
of pragmatism, illustrated by the fact that it was passed by the
government of Disraeli, despite the opposition which it had to centrali-

sation. The Home Secretary who introduced the Bill, Sir Richard Assheton Cross, was originally loathe to have any tightening of central government control. Why then was this legislation introduced?

Sir Edmund Du Cane, who was to become Chairman of the English Prison Commissioners, pressed the need for uniformity of administration but McConville (1981) has shown that the main justification was financial. Conservative back benchers were demanding that something be done to reduce rates and the government decided to achieve this through a redistribution of the burden of criminal justice expenditure from the rate payer to the tax payer. The lesson of how this legislation, which provided the context within which the prison services of the United Kingdom were to operate and to develop until well into the twentieth century, was introduced for reasons which had very little to do with penal principles is one which should not be forgotten by students of penology.

The Prisons Act 1877, which affected the prison system in England and Wales, received Royal Assent on 12 July 1877. The Prisons (Scotland) Act 1877 received Royal Assent on 14 August 1877 and both Acts came into force on 1 April 1878. The first substantive section of the Act relating to Scotland confirmed the underlying justification for the legislation:

> On and after the commencement of this Act all expenses
> incurred in respect of the maintenance of prisons to which this
> Act applies, and of the many prisoners therein, shall be defrayed
> out of moneys provided by Parliament.

So, the Conservative members of parliament and the rate payers had their way. All existing prisons were transferred to the Secretary of State and provisions were made for financial compensation from local authorities which had inadequate or insufficient prison accommodation.

A body of Prison Commissioners was to be set up to administer prisons on behalf of the Secretary of State. In addition to the Sheriff Principal of the County of Perth and the Crown Agent, who were to be commissioners *ex officio,* there was to be a maximum of three other commissioners appointed by Royal Warrant. The posts of inspector (by this time there were only two for the whole of Great Britain) were to remain but they were now to be simply assistants to the commissioners. The Secretary of State retained the right to appoint all governors, matrons, medical officers and chaplains. Other officers were to be appointed by the commissioners. The latter were required to prepare an annual report which would be laid before Parliament.

A Visiting Committee for each prison, consisting of commissioners of supply, justices of the peace and magistrates, was to be appointed. There was to be no restriction on any committee member from visiting any part of the prison or any prisoner at any time. They were to be required to visit the prison frequently and to hear any complaints made to them by prisoners. They had as yet no disciplinary function. In their first annual report (1879) the Prison Commissioners for Scotland described this inversion of role as one of the main features of the new legislation,

> insofar as under previous legislation the local authorities were
> the executive, administering the prisons, while the Government
> watched and inspected their administration; now the Government
> administers, while the local authorities in Scotland, in the shape
> of visiting committees, watch and inspect, the Government also
> inspecting for its own purposes.

It was somewhat disingenuous to suggest that while responsibility had been inverted the actual form of inspection would remain the same. Governments from 1835 had been content to use the government inspectors as agents for change who, in their published annual reports, were not slow to criticise local authorities and individual governors for tardiness in implementing recommended changes. This was not a role which local authorities were to be allowed to adopt in respect of government run prisons. Visiting Committees did not publish annual reports and their influence on the management of prisons was minimal from the outset.

One of the principal practical benefits of the new legislation was that it enabled the Secretary of State to transfer prisoners from one prison to another, a practice which had not normally been possible previously. This allowed for a more even distribution of prisoners among the available prisons. In addition to the General Prison at Perth the Commissioners took over direct responsibility for fifty-six county prisons in April 1878. Within one year of taking up office the Commissioners had reduced this number to forty-three. Three years later, on 31 March 1882, there were only thirty-five remaining and by 1888 this number had been reduced to fifteen.

All staff who had previously been employed in county prisons were transferred to government employment and became civil servants. At the end of March 1879 the Commissioners recorded a total of 504 staff in all prisons. Minimum entry age for males was set at twenty-four years and for females at twenty-two. At an early stage the Commissioners introduced uniform scales of pay throughout the country and arranged a scheme of periodic increases of pay to be awarded against good service certificates. According to the Act staff became liable to

> be distributed amongst the several prisons to which this Act
> applies in such manner as may be directed by the Secretary of
> State.

This was a major change in the conditions of service of staff and one which was to be of great significance in later years. The provision of prison quarters to accommodate staff, and their movement around the country led to a sense of isolation from the community at large and to a feeling of solidarity among staff who came to regard themselves as something of a breed apart.

The Prison Commissioners

Prison Commissioners: 1877-1929

	Chairman	Commissioners	
1877	Thomas Lee	T Folliott Powell	John H Burton
1880	Andrew B Bell	T Folliott Powell	John H Burton
1881	Andrew B Bell	T Folliott Powell	
1885	Andrew B Bell	Alex B McHardy	
1896	Alex B McHardy	Walter H Haddow	
1909	Lord Polwarth	Walter H Haddow	
1913	Lord Polwarth	James Devon	

During this period the Sheriff of Perth and the Crown Agent were Commissioners *ex officio*.

Throughout the last twenty years of the nineteenth century the English Prison Commission was dominated by Sir Edmund Du Cane, an arch-autocrat who ran the service in a virtually single-handed manner and who was considered by some commentators to have been 'the greatest figure in the history of the English Prison System' (Thomas, 1972). Du Cane's successor, Sir Evelyn Ruggles-Brise, directed the English service in a similar fashion during the first twenty years of the twentieth century. There is no comparative figure in Scotland.

The reason for this is probably two-fold. In the first place the architects of the Scottish prison system are to be found in the middle rather than at the end of the nineteenth century. The process of centralisation in Scotland was completed rather than begun by the Act of 1877 as was noted by the Scots Commissioners both in their evidence to the Elgin Committee of 1900 and in their tenth annual report:

> The management of the Scottish Prisons came under the control
> more or less complete of a central board in 1840, nearly half a
> century ago, and they have been in this respect widely different
> in their administration from the Prisons in England, which
> passed into Government control only twelve years since.

The second feature, which was also largely responsible for the separate identity of the Scottish system, was the fact that from the outset the prison service had been an integral part of the Scottish criminal justice process, locked securely into the close-knit legal system. The General Board of Directors, which took office in 1839, included among its nineteen members the Lord Justice General, the Lord Justice Clerk, the Lord Advocate, the Solicitor General, the Dean of the Faculty of Advocates and five sheriffs. The Managers of the General Prison, who were in office between 1860 and 1877 were, in addition to the Inspector of Prisons: the Sheriff Principal of Perth, the Crown Agent, and an advocate as secretary. Throughout the fifty-two years of its existence the Sheriff Principal of Perth and the Crown Agent remained members of the Prison Commission.

Thomas Lee, Sheriff of Perth, was appointed first Chairman of the Prison Commission for Scotland. In 1880 he was elevated to the judicial bench. The second chairman continued the legal tradition. Andrew Beatson Bell was an advocate and under him the Commission continued to exercise its role effectively but unobtrusively. The only occasion on which he seems to have found it necessary to show his teeth was in connection with the right of Scotland to convict labour in opposition to the wishes of Du Cane. This incident is dealt with later in this chapter.

The *eminence grise* of the Commission's first four years was Advocate John Hill Burton who had been appointed Secretary of the General Board in 1854 and who had been Stipendiary Manager between 1860 and 1877, moving on to the Commission where he remained until his death in 1881. Although unsalaried, Burton was sure enough of his position to, for example, argue successfully in 1878 against his colleague Folliott Powell who wanted to follow the English example and introduce the grade of Principal Warder (Scottish Record Office, HH57/30A).

The English Prison Service has been widely recognised for the military background particularly of its senior staff. Notwithstanding the presence of several military men after major wars, the situation was different in Scotland, where the link was more closely with the legal fraternity. Ironically the one man who, if anyone is to claim the title, was the leading figure in the Scottish prison system in the early part of the twentieth century was the exception to this rule. Alexander Burness McHardy, Commissioner between 1885 and 1896 and Chairman from then until his retirement in 1909, was both a military man and a protege of Du Cane. When Folliott Powell died in 1885 the Prison Commissioners for Scotland asked the newly appointed Secretary for Scotland, to whom they were now responsible, for permission to combine the roles of secretary and second commissioner. The Duke of Richmond and Gordon did not agree with the proposal and minuted to the Lord Advocate:

> I have consulted Sir Edmund Du Cane who knows most of the applicants whom he would recommend. He tells me Major McHardy, RE, is by far the best man on the list.

Like Du Cane and so many others in the English service McHardy held a commission in the Royal Engineers. Du Cane had brought him into the English Prison Service in 1877 and at the time of his appointment in Scotland he was Surveyor of Prisons in England. In their annual report for 1909 the Commissioners marked his retirement by recording their appreciation of McHardy's efforts on their behalf, and they repeated this in fuller fashion at their meeting on 5 November in that year:

> He has left unmistakenly the impress of his work upon the Prison System of Scotland. It is to be seen in the Prison Buildings themselves, many of which were entirely re-built or largely re-constructed in accordance with his plans and under his immediate supervision; these 'building' operations having been carried out mainly by prisoners working under the direction of

Officers of the Prison Staff, thereby not only effecting a very great saving in expense, but also affording prisoners a valuable training in building and construction work, qualifying many of them for honest employment after their liberation. Even more marked is the effect of his work in infusing into the Prison Administration of Scotland a spirit of reform.

A strict disciplinarian he yet ever strove to inspire the whole Staff with his own ideas of kindness, sympathy and consideration in the treatment of prisoners. He always took a broad view of his duties as Chairman of the Prison Commission and was never content to be a mere gaolor caring only for the safe custody of those in his charge, but made a wider study of problems of crime – its causes, treatment and prevention.

On 26 October 1909 the Honourable Walter George Hepburne-Scott, Master of Polwarth, was appointed Chairman of the Prison Commissioners. He had previously held office as Chairman of the General Board of Lunacy for Scotland. Polwarth continued to exercise the role of chairman in an unobtrusive manner. Like McHardy he took a broad view of his responsibilities and was prepared to make reference in his annual reports to features of the criminal justice process which were outside his immediate area of responsibility. He frequently referred to the benefits of probation as a method of reducing the increasing number of short term prisoners. In 1902 McHardy had travelled to the United States to study prison methods and in 1910 Polwarth went to Washington as the first official Scottish representative to the International Prison Congress.

The last individual to be appointed a Commissioner was Dr James Devon in 1913. His was an interesting example of poacher turned gamekeeper. He had previously been Medical Officer at Barlinnie Prison and in that role had been instrumental in organising classes in basic first-aid for warders and in extending these classes to other establishments. Prior to his appointment to the Commission Devon had little regard for his future colleagues and took the unusual step of expressing this publicly in the columns of the *Glasgow Herald*:

All the prisons in Scotland are under the control of a Board in Edinburgh consisting of two *ex officio* and two salaried members. The *ex officio* members are seldom, it may be never, within the prisons, and the management is to all practical purposes in the hands of the others. If, by any chance, one of these should be an incompetent person, the power of the other, administratively, would be supreme; and the bureaucracy would become an autocracy. There is no independent inspection of the work of the Board: the Commissioners report on their own work. They appoint, promote or dismiss all warders; they control and direct all other prison officials. Yet they cannot know local conditions as local men do; and they are not in a position to know much of the needs, other than physical, of the prisoners. They may arrange that the prison be kept right; they cannot arrange that the prisoner be put right, where there are as many points of difference in character and capacity between criminals as between, let us say, officials. (*29 January 1908*)

The Commissioners debated whether Devon should be disciplined or if they should respond publicly to this attack. In the end they decided to take no action and some five years later the same man was appointed as Commissioner to replace Walter Haddow.

This small group of men, Prison Commissioners for Scotland, administered the prison system at a time of great change. The central notion of the prison as a controlling mechanism of the state was confirmed and the notion of reformation of the individual through strict discipline, 'dressage', was reinforced. Yet within this context the Scottish Commissioners retained, frequently in the face of opposition from south of the border, important features of the Scottish system, such as the attitude to useful labour, to links with family and to preparation for release, which had been distinguishing features of the Scottish prison system since the first half of the nineteenth century.

Peterhead Convict Prison

The period of office of the Prison Commissioners was a time of considerable redistribution of the prison estate. When they came into office in 1878 they took over responsibility for fifty-seven prisons, including those in towns such as Greenlaw, Alloa, Campbeltown, Kirkcudbright, Dunblane and Dornoch. By the time they demitted office in 1929 there remained only twelve prisons, including most of the major establishments which are in use today.

Perth, of course, pre-dated the Commission. Building commenced at Barlinnie and Dumfries in 1882, at Peterhead in 1886, at Aberdeen in 1890 and at Inverness in 1901. The Borstal system had been introduced in Scotland with the purchase in 1911 of Blairlodge School at Polmont in Stirlingshire. The majority of prisons were built largely by prisoner labour.

The place of Peterhead in the prison system of today will be discussed in chapter six in connection with difficult prisoners. The story of its construction is worthy of fuller description not only because of its later significance but also as a well-documented example of how a prison came to be built. The new Commissioners received their Royal Warrants of appointment in August 1877. Within six weeks John Hill Burton was writing as follows to his new colleagues, who had not yet taken up office:

> It has been noticed that while Scotland contributes her share to the costs of maintaining (convicts) England has the benefit of the whole expenditure, along with any local service that may accrue in the shape of harbours or other works. It has sometimes been suggested that convict labour might be beneficially applied in fertilising the wastes of the Highlands and Islands or in supplying harbours of refuge or other safeguards for the navigation of the Northern Seas. Both these forms of production are of a kind not likely to excite local trade jealousy.
> (*Memorandum of 2 November 1877, Scottish Record Office*)

As has happened so often since, the pressure for a major penological change came not from any principle, philosophical or practical, but from a pragmatic consideration, in this case that Scotland was entitled to benefit from the labour of its convicts. This suggestion gained considerable support and the proposal which was most favoured was the construction of a harbour of refuge somewhere on the east coast of the country. In 1884 a parliamentary sub-committee was appointed to settle on the most suitable location. The short list was narrowed to Montrose or Peterhead and in due course the committee reported that:

> The most likely project for benefitting the shipping and fishing interests of the country at large, and at the same time profitably employing convicts, is the construction of a harbour of refuge at Peterhead, in Aberdeenshire.

The removal of all Scottish convicts from the English convict system would have entailed a significant reduction in the numbers available for public works there. Sir Edmund Du Cane saw that a considerable piece of his empire was in danger of disappearing and in August 1884 he curtly advised the Home Office that no convicts currently in the English system would be available to work at Peterhead until 1888 or 1889. The Home Office was aware of the game which Du Cane was playing and was not prepared to let him off the hook. It pointed out to him that in his evidence to the sub-committee he had said that there were between 600 and 650 Scottish convicts available for public works. It was further pointed out that Scottish sentiment on the issue could not be overlooked:

> Indeed it can fairly be said that the feeling in Scotland on the subject which can be very high at one time has been positively quiescent for some time past, in the full expectation that, after the Parliamentary Report of the Sub-Committee in favour of Peterhead, this question was practically settled. (*Memorandum from the Home Office to the Prison Commissioners, 9 August 1884*)

The Home Office then confirmed to the Treasury that between 600 and 650 Scottish convicts would be available for public works at Peterhead, of whom about 500 would make up the daily working parties. At the beginning of September 1884 the Treasury agreed in principle to the proposals. In early 1885 Andrew Beatson Bell, Chairman of the Scottish Commissioners, and Sir John Goode, Engineer-in-Chief for the construction of the proposed breakwater, visited several sites in the area and in March recommended that the prison should be built at Salthouse Point, adjacent to the harbour, while the quarry from which the granite for the breakwater was to be extracted should be some two and a half miles away at Boddam Castle, with a connecting railway between the two.

Having lost the battle over the work to be done at Peterhead, Du Cane attempted to influence the location of the prison, suggesting that it should be built at the quarry rather than at the breakwater. Bell, however, was not to be moved and insisted that the chosen site was the correct one. In May 1885 Du Cane was asked by the Home Office whether he had any final comment. His reply was somewhat petulant:

> I don't think anybody can doubt that the position involves some considerable risks and disadvantages; but if everybody concerned is prepared to accept and overcome them there is no more to be said. (*Correspondence with the Home Office, April 1885*)

The Prison Commissioners submitted an estimate of £99,519 for the construction of the new prison. The Treasury finally beat them down to £57,400 by insisting that corrugated iron rather than stone be used in constructing the prison chapel, that the height of the perimeter wall be reduced and that water closets should be replaced by dry closets. The land on which the development was to take place was owned by the Edinburgh Merchant Company and a figure of £5,000 was agreed for its purchase.

On 25 June 1886 the Peterhead Harbour of Refuge Act (49 & 50 Victoriae c.49) received the Royal Assent. According to the practice of the time when building new prisons, the first cell block was built by contract and the remainder by prison labour. On 29 June 1888 an Order in Council was approved,

> That the said Prison at Peterhead in the County of Aberdeen,
> with the whole buildings and grounds pertaining thereto, shall be
> a General Prison for the confinement of male prisoners sentenced
> to penal servitude.

The use of convicts on public works in Scotland was described by the Commissioners in 1889 as 'an entirely new departure in the history of criminals'. Staff were transferred from other Scottish prisons. As one might imagine there was a great deal of excitement in the small fishing town at the prospect of the arrival of the incomers. This was recorded in the *Peterhead Sentinel and Buchan Journal* on 10 August 1888:

> On Tuesday (7 August) the Peterhead Convict Prison – the first
> and only convict establishment in Scotland – received its first
> gang of convicts, who are now daily employed in work about the
> prison buildings. Their arrival caused considerable excitement in
> town, and for some days previously the railway station had been
> practically besieged day and night by crowds eager to see the
> prisoners . . .
> The convicts – twenty in number – were despatched from
> Perth General Prison on Tuesday morning . . . They travelled in
> a prison van – the only one of the kind in use in Scotland for
> railway purposes . . . At Peterhead station the arrival of the train
> was awaited by an immense crowd of all sorts of people, and
> there was tremendous crushing and pushing for good places.
> Since Wednesday the convicts have been daily at work in and
> near the prison buildings . . . Each gang at work is guarded by
> three warders, all of them armed with sword bayonets, while one
> carries a loaded carbine. These constantly keep their eyes on the
> prisoners, ready to deal with any symptom of an attempt at

escape. Much curiosity has been evinced to see the convicts at work, and yesterday forenoon quite a large number of telescopes and glasses were levelled at them from the town.

The convicts soon settled to their task. Their daily life was similar to what they would have expected in an English public works prison:

> They sleep in separate cells, but work in association; they are required to be industrious; and conversation, beyond what is absolutely necessary, is prohibited. They are provided with ample clothing, food, and allowed the use of library books in addition to the religious books with which every cell is furnished. (*Annual Report of the Commissioners, 1889*)

At the end of 1888 there were 114 convicts in Peterhead. Of these it was reported that 13 were serving their first sentence of imprisonment, 63 had undergone previous prison sentences and 38 had already served sentences of penal servitude. The mark system, common in convict prisons, was applied and a 'well behaved and industrious convict' might hope to be awarded sufficient marks to allow release after about three quarters of his sentence had been served.

The retention in Scotland of all prisoners convicted to penal servitude coincided with a fall in the numbers so sentenced. The Commissioners provided a double explanation for this fall: a decrease in serious crime in Scotland and a reduction in severity of the sentences passed by courts. This meant that convict numbers did not build up as quickly as had been hoped. By 1893 they had only risen to 330 and Admiralty engineers were expressing concern at the length of time being taken to construct the breakwater. Control of the quarry rested with the Admiralty who appointed a civilian quarry master. Some eighty were employed at the quarry with another seventy or so employed under master masons to dress the granite in the Admiralty Yard beside the prison.

During the early years of the century the annual average number of convicts in Peterhead was about 350, with a peak in March 1911 of 455. Even after completion of the breakwater prisoners continued to travel daily by the private prison train to labour in the granite quarry. From the time of its opening until 1939 officers carried cutlasses and prisoners were not normally allowed to come closer to any member of staff than a cutlass length. The quarry closed in 1957 and two years later the Admiralty Yard was handed over to the prison authorities.

Until this date officers appointed to guard prisoners in the external work parties carried rifles. The last recorded death of a prisoner by shooting was in July 1932 when three convicts attempted to escape from the Admiralty Yard. One of the escapers, a convict named Kynoch, was shot and killed by Warder Whyte. An inquiry into the shooting was held under the Fatal Accidents and Sudden Deaths Inquiry (Scotland) Act 1906, when the jury found that the prison officer had fired 'in the ordinary execution of his duties' and in accordance with prison regulations.

Peterhead Prison has, virtually from the date of its construction, been of symbolic pre-eminence in any consideration of the Scottish prison system: Scotland's only convict prison, a grim and depressing set of buildings on a headland jutting into the North Sea. As the twentieth century unfolded it recruited more and more of its staff from the local Buchan area. Their cultural roots were far removed from those of the prisoners, most of whom came from the central belt of Scotland. A sense of isolation which eventually became alienation was fostered, a fine irony for a prison which came into existence so that its prisoners could be employed on work which would benefit the community.

Report of the Elgin Committee (1900)

The major report on English prisons which was produced by the Gladstone Committee in 1895 had no application in Scotland although members of the committee visited Barlinnie and Perth Prisons for comparative purposes. The Prison Commissioners for Scotland had very little comment to make on the report at the time, other than to dismiss its proposal that two or more prisons should be selected as training schools for all ranks of prison staff on the grounds that staff in all prisons should be trained to an equal level of efficiency. The oft quoted dictum contained in paragraph 47 of the Gladstone Report, 'that prison treatment should have as its primary and concurrent objects, deterrence and reformation' had been a central tenet of official policy in Scotland since the Glasgow Bridewell had been extended in 1822 'for the punishment and amelioration of delinquents'.

Of much greater importance for a proper understanding of the development of the Scottish prison system at the turn of the century is the Report of the Elgin Committee of 1900. On 28 February 1898 a group of Scottish members of parliament met with Lord Balfour, the Secretary for Scotland, and presented him with an unsigned document,

Reasons for an Inquiry into the Administration of Scottish Prisons such as has been granted to the English and Irish Prison Services. The document went on at some length to describe the alleged inadequacies in the Scottish prison system. On 28 August 1899 Balfour responded by appointing a five man committee under the chairmanship of the Earl of Elgin and Kincardine to investigate the allegations. There were five terms of reference, although the committee took a broad view of these:

> We have constructed this reference to mean that the whole of
> prison life as it affects the prisoner was included in our Inquiry,
> and that nothing of the nature of prison treatment was excluded
> from our cognizance.

In its introduction the report dismissed any suggestion that the Prison Commissioners and their staff had been other than positive and humane in the administration of both the system and individual establishments. It regretted that the memorandum which caused the Secretary for Scotland to set up the committee was anonymous, thus preventing its authors from being examined. Despite this the committee considered that it had exhaustively studied all the allegations made:

> The results of such investigation will appear below, but it is our
> duty to say here that we found nothing to justify the very hostile
> denunciation of the whole administration of Scottish prisons; and
> that we regret the bitter spirit in which this paper was conceived
> and the veil of anonymity by which it was discovered.

The committee's first term of reference was to examine 'the provision made in Scottish prisons for the nursing and accommodation of sick prisoners'. In setting the argument which was to be followed, the report presented an interesting statement of the obverse of the principle of less-eligibility:

> A sick prisoner ought, we think, to receive at least as prompt and
> satisfactory treatment as he could have obtained had he not been
> in prison.

In other words, the prisoner was not to be put at a disadvantage in this respect because he was in prison, a sentiment very much in the spirit of the modern justice model of imprisonment.

In the committee's view the existing regulations allowed for this.

However one major difference between Scottish and English regulations was that the former allowed the removal of a serving prisoner to an infirmary or hospital either for the sake of the health of other prisoners or because he himself was in immediate danger. The committee considered this provision to be a significant advantage and recommended that its application should be extended. It was generally content with the resources available for the treatment within prisons of those prisoners who had minor illnesses. The report suggested that male 'nurse warders' should undergo a period of training in the Barlinnie Prison hospital and their female counterparts similarly in the female prison in Duke Street, Glasgow. It rejected the allegation in the memorandum that 'proper nursing arrangements are still entirely absent in Scottish prisons'. It was equally firm in its rejection of the allegation that the location of several sick prisoners in prison hospital cells without proper supervision led to these cells becoming hot beds 'of moral corruption' involving 'the gravest contamination or the grossest intimacies being contracted'. This section of the report contained one recommendation which was specifically intended to assist medical officers but which had the wider result of pushing prisons into the twentieth century more generally:

> We understand the Chairman of the Prison Commissioners to
> object to telephones, but they are now a recognised convenience
> for the transaction of business, and might, we think, be
> introduced with advantage into the general service of prisons.

The second term of reference of the committee was to consider 'the sufficiency of the accommodation provided in the prisons of Scotland for ordinary prisoners'. The original memorandum had specified three areas of complaint. The first was that the General Prison at Perth, 'the best and foremost prison of Scotland', was being all but abandoned. At that time two of the cell blocks were lying empty. The second complaint was that the provision of places for an additional 400 prisoners at Barlinnie was unnecessary as these prisoners could have been accommodated at Perth. Finally, objection was made to the 'unnecessary enlargement and extension of the badly situated, insanitary, antiquated, and long since condemned prison of Dundee, in order to complete the extinction of the model General Prison at Perth'.

In its report the committee acknowledged that there had been instances of overcrowding. They suggested two reasons for the increased number of admissions. '[In] years of good trade and good weather the numbers will rise' and this had been the case in the preceding years. At first sight this was an unusual assertion but the committee's reasoning was that so many offences were drink-related and drunkenness was more likely when people had money in their pockets. As evidence of this they cited the annual increase in the admission rate at the time of the Glasgow Fair holidays. The second reason, which was related to the first, was the increase in the number of statutory offences, most of which were likely to be committed by individuals under the influence of drink. To support its argument the committee compared the situation in Glasgow, with a population of 725,000, to that in Liverpool, with a population of 630,000. In Glasgow there had been in a recent year 19,000 arrests for drunkenness and 21,000 for breach of the peace and petty assaults. The comparable figures in Liverpool had been 4,339 and 800 respectively. One outcome of this discrepancy was that in 1897 the average length of sentence imposed in Scotland was 15 days compared to an average of 28 days in England.

The committee observed that such short-term prisoners 'who are here today and gone tomorrow' learned nothing from a period in prison and posed significant accommodation problems for prison authorities. The Commissioners had standing arrangements for transferring prisoners between establishments to relieve overcrowding but these were of little help when prisoners were serving such short sentences. The main areas of overcrowding were Glasgow and Greenock and the committee suggested that it might be necessary to build a new prison to relieve the latter area. (Within three years the Commission had taken up this suggestion with the construction of Greenock Prison.)

The main reserve of accommodation in the system was in the General Prison at Perth. The report rejected the suggestion that this should be used to relieve overcrowding in the west of Scotland because of the brevity of most prisoners' sentences. As far as prisoners serving longer sentences were concerned the report supported the stance taken by the Prison Commissioners, which was that one of the main objects of the existing system of allocation and the justification for building a new general prison at Barlinnie was to keep the long-term prisoner close to his home environment: 'this is probably of greater importance to him than to the man with a short sentence of a few days only'.

This is a topical observation in the light of present policy and practice. Since the end of the Second World War a basic principle of the national classification system in the Scottish Prison Service has been to separate long-term prisoners from those serving short sentences and to put the long-termers to prisons where they might receive some form of training, regardless of geographical location. There is now a body of opinion which suggests that the primary consideration in allocation should be to keep the prisoner as close as possible to his home environment; that is, a return to the principle applied at the time of the Elgin Committee of Inquiry.

The committee was equally dismissive of the argument in the memorandum that 'the badly situated, insanitary, antiquated, and long since condemned prison of Dundee' was being expanded 'in order to complete the extinction' of Perth Prison. The report was at pains to emphasise that the Dundee Prison was well-appointed and that the re-building, which was undertaken largely by prisoner labour, provided good training for the prisoners involved. It was admitted that the location of the prison was far from ideal but confirmed that a city as large as Dundee could not be left without a prison.

The report gives the impression of less than total enthusiasm for its own argument and in the light of subsequent events it would appear that the Commissioners were indeed expanding Dundee Prison at the expense of Perth. Given the relative sizes of the two centres of population this move would have been in keeping with the general strategy of keeping convicted prisoners as close as possible to their home area. By the early 1920s the numbers in Perth Prison had been run down to such an extent that it held only prisoners awaiting trial. As soon as possible after sentence they were transferred to Dundee. However, plans to close Perth hit an unexpected snag and within a few years the future of the two prisons was reversed. The annual report of the Commissioners for 1928 tells the story:

> Dundee Prison was closed on 4 October. This was the result of an offer from the Town Council to purchase the prison and use it, partly as improved police premises and legalised cells, and partly for an extension of the Corporation Tramways Department. In March 1922 it was arranged that Perth Prison, so far as ordinary prisoners were concerned, should be practically closed and all prisoners transferred to Dundee. This was done as a measure of economy; but it was impossible to remove the Lunatic Department from Perth Prison, and it was found that greater economy would result from the closing of Dundee Prison and the transfer of Dundee prisoners to Perth.

Ironically, within ten years a new Criminal Lunatic Asylum was under construction at Carstairs, Lanarkshire. The grounds on which the Commissioners had been reluctantly forced to retain Perth Prison were removed but by that time the die had been cast.

The third area of investigation for the Elgin Committee was 'juveniles and first offenders, and to what extent they should be treated as classes apart'. This term of reference, now referred to as classification of prisoners, is as important today as was the previous one of allocation. Present thinking in the Scottish prison system in this respect also favours a return to the principles being applied in the service at the turn of the century.

The Elgin Report concluded that little change was required in the existing arrangements. In his evidence McHardy, Chairman of the Prison Commissioners, indicated that some thought had been given to locating all juveniles in Cupar Prison but that no action had been taken because the numbers involved were so small. A juvenile prisoner was defined as one who was sixteen years old or less. In 1899 the total number in custody in the country was twenty-one, of whom five were under sixteen years of age. According to the *Minutes of Evidence of the Inquiry (Command 219)*, McHardy indicated that governors were allowed to exercise discretion as to which young prisoners they kept apart from the main population:

> Well, we had the age of sixteen put in our rules and regulations,
> but I myself observed sometimes in prison miserable little
> creatures who were supposed to be seventeen, eighteen, and so
> on, and with the concurrence of others we have not specified in
> our last regulations what a juvenile is; the Governor determines
> whether he is a juvenile or not. That is with the intention of
> giving the poor creature, though past the age, a chance of being
> treated as juvenile.

The committee supported the Commissioners in preferring this flexible form of separation to the more general suggestion that all prisoners under the age of twenty-one should be kept separate on the grounds that 'it is notorious that between the ages mentioned [eighteen and twenty] there are not a few who can only be described as habitual criminals already'. The position adopted by the Elgin Committee in support of the Scottish Prison Commissioners in this matter went in the face of general penal enthusiasm at the time for a rigid separation of prisoners based on age alone. In due course the Commissioners had to concede to pressure from the government and in terms of the Prevention of Crime Act, 1908, the first Borstal institution was opened near the village of Polmont in December 1911.

The report used a similar argument in rejecting a rigid separation of first offenders from others who had previous prison experience. Any separation was best done on the basis of individual assessment, not least because it was difficult to decide with any certainty who was a genuine first offender; 'the only fact in which they resemble one another is that they have not before been detected'.

These two items are germane to the discussion which is going on within penology today about the validity of the present system of prisoner classification in its distinction between under-21s and adults, between first offenders and recidivists, and between short and long-term prisoners.

The Elgin Committee had also been asked to consider 'the sufficiency of prison dietary'. The Professor of Materia Medica at the University of Edinburgh was medical adviser to the Prison Commissioners. During his absence in India the Commissioners had asked his replacement to report on the matter of prison diet. He had done so in 1899, concluding that many prisoners, particularly the able-bodied who were serving less than four months, were underfed. He had recommended that dietary classification should be based not on length of sentence but on the particular needs of the prisoner, especially in relation to the work he was expected to do. The Commissioners had accepted these recommendations and this action satisfied the Elgin Committee.

Finally, the committee had been asked to examine 'prison labour and occupation, with special reference to the physical condition and the moral improvement and training of the prisoners'. Reference has already been made in this text to the Scottish tradition of 'useful' as opposed to purely penal labour. McHardy pointed out in his evidence an important difference between Scotland and England:

> Probably I think the greatest difference which stands out and
> meets everyone going into the English and Scotch prisons is that
> in England they have the treadmill, and they have been
> accustomed all along to have that means of enforcing what they
> call first-class hard labour.

Since the time of Brebner, prison administrators in Scotland had steadfastly refused to put prisoners to penal labour, with the exception of a period in the middle of the nineteenth century when pressure from central government led to the introduction of the crank machine. In fairness to McHardy, he did not overstate his case:

> There is no unproductive labour, but there is a lot of it not very productive.

The Commissioners were restricted by the government's insistence that labour in prisons should not interfere with independent commercial enterprise and that work should be sought principally from government departments. The Elgin Committee suggested that such a blanket restriction was unnecessary and observed that prison labour would be more rewarding if it were related more directly to commercial needs. The Commissioners took a pragmatic line in their evidence to the committee:

> It will be seen that all the labour is industrial, but there is undoubtedly a large amount of it under the heading of picking which is of a very low class. It may, however, be remarked that it is necessary to have in prison a certain amount of very simple labour for the employment of the large numbers committed for drunkenness and breach of the peace, who, when at liberty, are idlers and have never learned a trade. There are many drawbacks to the development of useful trades in prison. The principle the Commissioners have acted on is that the Government is not anxious to develop manufactures in the ordinary sense which the term now implies – namely, large collections of machinery adapted for the production of specific articles. Instead of erecting machines of the latest type, doing the work of many hands, the Commissioners have to discover on what work manual labour alone can be employed without the introduction of any machine to facilitate it.

The Commissioners went on to comment that the most useful work they had to offer was on the many building operations within establishments since this was the sort of work which prisoners were more likely to find after release.

The Elgin Committee's comments on this section of the report concluded with a refreshingly honest observation:

> It must, however, be added that no one ranks very highly the educative and reformatory influence of prison labour.

This pragmatism contrasts strongly with the view which has held sway over the last twenty or so years. This has been, as Dobash (1983) points out, that prisons should be industrial centres providing high quality goods for both the public and private sectors, under the direction of a central organisation which includes product development and marketing branches. Dobash argues, however, that this structure has more to do with a reinstatement of the earlier goals of confinement, linking prison labour with capital for the purpose of creating surplus value, than with any notion of rehabilitation.

The Elgin Committee dealt with one other matter which was not directly within its terms of reference. It commented on the fact that many of the problems which confronted the management of prisons required 'experience in medical requirements and practice' for their solution. It suggested that it was not sufficient for the Commissioners to have a medical adviser but rather that one of their number should have medical qualifications. It went on to comment that the expense of an additional commissioner with medical qualifications might be recouped by the abolition of the post of inspector which it considered to be 'quite anomalous' since the post holder performed many of the duties of a commissioner without any of the authority. The post of inspector eventually survived the Commission itself, remaining in its internal form until the May Report in 1979 confirmed the view of the Elgin Report about internal inspection. The recommendation that one commissioner should be medically qualified was adopted, not by an addition to the membership but by the appointment of Dr James Devon to the Commission in 1913.

It should be noted that there was one important area of concern which the report did not address. Several matters raised in the original memorandum of complaint referred to staff difficulties. In the preamble to its report the committee observed:

> It was not within the scope of our reference to investigate any feeling of dissatisfaction which might appear to exist among members of the prison staff. Accordingly we express no opinion upon this question, but we cannot ignore the fact of the existence of dissatisfaction in certain quarters.

Inspectors of Prison

With the increase in central control of the prison systems in the United Kingdom the need for an independent inspectorate, which had originally been established in order to set up consistent standards in the various local prison authorities, had become less obvious. Indeed, central government, which had been more than willing to encourage the early inspectors to take a highly public stand even in matters which were outwith their immediate terms of reference and to be critical at a personal level of local authorities and individual governors, became the more reluctant to allow this in proportion to its own increased responsibility.

By 1857 the Inspector of Prisons for Scotland, in addition to the most northern counties of England for which he had held responsibility for some years, had been given charge of prisons in the counties of York and Lancaster, changing his title to Inspector of Prisons for the Northern District. In 1870 Captain T Folliott Powell, until then Governor of Chatham Convict Prison, was appointed Inspector of Prisons for the Northern District and in that capacity became one of the four Managers of the General Prison. Following the 1877 Act he was appointed a member of the Prison Commission for Scotland and gave up his appointment as Inspector. The new Commission wished to appoint two inspectors for Scotland. The Treasury thought that only one was required. Unusually, the Treasury gave way:

> . . . my Lords have agreed only with much hesitation to the
> appointment of two inspectors . . . They have accepted the
> reasons offered for the immediate appointment of two Officers
> but they continue to be of opinion that the circumstances relied
> on are temporary in their nature and that one of these
> appointments ought to be made on the understanding that at the
> end of three years is may be withdrawn without giving a claim
> for compensation. *(Letter to Commissioners, 21 January 1878)*

In April 1878 the Secretary of State appointed without condition Mr Stuart Johnson and Major W G B Willis, 'two gentlemen who have had large practical experience in the English convict service'. Willis was allocated the eastern prisons and Johnson the western. Their reports were published as appendices to the annual reports of the Prison Commissioners.

Johnson died in 1894 and the Commissioners decided that in view of the reduced number of prisons Willis should be the sole inspector. The latter remained in post until 1903. Despite the length of his tenure, his influence on the service was not significant and he regarded himself primarily as a servant of the administration. In his final report he allowed himself some personal comment:

In looking back twenty six years on prison service in Scotland, I have seen many changes. The most observable is, perhaps, the marked alteration in the prisoner class. There is less brutality and more civilisation, due, I think, in a great measure to far less severity, more sympathy, and firm, but just, rational treatment. Another gratifying alteration is, I am glad to say, the status of the prison warder. This has greatly bettered from what it was twenty six years ago. It has improved in position, and chances of advancement, in regard to comfort, good quarters, social amusement, and endeavour to counteract as far as possible the monotony of the duties.

When Willis retired in 1903 the Commissioners agreed with the Treasury that the post should not be filled. It was subsequently decided that the Secretary to the Prison Commissioners, who at the time was David Crombie, should be appointed Inspector of Prisons in terms of the 1877 Act. From that point publication of a separate annual report ceased. Inspection continued in an internal and intermittent fashion in the Scottish Prison Service until, following a recommendation contained in the Report of the Committee of Inquiry into the United Kingdom Prison Services in 1979 a 'distanced' inspectorate was established in January 1981.

Levels of Imprisonment

Scottish courts have a record of sending comparatively high numbers of offenders to prison for relatively short sentences. Representative average daily numbers of prisoners in custody during the period of office of the Prison Commissioners were:

    1879: 3137
    1899: 2749
    1928: 1639

The reduction in these levels, while due mainly to political and social factors, was certainly influenced by the strong public stand taken by the Commissioners. They complained regularly, for instance, at the consistently high rate of committals. The average for the last quarter of the nineteenth century was between 11 and 13 per 1,000 of the population. In their annual report for 1913 the Commissioners observed that the rate had decreased to 9.95 compared to the level of 10.23 in 1912. The comparable figure for England in the same year was 4.82. The Elgin Report had noted that the average length of sentence in Scotland was 15 days compared to 28 in England. By 1903 this had increased marginally to 18 days; by 1913 it had altered to 17.23 days.

The Commissioners were not slow to voice their unease at the large number of offenders being sent to prison for short periods:

> The Commissioners still believe that much more effort should be made to deal with first offenders in other ways than by committing to prison, particularly for short sentences . . . There is a marked increase in sentences of five days, and a decrease in sentences of from ten days and upwards . . . The Commissioners have often expressed their views as to the futility of short sentences, and so have many other authorities upon the subject, but nevertheless they continue to increase . . . Thousands are annually committed to prison in default of payment of a fine for comparatively trivial offences, and thus for the first time make their way automatically into prison. (*Annual Report, 1914*)

With unfailing regularity annual reports commented on the high numbers of prisoners sentenced for offences related to drunkenness. In an appendix to the report for 1889 Sir Douglas MacLagan, Medical Adviser to the Commissioners, complained at the intolerable strain being placed on prison medical officers who had to deal with these persons who were invariably 'utterly broken down in constitution, barely recovered from the direct effects of debauch'. At the same time, it would be wrong to give the impression that drunkenness related only to minor offences:

> While it requires no investigation to realise that the excessive numbers of committals for drunkenness and breach of the peace, which account for 40,000 out of a total of 56,500, were brought about by abuse of alcohol, it is nearly certain that also in cases of more serious crime drink is often an important factor. At a recent inspection of Barlinnie Prison, Glasgow, which contains the largest population in one prison, an examination was made into 245 cases of the prisoners with longest sentences, and who therefore might fairly be presumed to be the greatest criminals. According to their own statements, which have been in some cases verified, 171 of them were more or less affected by liquor at the time when the crime was committed, whilst only 74 were sober. (*Annual Report, 1899*)

The Prison Commissioners did not confine themselves to negative complaints about the high level of imprisonment. In succeeding annual reports they pressed the advantages of alternative forms of sentence. They were early supporters of probation, extolling the virtues of the new system of Probation Guardianship, 'whereby the operation of the sentence is suspended provided that the offender behaves well under supervision', and urging that the scheme be given statutory power. The Probation of Offenders Act was duly introduced in 1907 and two years later the Commissioners were urging that greater use should be made of the Act and that regular probation officers be appointed throughout the country.

They returned to the charge in their report in 1922 and seized on the problem which continues to bedevil our system for dealing with offenders today, the fact that there is little fiscal incentive for a local authority to provide resources to keep an offender out of prison:

> It is too often forgotten that probation properly worked is nevertheless very economical as compared with the high costs of imprisonment at the present time when every prisoner costs £84.7s.5d. per annum or 4s.7d. for every day's imprisonment. It is obvious that the expenses of a probation officer would soon be met if he succeeded in keeping a reasonable number of persons out of prison; but this aspect of the question does not appeal greatly to those whose duty it is to appoint and pay probation officers, in as much as they bear no direct share of the cost of imprisonment.

It is worth noting in passing the refreshing willingness on the part of the Commissioners to comment in public about criminal justice issues which went far beyond their own restricted field of immediate concern. While hardly bed-time reading, their annual reports compare favourably with the statistic-ridden presentations of their modern successors. This degree of candour may well have contributed to the legislation of 1928 by which the Commission was abolished.

After-Care of Prisoners

The Scottish Prison Commissioners were concerned not only with reducing the existing prison population and with keeping offenders out of prison but also, following in the footsteps of William Brebner, with providing support for prisoners after they were released and legally no longer the responsibility of the prison system.

It is by seeking to organise more after-care and guardianship
of prisoners that we should perhaps aim at further development.
At present this cannot be done officially, but a good deal might
be done unofficially if the various churches and discharged
prisoners' aid societies could organise bands of workers who
would make a point of befriending without patronising
discharged prisoners committed to their care. In time this might
develop into more official guardianship such as we have already
for inebriates discharged on licence. (*Annual Report, 1910*)

Within two years the Commissioners had taken their efforts a step
further by appointing an agent whose job it was to find employment for
released convicts. In 1919 the Secretary of State instructed the Commissioners 'to enquire into and report upon the workings of the
Probation Acts in Scotland and to endeavour to promote the wise
employment of this method of dealing with offenders'. The outcome
of this inquiry was the establishment of the semi-official Scottish
Central Association for the Probation and Supervision of Juvenile and
Other Offenders of which the Secretary of State himself was to be
president. The Association received an annual grant from the Treasury
out of which it was entitled to make grants to aid the payment of
probation officers, as well as providing assistance to discharged convicts and borstal licence holders. This body remained in existence until
1930 when its functions were taken over by the Scottish Juvenile
Welfare and After-Care Office and the salaries of its two paid
employees were taken out of the Prisons budget.

The whole thrust of this field of activity of the Prison Commission
can be summed up as a plea for a closer relationship between the
various elements of the criminal justice process.

The remedy appears to lie in a much closer co-ordination
between the various Courts and departments responsible for the
administration of justice in the country, and a wider spread of
information as to the different methods of treating offenders and
criminals. (*Annual Report, 1913*)

This remains a live issue today. Informed commentators are coming
more to the notion that the real crisis facing the prison system is not one
of poor facilities or shortage of resources but rather a problem
discussed in succeeding chapters, concerning its proper relative organisational position.

5 Care or Control
Features of Imprisonment since 1929

An important part of the debate about the purpose of imprisonment which has waxed and waned over the last sixty years has been whether priority should be given to the need to control prisoners or to the need to care for them, whether these two considerations are exclusive or whether they can be complementary. Provision of education and welfare services has grown throughout this period and particular attention has been paid to the needs of young offenders and of women prisoners. This has contrasted with increasingly complex security arrangements, which can be traced to a series of spectacular escapes from English prisons in the 1960s.

Education
From the middle of the nineteenth century there had been a tradition of at least minimal education provision in most Scottish prisons. In the smaller prisons this had often been provided by the chaplain and until alterations introduced by the Prisons (Scotland) Act 1989 the chaplain remained in theory responsible for oversight of education in penal establishments. Many larger prisons had officers who were nominated specifically to teach. Educational provision was set on a more formal footing with the introduction of the Borstal system at Polmont Institution in 1911 and this later expanded into adult prisons. Officers were still encouraged to come into establishments in their free time to pass on whatever skills they possessed. Not surprisingly management encouraged this altruism among staff:

> The Department are of the opinion that this measure of
> association, by reducing the monotony of prison routine,

exercises a wholesome effect on the prisoners and gives them a fresh interest, and their thanks are particularly due to those officers who devoted their own time to the supervision of the exercise of these privileges.
(*Annual Report of the Prisons Department, 1932*)

By 1938 there were two full-time teachers at Polmont in addition to one officer/teacher. Local authority teachers gave classes at Barlinnie, Edinburgh and Greenock Prisons. The expansion of educational provision was halted by the outbreak of war but the Report by the Scottish Advisory Council on the Treatment and Rehabilitation of Offenders noted in 1949 that it was back on course. By 1953 the Prisons Report commented that local education authorities provided evening classes in all establishments holding long term prisoners. In that year the financial arrangements whereby local authorities were reimbursed the pro rata cost of teachers' salaries, which remains today, was introduced. 1973 saw the appointment of the first full-time education officer at an adult establishment, Edinburgh Prison.

In 1990 all but the smallest establishments have extensive education units, staffed by qualified teachers, seconded from local authority education departments. Subjects range from remedial learning to university degree level courses. City and Guilds or vocational training modules are offered in a wide range of skills. Increasing emphasis is being placed on social and life skills development in collaboration with prison officers, social workers and other specialist staff.

Welfare

Reference has already been made to how the Scottish Juvenile Welfare and After-Care Office came into being in 1930. It became common for the staff involved to visit future clients during the course of their sentences and the need for welfare staff to work exclusively within establishments came to be recognised, as was recorded in the *Prisons in Scotland Report* for 1961:

The expansion of the prison welfare service forecast in paragraph 173 of last year's report took place in the autumn, when arrangements were made to cover the requirements in every Scottish prison. A second full-time officer was assigned for duty at Barlinnie Prison and a full-time officer at Edinburgh Prison: visits were made to the other prisons regularly or as occasion required. Governors reported that relief from anxiety rendered prisoners amenable to prison discipline and training. This relief and the details supplied by welfare officers as to prisoners' circumstances and requirements also helped officers responsible for after-care on release in their efforts to secure a lasting rehabilitation.

In 1965 responsibility for after-care of former prisoners was taken over by the probation service. The separate prison welfare system continued in existence and expanded until 1972. In that year the Report of a Working Party on the Manning of Social Work Services in Penal Establishments in Scotland recommended that responsibility for the welfare of prisoners should be taken over by the local authority social work departments in keeping with the principles of generic social work. This change duly took place in November 1972. Local authority social workers continue to be employed in penal establishments and the cost of providing this service is borne by the Scottish Home and Health Department.

These developments initially proved to be a mixed blessing for the prison service. On the one hand the creation of social work 'units', staffed by persons who were in the system but not of it, served to underline what was seen by some at the time as the dichotomy of 'care versus control' and to suggest that 'care' could only be undertaken by professionals from outwith the service. At the same time, prison officers became increasingly concerned as they perceived their role being restricted, and worried that the introduction of 'caring' staff would leave them with only a control function. In an attempt to address this problem a further working party was set up. In 1989 it produced a National Framework for Social Work in penal establishments. This document laid out the ideal of a shared enterprise between social workers, prison officers and other interested professionals.

The principle of 'through care', which recognises the need to support and encourage the offender by a continuum which begins before sentence, remains while he is in prison and continues after release, is as important today as it was in the days of William Brebner and is still recognised as an ideal.

Young Offenders

The problem of how society should deal with its young adult deviants is not a new one. The cry of Shakespeare's Bohemian shepherd in 'A Winter's Tale' has evoked many a sympathetic response over the years:

I would there were no age between ten and three and twenty,
Or that youth would sleep out the rest;
For there is nothing in the between
But getting wenches with child,
Wronging the ancientry, stealing, fighting.

In the Glasgow Bridewell in the first half of the nineteenth century Brebner introduced a system of classification which separated juvenile prisoners from adults. He also expended considerable effort in setting up a House of Refuge to which these youngsters could be admitted on release as a means of keeping them apart from bad influence. This model of separation was continued with the opening of the General Prison at Perth in 1842.

The first formal proposal in Britain that there should be separate institutions for young adult prisoners was made in the Gladstone Report in England in 1895. This report suggested that the ages between sixteen and twenty-three years were crucial in the maturation of habitual criminals. The Gladstone Committee was aware of the regime at Elmira Reformatory in New York, which was based on the principle that young people should be reformed rather than punished and it was an experiment along these lines which it recommended. This proposal found official acceptance and in 1900 part of the convict prison near Rochester in Kent was set aside to provide a reformatory regime for young offenders. The prison was situated in the village of Borstal. The name of the village became associated with the type of institution and was subsequently enshrined in statute with the enactment of the Prevention of Crime Act in 1908.

In their evidence to the Elgin Committee in 1900 the Prison Commissioners for Scotland indicated that they had previously given thought to converting part of the prison at Cupar exclusively for juvenile offenders. They went on to indicate that they were not attracted to the notion of a statutory distinction based on age alone. Maturity or lack of it was often defined by other features and for that reason the Scottish Commissioners preferred to leave governors with a degree of flexibility in deciding which young offenders should be kept apart from adults.

The Commissioners eventually found the tide of official enthusiasm impossible to resist and in 1911 purchased Blairlodge School, 'a large private boarding school for gentlemen's sons situated at Polmont, Stirlingshire', to house this category of young prisoners. The enabling statute had authorised the Secretary for Scotland to find a suitable name to replace 'Borstal'. The new establishment was named Polmont Institution but from the time of its opening on 18 December 1911 it was known to everyone as Polmont Borstal. In their annual report for that year the Commissioners described the new institution:

> The buildings are very extensive, and comprise a large central covered hall and gymnasium, surrounded by spacious class-rooms in the form of a hollow square, and above which are two floors of single bedrooms, in each of which a boy can be accommodated, and a good house for the Governor. There is also a large dining-hall, a chapel, swimming bath, workshop, and a very good farm steading, besides various other buildings, some of which have been converted into houses for married warders, and rooms for bachelor warders. The whole buildings are lighted by electricity; the boilers and engines were in good order, but it was necessary to re-wire the whole building. Much yet remains to be done to put the buildings and grounds in good order and complete occupation, but this will afford useful and constructive work for the inmates for several   years to come. The grounds extend to thirty acres. Parties of boys are now engaged at joiner work, mason work, blacksmith work, plumbing, painting, also gardening and labouring. The classrooms and dormitories have the windows barred, but there are no walls outside or round the grounds, and, of course, no armed guards, as it is not a convict prison. In order to prevent escape reliance is placed on the good behaviour of the lads and the vigilance of the warders instructing the working parties. A professional schoolmaster carries on school in the evenings, and a gymnastic instructor gives instruction in physical drill and gymnastics. It is anticipated that the numbers in the Institution will grow rapidly, notwithstanding that only those are eligible to be sentenced who are over sixteen and under twenty one years of age, and who are convicted on indictment.

Impressive as is the description of the new institution and what went on within it, the most telling comment in the above extract comes in the final sentence. Whenever the courts are provided with a new option for disposal it immediately becomes not an alternative but an addition, with the consequence that the number of offenders receiving custodial sentences increases. This reality was recognised even by Alexander Paterson:

> Wherever prisons are built, Courts will make use of them. If no
> prison is handy, some other way of dealing with the offender
> will possibly be discovered. (in Ruck, 1951)

The sentence of Borstal training was to be passed on an offender if 'by reason of his criminal habits or tendencies, or association with persons of bad character, it is expedient that he should be subject to detention for such term and under such supervision and discipline as appears most conducive to his reformation and the repression of crime'.

Between 1922 and 1946 the English Prison Commissioner who had particular responsibility for the Borstal system was Sir Alexander Paterson. He organised Borstal institutions as pale reflections of public schools. Staff were taken out of uniform, education was emphasised, house masters and matrons were appointed. Paterson summed up his philosophy as follows:

> Borstal training is based on the double assumption that there is
> individual good in each, and among nearly all an innate
> corporate spirit which will respond to the appeal made to the
> British of every sort to play the game, to follow the flag, to stand
> by the old ship.

The Criminal Justice (Scotland) Act 1949 established a new criterion for Borstal trainees, 'that it is expedient for his reformation and the prevention of crime that he should undergo a period of training in a Borstal Institution'. The same Act provided for the introduction of detention centres, which were to be used, according to the Minister who introduced the Bill in parliament, 'for those who require not so much training and guidance as to be pulled up sharply and to be made to realise that they've done wrong'.

In the post-war years there had been growing judicial opinion opposed to the view of the prison authorities that lengthy training was all that was necessary for young offenders. It is probably true that the acceptability of military detention during the war years created a climate which paved the way for the provision of detention centres. The Labour Home Secretary who introduced the provision was the first to refer to it as 'a short, sharp shock'. (In its original context in *The Mikado* this phrase actually refers to capital punishment.)

It was not until eleven years after the passing of the Act that the first Scottish detention centre was opened at South Inch House, the former Criminal Lunatic Department at Perth Prison, in June 1960. A second detention centre was opened at Friarton near Perth in 1963. In 1967 all detention centre training in Scotland was concentrated at the newly opened institution at Glenochil. The detention centre, like the Borstal institution which preceded it, was a child of its time, providing a socially acceptable model of disciplined institutional life for young convicted offenders.

In 1960 the Scottish Advisory Council on the Treatment and Rehabilitation of Offenders published a report which indicated that prison was never a suitable disposal for those under the age of twenty one and that a disposal, separate from Borstal and detention training, which would be both punitive and deterrent, was required. This recommendation was taken up in the Criminal Justice (Scotland) Act 1963 which provided for the establishment of Young Offenders' Institutions. The report from the Advisory Council had suggested that only one such institution would be required. In the event this was a significant underestimate. The first Young Offenders' Institution was opened in Edinburgh in 1965. In the same year Dumfries Prison was converted to become a Young Offenders' Institution and in the following year a hall in Barlinnie Prison had to be converted as a third such institution. The experience following the introduction of the borstal provision was being repeated. If courts were provided with a new option they would be quick to use it.

In 1969 the Scottish Home and Health Department published a consultative memorandum which concluded that the provision of three separate types of institution for offenders under the age of twenty one was both wasteful of resources and an inefficient method of operation. The memorandum proposed that the three sentences of detention in Borstal, detention centre and young offenders' institution should be replaced by a single generic sentence; that the court should stipulate the length of sentence; and that subsequently the prison administration should determine in which location and under which regime the sentence should be served. The notion that there was an ideal length of time for training in a Borstal or a detention centre was thus to be abolished. Custodial sentences were to be as short as considerations of criminal justice and crime prevention would permit.

It was eventually decided that Scotland should not act until the Advisory Council on the Penal System had published its report on Young Adult Offenders. The principal recommendation of this report, which was published in 1974, was that a 'custody and control order' should be introduced which would provide a continuum between the institution and supervision in the community. This recommendation was never implemented.

In retrospect, it was unfortunate that Scotland delayed action on the 1969 memorandum. This may have been inevitable, given the subsequently voiced opinion that it was 'retrograde in advance of its time'. In the event, the proposed alterations were incorporated in the 1978 Criminal Justice (Scotland) Bill which proposed the abolition of the three separate sentences and the introduction of a single generic sentence. This Bill was never enacted and when its successor was introduced in 1979 by the newly elected Conservative government it had been altered to include a separate provision maintaining the 'brisk discipline' of the detention centre.

The provisions of the Criminal Justice (Scotland) Act 1980 in respect of young offenders came into force in November 1983 and Polmont, Castle Huntly and Noranside Borstal Institutions were redesignated as young offenders' institutions. One fairly immediate outcome was a significant fall in the total number of young offenders in custody, the obverse of the consequences of the 1908 and the 1963 legislation.

The recommendations of the 1969 memorandum were at last fully implemented through the Law Reform (Miscellaneous Provisions) (Scotland) Act 1985 which provided for a generic young offender sentence for young adults under the age of twenty-one.

Between October 1981 and February 1984 five inmates died whilst serving sentences at the complex at Glenochil, which included a young offenders' institution and a detention centre.

In November 1984 the Secretary of State established a working party 'to review the precautionary procedures adopted at Glenochil Young Offenders' Institution and Glenochil Detention Centre to identify and supervise inmates who might be regarded as suicide risks; and to make recommendations'. During the course of the review two further self-inflicted deaths took place, one in each of the institutions.

The Chiswick Report (1985) contained sixty-three recommendations, the majority of which were accepted by the Secretary of State. The working party took a broad view of its remit and extended its deliberations to the general regime and management at Glenochil as well as giving some thought to the wider criminal justice process for those under the age of twenty-one. It began by discussing the need to achieve a proper balance between procedures that reduced the risk of suicide to a minimum yet were compatible with an acceptable way of life in a penal establishment. A basic requirement, it suggested, was that there should be an appropriate balance between a prison officer's concern for discipline and his interest in the welfare of inmates. The report went on to make a series of recommendations which, it suggested, would assist in both the identification and the management of inmates who were at risk. It discussed medical and nursing requirements.

The report also turned its attention to more general aspects of the regime at Glenochil. It recommended that the Young Offenders' Institution should be broken down into smaller units, that staffing should be on a group basis and that there should be a scheme whereby personal officers were allocated to each inmate. It was suggested that officers should be specially selected and trained for work with young offenders, that female officers should be employed at Glenochil and that staffing of the two institutions at the complex would be separate. The working party paid particular attention to the need for a clear statement of the aims and nature of detention centre training. It drew up an extensive list of features which it suggested should prevent offenders being sentenced to detention centres. A further set of recommendations dealt with the need for close contact between an inmate and his family. Finally, the working party recommended that a planning and development unit should be set up within the prison service headquarters and that consideration should be given to the need for a review of the criminal justice system as it applied in Scotland to those offenders who were under the age of twenty-one.

It is probable that the next subject on the agenda with regard to this group of prisoners will be whether a distinction between those offenders who are under the age of twenty-one and those who are 'adult' remains valid. This distinction was introduced in the early years of this century when twenty-one was the age of majority. This is no longer the case. If any age can be said to be that of majority it is now arguably eighteen years. The Prison Commissioners for Scotland were reluctant to introduce a separate regime for juvenile offenders based solely on an age criterion, preferring a more flexible arrangement which would allow them to place mature youngsters in adult establishments while keeping those who were older but immature separate from mature criminals. Their opinion was supported by the Elgin Committee in 1900. There have recently been suggestions from various quarters that consideration should be given to extending a system similar to that of Children's Hearings to take in offenders up till the age of eighteen. The

Chiswick Committee may well have had issues such as these in mind when it recommended that consideration should be given to a review of the criminal justice system for offenders under the age of twenty-one years.

Female Offenders

Until the early part of the nineteenth century there was very little segregation of any prisoners in Scottish jails; untried mixed with convicted, young with old, male with female. William Brebner was the first to introduce separation of male prisoners from female. This was taken up by the first Inspector of Prisons who encouraged local authorities both to provide separate accommodation for female prisoners and to put them under the exclusive control of female staff. This was the pattern adopted when the General Prison at Perth opened in 1842. A matron was placed in charge of the female section, reporting directly to the governor.

One of the most striking features of prison history in Scotland has been the significant reduction in the proportion of female to male prisoners. This has decreased to such an extent that one now considers imprisonment almost exclusively in a male context. It was not always so. When the General Prison opened at Perth in 1842 over one in three prisoners in Scotland were female. The proportion now is just over 3 per cent.

Prison Population

	Male	Female	Total
1843	1574	877	2451
1938	1247	124	1371
1966	3832	117	3949
1987	5259	187	5446

How is this reduction to be explained? There is probably no one simple answer but rather a combination of sociological influences. The nature of the crimes and offences which most commonly lead to imprisonment in today's society, violence, house-breaking, theft, are more likely to be committed exclusively by males than were the predominant offences of a century and a half ago, such as drunkenness and immorality. Account would also have to be taken of possible bias in police investigation of offences, in their prosecution and in the sentencing practices of courts. This is deep water on which to embark without proper research. Given the attention which is frequently drawn to the comparatively high rates of general imprisonment in Scotland there may be value in undertaking research to examine the female statistics. Such a project might well turn up results which could be usefully applied to the way in which male offenders are dealt with.

By 1938 convicted female prisoners were concentrated in Edinburgh, Duke Street (Glasgow) and Greenock. In 1955 Duke Street prison was closed and all convicted female prisoners and Borstal trainees were accommodated in Greenock Prison. In the early 1970s a new generic penal institution was built at Cornton Vale near Stirling. When this was completed all convicted women were transferred there.

Security

In the early 1960s a series of spectacular escapes from English prisons occurred. It has been argued (Thomas, 1972) that these escapes were merely the culmination of the general confusion which existed among prison staff at all levels as to the primary aim of the service, which is secure custody, a confusion which had its roots in the Gladstone Report of 1895. Be that as it may, the final straw was the escape of the spy George Blake from Wormwood Scrubs Prison on 22 October 1966. Two days after this incident the Home Secretary set up a committee of inquiry under the chairmanship of Lord Mountbatten. The report of the committee was published in December 1966. It was a remarkably precise document which addressed itself directly to its terms of reference:

> The Mountbatten Report provided a single-minded and
> straightforward analysis of an essentially simple logistic problem
> based on direct experience of the situation which existed. It
> presented clearly documented evidence about the matters under
> review and produced unambiguous and uncompromising
> answers at a practical level. (King & Elliott, 1977)

J E Thomas has suggested that the recommendations in the report involve a return, in matters of detail as well as of principle, to the pre-Gladstone prison service. It is undoubtedly true that the English Prison Service has become more directly concerned with its security obligations over the last twenty years than it was in the years immediately preceding Mountbatten.

The inquiry was conducted almost entirely in England and was concerned with the prison service in England and Wales. The members of the committee made only a short visit to Inverness Prison to look at arrangements in the unit there. The Scottish Office did, however, consider which of the recommendations contained in the report might be taken up in Scotland. It concluded that the number of prisoners requiring the super-secure conditions envisaged for Mountbatten's maximum security prison would not justify a separate Scottish establishment although the Home Office was advised that Scotland might wish to take up six places in the proposed new prison to be built on the Isle of Wight.

In the event this recommendation that the most dangerous prisoners should be concentrated in one maximum security prison was not acceptable to the Home Office. In the traditional mode of dealing with such matters a further committee under the chairmanship of Professor Leon Radzinowicz was set up. *The Report of the Advisory Council on the Penal System on the regime for Long-Term Prisoners in Conditions of Maximum Security* duly produced the acceptable recommendation that this type of prisoner should be dispersed throughout a number of prisons holding long term prisoners.

The Mountbatten Report recommended that greater emphasis should be placed on security when staff were being trained and that there should be a new specialist course for staff undertaking special security duties. It also suggested the appointment of special security officers in each closed prison and recommended that a manual of security guidance should be prepared. These recommendations were all implemented by the Home Office, as was the appointment of a Chief Superintendent from the Metropolitan Police as security adviser in prison service headquarters.

These recommendations were given short shrift by the Scottish Office which decided that the separate appointment of a security officer would lead to a confusion of responsibility with the Chief Officer in a prison, particularly with regard to supervision of security duties to be undertaken by staff.

> In these circumstances we would not favour a specialist course
> on security in Scotland and we consider that the emphasis
> already given to security in training syllabuses is adequate.

A key proposal in the report was that the service in England and Wales should have a new professional head with the title of Inspector General. Not for the last time, an official inquiry commented on the gap which had grown up between headquarters and 'the field', that is, establishments. Without attributing this directly to the abolition of the Prison Commission, which had taken place in England and Wales only in 1963, Mountbatten highlighted the need for clear leadership in the prison service and suggested that this might best be achieved by the appointment of an Inspector General. In response to this the Scottish Office showed a certain smugness, taking the view that this recommendation had been influenced by the fact that the post of Inspector had been resurrected in Scotland two years earlier after a gap of some years.

> In a sense this may be something on which we in Scotland are already ahead of England. We have had an Inspector of Prisons for the last two or three years, and it may be that the Mountbatten Inquiry learnt something from this. We shall be continuing with our Inspectorate, but we should certainly welcome visits by the 'supremo', who may also learn from Scottish experience as well as teaching something. We will welcome his presence, but we shall maintain our own Inspectorate system. (Under Secretary of State, 16 February 1967)

Despite these expressed reservations on the part of the Scottish Office at the time, the Mountbatten Report did much in Scotland as well as in England to concentrate the minds of those responsible for the prison service on their primary task, that of security. Those actually working in prisons had never lost sight of that task.

> The officials, in short, know on which side their bread is buttered. Their continued employment is tied up with the successful performance of custody and if society is not sure of the priority to be attached to the tasks assigned to prison, the overriding importance of custody is perfectly clear to the officials. (Sykes, 1971)

The overriding importance of custody may have been perfectly clear to those working in prisons, although Mountbatten questioned whether this was so in all cases in England. It had undoubtedly been lost sight of by senior administrators, and the extent to which legislators subscribed to the social welfare model of imprisonment was underlined in the parliamentary debate on the Mountbatten Report by a future Lord Chancellor of England:

A point of criticism of the Report is that the prison service has not yet been properly slotted into the need for social work generally. Prison Warders may be said largely to be a service apart. Perhaps they will always be. However, there ought – and this is a general problem of social policy with which the Rt Hon Gentleman and his colleagues must concern themselves – to be a larger organisation of social workers in the community with a closer liaison between the Prison Service and other forms of social work which may be allied to it. Probation Officers are an obvious example. There should also be a breaking down of the isolation which exists between the Prison Service and other forms of social work; the provision of adequate training courses on which they will meet other social workers, and so on. (Quintin Hogg, 16 February, 1967)

This continued reference to the prison service and 'other forms of social work' showed that opinion at least in England had almost ceased to relate the prison system to the criminal justice process. This was not true to such a degree in Scotland where the criminal justice orientation left by the Prison Commissioners still carried some weight.

One practical recommendation made by Mountbatten which was quickly adopted and which remains in force today was the allocation of each prisoner to one of four security categories, ranging from those whose escape must be prevented at all costs (category A) to those for whom no physical security was necessary (category D).

The May Report, 1979

The last departmental report to be taken account of during this period, apart from those related directly to pay and conditions of staff which will be dealt with later, is that of the Committee of Inquiry into United Kingdom Prison Services, the May Report of 1979. The prison system in England had come under considerable pressure in the 1970s, a pressure which related to increasing numbers of prisoners, to increasing staff militancy and to demands for increased rights for prisoners. One newspaper report summarised the decade in this manner:

Proclamations that there is a crisis in British prisons have been at fever pitch for the whole of the past decade. In 1970 the Howard League said that prisons were 'faced with a crisis'. In 1973 the Prison Officers' Association (POA) headlined a magazine editorial 'Crisis Point'. In 1976 'The Times' headlined three

special features 'Crisis in Prisons'. In March 1977 the House of
Commons, debating penal policy, rang to the word 'Crisis'.
(*Observer*, 4 November 1979)

The feature of greatest concern to those working within the system was
the deteriorating state of industrial relations. This found a particular
expression in England and Wales in a long-running dispute between
the Home Office and the Prison Officers' Association about payment
of one special allowance, the continuous duty credit. In the absence of
agreement the POA threatened widespread industrial action in England and Wales from 5 November 1978. It should be noted that
Scotland was not at all involved in this particular dispute. On 27
October 1978 the English Prison Governors' Committee sent an open
letter to the Home Secretary which began:

> Total breakdown is imminent in the prison system. Prison
> Governors believe that it is our duty to publicly warn Ministers
> of the gravity of the situation we face. There is little time left.

The letter went on to argue that the root of the problem was an outdated
and unworkable industrial relations structure, exacerbated by a
'deplorable lack of leadership from the Home Office'.

> We consider that the present chaotic situation demands a
> rigorous public enquiry into industrial relations within the Prison
> Service.

The Home Secretary responded to this letter with a speed and in a
manner which privately surprised even the prison governors. On 6
November 1978 staff representatives were called to the Home Office
and advised that a committee of inquiry was to be set up and draft terms
of reference were discussed. On 8 November officials of the Scottish
Home & Health Department, clearly taken unawares by the speedy
turn of events, called a similar meeting in Edinburgh. The initial
reaction of the Prison Officers' Association was hostile since their
main demand was for a settlement of the immediate pay dispute rather
than a wide-ranging review of the prison system. They insisted that the
inquiry should be in two parts and that matters relating to pay should
be dealt with in the first phase.

On 17 November 1978 the Home Secretary announced the terms of
reference of the proposed inquiry.

My Rt Hon Friends, the Secretaries of State for Scotland and
Northern Ireland, and I have appointed Mr Justice May as
Chairman of the Committee of Inquiry into the United Kingdom
Prison Services with the following terms of reference.
To enquire into the state of the prison services in the United
Kingdom; and having regard to:

a.   the size and nature of the population, and the capacity of the prison
     services to accommodate it;
b.   the responsibilities of the prison services for the security,
     control and treatment of inmates;
c.   the need to recruit and retain a sufficient and suitable staff
     for the prison services;
d.   the need to secure the efficient use of manpower and
     financial resources in the prison services;

To examine and make recommendations upon:

i.   the adequacy, availability, management and use of
      resources in the prison services;
ii.   conditions for staff in the prison services and their
      families;
iii. the organisation and management of the prison services;
iv.   the structure of the prison services, including
      complementing and gradings;
v.   the remuneration and conditions of service of prison
      officers, governors and other grades working only in the
      prison services, including the claim put forward by the
      POA for certain 'continuous duty credit' payments, and
      the date from which any such payment should be made;
vi.   allowances and other aspects of the conditions of service
      of other grades arising from special features of work in the
      prison services;
vii. working arrangements in the prison services, including
      shift systems and standby and on-call requirements;
viii. the effectiveness of the industrial relations machinery,
      including departmental Whitley procedures, within the
      prison services.

In establishing a committee with such far-reaching terms of reference
the Secretaries of State were making inevitable the dissatisfaction
which was voiced when the committee eventually reported. The
original impetus for the inquiry had been a problem on a detailed
matter of pay for prison officers in England which had been extended

by governors into a plea for an inquiry into industrial relations. This was recognised by the opening sentence of the eventual report:

> The Inquiry was set up on 17 November 1978 after a long period of deteriorating industrial relations especially in England and Wales.

No doubt remembering the speed with which Mountbatten had reported, Merlyn Rees, the Home Secretary, asked the committee to report by the end of March 1979. In this hope the committee, whose full membership was announced on 28 November 1978, asked that all written evidence be submitted to it by Christmas. This target was impossible to meet and, as the evidence began to accumulate, the committee realised that its whole time scale was impracticable. If it was to attempt any proper assessment of the prison system it would require a longer period for deliberation. The Home Secretary accepted this reality and announced in February that the committee hoped to report by summer 1979. As far as prison staff were concerned the major issue for the inquiry remained that of pay and the committee was pressed to produce an interim report dealing with this topic. The committee resisted the pressure, arguing that it was impossible to separate the question of pay from all the other issues.

The May Report was finally published on 31 October 1979. In its conclusions it drew attention to the problems caused by overcrowding. It recommended that alternative disposals be sought, particularly for petty offenders, but concluded that for the foreseeable future a substantial prison population was likely. As far as Scotland was concerned the problem was one of uneven distribution of prisoner population. The committee noted that, whereas the total excess of population over places was 1 per cent, 30 per cent of all prisoners were in shared cells.

In a chapter on objectives and regimes the report acknowledged that the first objective of imprisonment is secure custody but insisted that it should also have a constructive aspect. It accepted that 'the rhetoric of treatment and training' had had its day. The humane containment and justice models were, argued the report, unacceptable in that their emphasis was too negative. Its preferred solution was what it described as 'positive custody' (para 4.26). The objectives of the prison service should be stated in the following manner:

> The purpose of the detention of convicted prisoners shall be to keep them in custody which is both secure and positive, and to

that end the behaviour of all the responsible authorities and staff towards them shall be such as to:

a. create an environment which can assist them to respond and contribute to society as positively as possible;
b. preserve and promote their self-respect;
c. minimise, to the degree of security necessary in each particular case, the harmful effects of their removal from normal life;
d. prepare them for and assist them on discharge.

The dismissal by the committee of the justice model and of humane containment, as proposed in evidence by King and Morgan (1980), was based on a failure to understand the principles on which these models are founded. It is quite wrong to suggest, as the report did, that these models imply that prison staff must work in a moral vacuum. The committee confirmed its failure to understand these models fully by describing them as a means without an end which would result in making prisons into human warehouses for both prisoners and staff. One might just as easily make the same criticism of the failure to apply properly the principles of the rehabilitative model in the existing penal process. It is difficult to avoid the conclusion that May did merely wish to change the rhetoric of treatment and training without changing the underlying philosophy. The report states as much in paragraph 4.27:

... we intend that the rhetoric alone should be changed and not all the admirable and constructive things that are done in its name.

This is old wine in new bottles.

The extensive chapter of the report dealing with the organisation of the prison system refers almost exclusively to England and Wales. The Scottish organisation is dismissed in a phrase:

we have received no evidence suggesting a present need for further change, nor have we ourselves observed any such need. (paragraph 5.2)

This conclusion is surprising in view of evidence given to the committee by the Scottish Prison Officers' Association which detailed the need for 'radical changes in the structure of the Prison Services' and from the Scottish Prison Governors which argued that much of the unrest within the service was due to the existing organisational structure.

On the question of inspection of the prison services the report accepted that it would be impossible to have an independent inspectorate in the strict sense of that word since reports would have to be submitted to the Secretary of State, who was the individual with constitutional responsibility for managing the prison service. What was recommended instead was an inspectorate which would be distanced from the prison service itself, headed by a Chief Inspector who should be either an individual independent of the civil service entirely or a former senior prison governor.

In due course the Secretary of State for Scotland took the first of these options, both in 1981 when he appointed a past Chairman of the Parole Board for Scotland in the face of strong opposition from prison governors and again in 1985 when he appointed a retired engineer. In 1989 he ignored the recommendation of the May Report by appointing as Chief Inspector a senior civil servant in the Scottish Office, who was on the point of retiring.

This new arrangement represented a return to the form of inspection which existed before 1877 although it has to be said that the calibre of report published to date by the modern inspector is somewhat inferior to that of his historical predecessors in terms of breadth of discussion of penal issues and causes of offending. In this section of its report the May Committee took the opportunity to point out that the legal position of those prison visiting committees appointed by local authorities had not been regularised after the changes brought about by the Local Government (Scotland) Act 1973, a fact which the committee took to be a reflection on the lack of importance attached to visiting committees.

In the matter of physical resources the May Report made two specific references to Scotland. It expressed surprise at the remarkable degree of structural neglect at Peterhead Prison and recommended that there should be substantial redevelopment on the same site. It also referred to the new prison at Shotts in Lanarkshire, originally planned to hold 1,000 prisoners but at the time of the report holding no more than sixty, as 'a truncated monster' and recommended that it should be expanded. The report further took the view that the application of the European and United Nations Standard Minimum Rules should mean the abolition of enforced cell-sharing and the provision of toilet facilities in all cells.

The rest of the report dealt with the roles and training of staff, pay and industrial relations. These will be discussed in a later chapter.

The May Committee argued that its recommendations should be accepted as a package but the response of the government was less than whole-hearted. An editorial in *The Scotsman* newspaper on 1 November 1979 was not surprised.

> This traditional public indifference to what goes on inside prisons (except when prisoners are alleged to be pampered) no doubt helps to explain why Mr Whitelaw, while he jumped into immediate acceptance of the pay recommendations by the Inquiry, was much more cautious about the prison-building and prison-reform programmes that were simultaneously recommended.

The first response from the Scottish Home & Health Department was to set up a May Report Unit which consisted of two administrative class civil servants. In late 1980 several internal working groups were established to consider various aspects of the report such as Objectives and Regimes, Organisation and Management, Physical Resources, Staff Roles, Training, Industrial Relations, Staff Mobility, Transfers and Promotions. The remit of all these working groups was to report to the Prison Service Management Group. The majority of them did so by mid 1982. In many instances the reports of these groups disappeared without trace; elements of others were taken up with the Scottish Prison Service Whitley Council.

It would be incorrect to paint a totally negative picture of the outcome of the May Report. There were organisational changes in the Home Office. Distanced inspectorates were introduced in Scotland and in England, although one might question whether the Scots one at least is operating in the manner envisaged by May. It is hard to avoid the conclusion that May's main achievement was to settle the original problem which was one of pay for prison officers. (Within twelve months of the publication of the report prison governors had negotiated a separate pay settlement with the Treasury.)

In dealing with the separate and much more fundamental issue of the objectives of the prison services within a criminal justice context the May Committee failed to shed any new light. The majority of issues which it suggested required further investigation were dealt with in the time-honoured bureaucratic fashion, by setting up a further set of committees which sat until the original issue had been forgotten, and whose own reports were eventually quietly filed.

Since the final act of centralisation of the prison systems in 1877 there have been major inquiries, largely to do with pay and conditions of service for staff, every quarter century or so. The first two of these, Gladstone in England in 1895 and Elgin in Scotland five years later, took a more fundamental look at the prison system. The Stanhope Report in 1923 was concerned with pay and conditions and was generally considered to have been unsatisfactory. The Wynn Parry Report in 1958 was similarly concerned with pay and conditions and was generally seen as having been successful. History is likely to view May as also having been concerned primarily with pay rather than wider issues; one suspects that it will be linked more with Stanhope than with Wynn Parry.

6 Good Order Under Stress
Difficult Management: Difficult Prisoners

In respect of prisoners the task of prison management can be, and in this book is, expressed in three main categories: custody, good order and opportunity. First, the prison service has a fundamental responsibility to ensure that prisoners are held in custody until expiry of sentence or until such time as the Secretary of State sets an earlier date for release. Second, prisons should provide a safe environment both for staff and for prisoners. Third, the resources and facilities available in prison should be organised and presented to prisoners in such a way as to encourage them to make full use of these opportunities with a view both to using their time in prison constructively and to preparing themselves for release. In this chapter we are discussing the second of these categories:

> If custody is elevated to the first rank in the list of tasks to be accomplished by the prison, the objective of maintaining internal order is a close second. (Sykes 1971)

The responsibility of maintaining internal order is placed on the prison service by the Secretary of State, who is responsible to parliament for the administration of prisons; by society, on whose behalf prisoners are held captive; and not least by prisoners themselves. For if anarchy exists in a prison, if staff do not exercise control, then a minority of prisoners will take control and that will be bad news for the majority. Most prisoners most of the time accept the necessity of control and good order in prisons.

In 1837 the newly appointed Inspector of Prisons for Scotland had already noted one important feature about prisons:

In a Prison, as in many places in the outer world, there are
commonly a few desperate fellows who set all ordinary means of
control at defiance, and who are only to be restrained by physical
means. But, under good regulations, the great majority of
prisoners are quite tractable and make no attempt to escape; and
a skilful Governor soon becomes acquainted with their different
characters.

The alleged reasons given for serious incidents of unrest in prisons
have not changed significantly over the last 150 years. In 1861 there
was a major riot in Perth Prison involving a recently sentenced group
of long term prisoners and troops had to be called from the city to quell
the disturbance. In their annual report for 1862 the Managers of the
General Prison attributed this riot directly to the increased length of
sentences being passed by the courts:

We have kept in view, however, that with the progress of
time . . . a new class of prisoners are generally coming into
existence, namely, those who have been for a long period in
detention, and who, owing to the effect of protracted
confinement, both on the body and the mind, require a method of
treatment not necessarily applicable to prisoners whose privation
of liberty has been more recent.

Moving to more recent times, a serious riot took place in Barlinnie
Prison in late 1934. A committee of inquiry under the chairmanship of
Sir George Rankin reported on the incident (1935). It found that the
riot had been sparked off by unrest over what to an outsider might
appear as relatively minor concessions which prisoners had come to
expect.

The main recommendation which I desire to make upon this
aspect of the case is that in my judgement the time has now
come when the Prisons Department may with advantage review
and settle the whole question of 'privileges' in Scottish
Prisons . . . There will be a distinct advantage if too great
discrepancy as between the practice at one prison and the
practice at another can be avoided, as prisoners are quick to
make comparisons between the routine at different prisons and
discontent may easily be caused in this way.

In the course of the 1980s the Scottish Prison Service experienced a number of major incidents which were traumatic in terms of their number and ferocity. While the whole question of recent unrest in Scottish prisons requires careful examination, it should not be considered as an entirely new phenomenon, nor outwith its wider context. The foundation of any prison system is that one group of human beings deprives another group of human beings of liberty. In such an environment it is no surprise that from time to time major incidents of unrest occur.

Another cautionary note is in order. We should not be too hasty in identifying a prisoner as 'difficult' or 'dangerous'. Very often prisoners, particularly those in the early years of adulthood, require time to accept the prospect of many years of incarceration. A negative response from such a prisoner need not necessarily be translated into violence if properly managed:

> . . . a lot of people question the ethics of labelling a specified
> individual as dangerous in order to justify special measures of
> control. Their arguments vary. Some hold that labelling a man as
> dangerous can make him more so, even make a dangerous man
> out of a non-dangerous one. The way in which he is treated by
> police and prison staff can make him respond aggressively to any
> attempts to control him, or indeed other forms of frustration
> when he is at liberty again. This is not, however, an argument
> against labelling anyone as dangerous, but against careless
> labelling and certain techniques of inmate management.
> (Walker, 1980)

The problem of how to manage these 'few desperate fellows' in prison is not unique to Scotland. The Correctional Service of Canada has responded to this problem by establishing Special Handling Units in which the prisoners who present the greatest management problems are held in very restricted regimes. In the United States of America the Federal Bureau of Prisons has two models which lie at either end of the spectrum of available options. The Federal Correctional Institution in Butner, North Carolina, has developed a regime modelled directly on that proposed by Norval Morris (1974), which called for a secure, humane environment in which a prisoner, aware of his release date and a graduated release plan, could focus attention on acquiring self-knowledge and self-control.

At the other end of the spectrum is Marion Federal Penitentiary, Illinois, whose regime amounts to straightforward warehousing. The danger in Marion is that staff and prisoners have become so entrenched in their isolation that the negative regime becomes self-perpetuating. The challenge of not allowing this to happen in the management of its most intractable prisoners may well be the measure of the humanity of a prison system. In England and Wales the Home Office Prison Department has experimented with a series of models designed to cope with the prisoner who presents serious management problems. The latest of these are based on recommendations made by the *Report of the Control Review Committee (1984)*.

The Scottish Context

One of the great debates in the prison service in England and Wales over the last twenty-five or so years regarding the custody of those prisoners who require to be held in conditions of maximum security has centred around the relative merits of whether they should be *concentrated* in one location or *dispersed* in several. The Mountbatten Report on prison security in 1966 recommended that such prisoners should all be concentrated into one super-secure prison. The Radzinowicz Report on long term imprisonment two years later recommended that these prisoners should be dispersed around several prisons. The latter recommendation was based on the situation which committee members discovered in the federal system in the United States. (It is now clear that the apparent dispersal system which they found in operation was merely a hiatus between the closure of Alcatraz and the opening of Marion Penitentiary.) The policy of dispersal was adopted in England and Wales and has been in operation since then although there are indications that the principle of concentration may be coming back into favour.

Because of the small number of prisoners involved and also because there were not the same pressures which led to the setting up of the Mountbatten Inquiry in England, Scotland never had to make a clear choice between the two models of concentration or dispersal. It continued, as it had done since 1888, to locate its most difficult and violent prisoners in Peterhead Prison. This enforced restriction of choice turned out to have unforeseen benefits for it obliged the organisation to focus on the two issues which are fundamental in coping with the problem of difficult and violent prisoners. These are the relationship between staff and prisoners and the separation of the latter into small groups.

There has never been any argument in Scotland, at least in theory, that the key to the smooth running of a prison is the relationship between the prison officer and the prisoner. Since the early 1960s the most frequent expression of this has been through some form of group officer system which has involved one or more officers being given responsibility for a group of about ten prisoners. There has been increasing appreciation that there are particular benefits to be gained from developing this kind of arrangement for prisoners who pose special problems.

The Scottish prison system has traditionally allowed large numbers of prisoners to congregate at work, recreation and exercise. One consequence of this arrangement is that from time to time individual prisoners can seriously disrupt the smooth running of an establishment. The normal forms of official response to prisoners who refuse to conform to rules and regulations have been loss of remission or of other so-called privileges such as association, recreation or earnings, for a limited period. In extreme cases a governor can request application of the provisions of Prison (Scotland) Rule 36:

> If at any time it appears to the Visiting Committee or the
> Secretary of State that it is desirable for the maintenance of good
> order or discipline, or in the interests of a prisoner, that he
> should not be employed in association with others, the Visiting
> Committee or the Secretary of State may authorise the Governor
> to arrange for him to work in a cell, and not in association for a
> period not exceeding one month from the date of each
> authorisation.

With the increasing freedom of association accorded to prisoners in the years after the end of the Second World War these forms of individual control, including Rule 36, were found insufficient to manage the very small group of prisoners whose level of protest was most explicit, particularly at Peterhead Prison. This was despite the fact that all prisoners at Peterhead were, and remain today, in single cell accommodation.

Unrest increasingly took the form of violence against both staff and other prisoners. The introduction of the Murder (Abolition of the Death Penalty) Act 1965 meant that the ultimate penal deterrent in the United Kingdom became imprisonment. In the opinion of some people the abolition of capital punishment did nothing to check the level of prison violence. For a decade before the passing of this legislation the

Scottish Prison Officers' Association had been consistently arguing that its members were in an increasingly vulnerable position. At the departmental Whitley Council in 1956 it had pressed for the construction of a separate unit to house those prisoners in the event of 'no-hanging' legislation being introduced. The Home and Health Department responded by stating that it shared the concern of the staff and accepted the need for a special establishment to house the troublesome element in Scottish prisons.

The Inverness Unit

A departmental working party, on which staff had a strong voice, and which had been set up to review arrangements for the classification of prisoners, recommended in early 1966 that a unit to hold particularly difficult prisoners should be set up within Inverness Prison. The unit was seen as one measure to reduce the likelihood of assaults on staff. The system of group isolation was intended to contain any prisoner who was 'violent, subversive or recalcitrant' until such time as he demonstrated his fitness to return to his normal prison of classification.

The expected profile of such prisoners would include a record of subversive behaviour, usually accompanied by violence against other prisoners and/or staff. Not uncommonly there would be involvement in factional feuds among prisoners. The prisoner concerned would probably have spent a number of periods in segregation in his prison of allocation. The routine in the proposed unit was to be a spartan one, consisting of hard work, strict supervision and limited 'privileges'. Governors would recommend prisoners for transfer to the unit and all transfers would be approved by the Home and Health Department. Subsequent response was to be reviewed by an internal board.

The recommendation was accepted by the Department and in October 1966 the new unit was opened in A Hall, the main accommodation block in Inverness Prison. Two years later the Segregation Unit, as it had become known, was relocated in the smaller B Hall.

With hindsight it seems clear that in setting up this unit two incorrect assumptions were made. The first was that the existing staff in Inverness Prison, a small local establishment holding short-term prisoners, would be able to operate the unit without special training. The second was that it would be suitable for all 'violent, subversive or recalcitrant' prisoners. The unit, far from having the desired effect on some prisoners, appeared to exacerbate their unruly conduct. The more restrictive the regime in which they were held, the worse their behaviour became. One result of this was that some prisoners were held in the unit for periods considerably in excess of the originally estimated average of four months.

This unhappy situation led to a series of major incidents in the unit between 1969 and 1972. In April 1969 complaints were voiced at the annual conference of the Scottish Prison Officers' Association about relaxations which were being made to the spartan regime in the unit.

There were several incidents in the unit in November 1969, following one of which all prisoners were relocated in the punishment block of the prison. The Inspector of Prisons carried out an investigation into these incidents. He found that staff strongly resented the fact that prisoners were being kept in the unit beyond the period when, by their behaviour and conduct, they could have been returned to their prison of classification. The Inspector recommended a significant physical alteration to the unit which involved erecting a grille corridor within each cell area to separate prisoners from staff. Work was put in hand to improve the security of the former punishment block and ancillary accommodation as well as incorporating the changes proposed by the Inspector of Prisons. The upgraded Segregation Unit was opened in April 1971.

On 28 December 1972 there was a serious incident of violence in the unit when four prisoners, all of them regarded as very dangerous, launched an organised attack on staff during an evening period of recreation in association. The fifth prisoner was indisposed and in his cell at the time. They were subdued after a battle in which one officer lost an eye, others sustained stab wounds and two prisoners were injured. The four prisoners were subsequently convicted of assault to severe injury and attempting to escape; each was sentenced to a further six years' imprisonment.

A decision to set up the Special Unit in Barlinnie Prison had already been taken and, when it opened in early 1973, three of the prisoners from the Inverness Unit were transferred to it. The two others from the unit were returned to their prison of classification. Between February and June 1973 ten out of the forty-three staff in post at Inverness Prison at the time of the December incident left the prison service.

Although no prisoners were transferred to the unit after the incident in December 1972, the official position was that the unit was never formally closed and was available for use. This position was confirmed by the Under Secretary of State in October 1973. In June of that year representatives of the Scottish Prison Officers' Association had met the Minister and asked among other things that in future all prisoners in the unit should be held under 'Rule 36' conditions; that is, with no association.

A review of staffing and procedures was begun in consultation with the SPOA. Despite the fact that the unit was technically available for use governors were aware that this review was going on and were discouraged from identifying prisoners for possible transfer to the unit. The review was completed in 1976 and new regulations for the unit were drawn up. Its purpose was defined as follows:

> The Unit will be used for the secure custody, for a limited period, of prisoners who, despite repeated employment of appropriate correctional methods within their establishment of classification, continue to exert by their behaviour and attitude a marked subversive influence and flagrant refusal to co-operate in the course of the normal daily routine in the work of the establishment.

In the course of the 1970s the Inverness Unit took on what was almost a symbolic significance both inside and outside the Prison Service. In response to press requests for comment the Secretary of State issued a public statement on 2 February 1978 which began as follows:

> In view of the recent publicity given to the Segregation Unit at Inverness Prison and the suggestion that it may be brought into use again I want to make it quite clear that there is no intention of placing prisoners in the unit at this time.

In May 1978 another departmental working party recommended that the unit should be made available for immediate use. A public campaign was mounted, largely supported by the press, in opposition to any further use of the unit. This was energetically countered by the SPOA. In November 1978 a special delegate conference of the Association decided to implement a form of limited industrial action in protest against the continuing failure to admit prisoners to the unit.

Later that same month representatives of the SPOA presented three resolutions from that conference to the Under Secretary of State. First, they said, there was a need for alternative units to deal with unruly and violent prisoners. The Minister agreed that his department should enter into informal discussions with the Prison Governors' Committee and the SPOA on this matter. Second, there was a need for further visits by the media to penal establishments. On 14 November 1978 forty members of the press had taken part in a visit to the Inverness Unit. Third, a standing committee should be set up to consider the allocation and treatment of violent and unruly prisoners. The Minister agreed that such a committee should be established and that its membership should include representatives of the governors, the SPOA and the Home and Health Department as well as a psychiatrist and an independent layman. In December 1978 one prisoner was transferred to the unit. Since then it has been in regular although not continuous use.

In July 1984 the European Commission on Human Rights rejected a complaint by a prisoner that his period of detention in the unit constituted a breach of Article 3 of the European Convention on Human Rights which states that 'No one shall be subjected to torture or to inhuman or degrading treatment or punishment'.

The relatively smooth operation of the Inverness Unit during the last ten years owes much to the lessons which were learned in the early years. Before it re-opened all staff in Inverness Prison were given training in what to expect during their periods of duty in the unit and how they should respond. The central monitoring body has provided a safeguard for prisoners located in the unit and a support for staff. Although a detailed routine has been agreed for the operation of the unit and is strictly adhered to, what amounts to an informal and unwritten contract is agreed between staff and prisoners. Those among the latter who wish little contact with staff have their wish granted, receiving only the necessary supervision and physical care. On the other hand many prisoners sent to the unit appear to regard their stay there as 'time out' from the pressures of their normal prison existence and take the opportunity to discuss their problems at length with staff.

In March 1979 the Secretary of State established a standing committee to consider the allocation and treatment of unruly, violent and/ or subversive prisoners. The terms of reference given to this committee were:

> To advise the Department on the allocation and management of prisoners referred to it by the Department because of difficulties created by their unruly, violent and/or subversive behaviour.

> In the case of prisoners detained in the Inverness Unit, to advise, on the basis of periodic reports from the Inverness Prison Assessment Team, on their management and, in particular, their transfer from the Unit in accordance with the Rules governing the Unit.

> The Committee may, if their experience suggests that alternative
> regimes or units are desirable for the management of violent,
> unruly and/or subversive prisoners, make recommendations on
> the subject to the Department.

The new committee was to consist of two representatives each from the
Prison Governors' Committee and the SPOA, an officer of the
department, a psychiatrist and a lay member. At the first meeting of the
committee, in June 1979, the lay member was elected chairman. In
practice the committee has concerned itself almost exclusively with
those prisoners located in the Inverness Unit.

It is very rare for a prisoner to be sent to the Inverness Unit other
than from Peterhead Prison. To a great extent its future use in its
present form will be inextricably linked to the continuing use of
Peterhead Prison for the detention of prisoners who present difficulties
to management. Whatever the reality of its present operation it cannot
shake off the image of the 'cages', given it as a result of the grilled
corridor outwith the cell area, and the reputation which remains a
legacy from the early years of its use (Boyle, 1977).

The Barlinnie Special Unit
In May 1970 representatives of the Scottish Prison Officers' Association met with the Parliamentary Under Secretary of State to discuss the
safety of prison staff. Following that meeting the Minister agreed that
a working party should be set up 'to consider what arrangements
should be made for the treatment of certain inmates likely to be
detained in custody for very long periods or with propensities to
violence towards staff'. The working party, which included departmental officials and a psychiatrist as well as representatives of the
governors and the SPOA reported in 1972, making sixteen recommendations. The first and last of these were respectively:

> A Special unit should be provided within the Scottish Penal
> System for the treatment of known violent inmates, those
> considered potentially violent and selected long term inmates.

> The traditional officer/inmate relationship should be modified to
> approximate more closely to a therapist/patient basis while
> retaining a firm but fair discipline system.

A further recommendation was that the unit should be purpose built within the grounds of Perth Prison. This was subsequently found not to be feasible on technical grounds. At that time the former female block within Barlinnie Prison in Glasgow was vacant and it was decided that the new Special Unit should be located there. In November 1972 the initial staff volunteers and the appointed governor began an eleven weeks' training course consisting of five weeks at Polmont Officers' Training School and six weeks spent between Grendon Underwood Prison, Broadmoor and Carstairs State Hospital. On 5 February the unit was opened and within a short period five prisoners had been admitted, including three from the Inverness Segregation Unit.

Following the Scottish tradition of what may be euphemistically described as pragmatic regime development, the unit was allowed largely to create its own ethos. In the early years a strong sense of community, encompassing both staff and prisoners, developed. This was due in some measure to the external criticism which the unit attracted. One Scottish Sunday newspaper complained of the 'expensive kid glove treatment' being accorded to prisoners in the unit.

The SPOA has always, officially at least, regarded itself as one of the prime movers in the establishment of the Special Unit and the General Secretary of the Association was soon publicly defending the concept of the unit against such criticism. Privately staff in the unit complained at the treatment which they received at the hands of staff in the main prison of Barlinnie and, together with criticism coming from other parts of the service, there was an early crisis of confidence within the unit.

The virtual absence of restriction on visits led to a steady stream of interested individuals, several of whom attended on a regular basis. Within the secure perimeter prisoners had relative freedom of movement for most of the day. In the absence of organised work some of them took up painting, sculpting and writing which in turn generated further external interest.

It could be argued that in its early days an error of judgement was made in allowing too strong a spotlight to be turned on the Special Unit initiative. This resulted in a polarisation of views about its relative value. Conscious of this, the Scottish Home and Health Department embarked in the mid and late 1970s on a deliberate policy of reducing the publicity which it attracted. This in turn led to suggestions that the Department was embarrassed by its perceived success in managing prisoners who had previously been highly disruptive. As a result the government felt obliged to express public support for the unit on several occasions. In December 1979, for example, the Under Secretary of State gave the following reply to a question in the House of Commons:

> I have already made it clear on a number of occasions that it is
> the Government's intention that the Special Unit should continue
> to operate as it has in the past and in the way that was intended
> when it was first set up.

The Barlinnie Special Unit can hold a maximum of eight prisoners. All will be serving long sentences and are typically potentially violent, volatile and intelligent. Prisoners with serious psychiatric problems or drug dependency are not admitted. Potential candidates are initially recommended by the governor of the prison of classification. An assessment of suitability is carried out by a group of staff from the unit and the implications of transfer are discussed with the prisoner. If the assessment is favourable the case is referred to the Secretary of State for approval.

An early difficulty was the suspicion that some prisoners elsewhere in the system regarded the unit as a soft option and took the view that if they created maximum unrest, often by assaulting staff, they were more likely to be transferred there. The method of assessment and selection has attempted to exclude such motives for transfer and such allegations are rarely voiced today. With the exception of the governor all staff in the unit are volunteers. They also go through an assessment period and a screening process before being recommended for work there.

The main community activities centre round a series of regular meetings. The most important of these is the formal weekly community meeting. Those present elect a chairman and a record is kept of the discussion. Security and staffing issues may not be raised but other matters are open to full debate. Domestic questions are decided at the meeting. Other issues are referred to the governor or to headquarters as necessary. There is no formalised system of punishment. A serious breach of rules may result in transfer from the unit. When internally agreed procedures are broken the prisoner concerned has to explain his actions to other members of the community.

There is no structured programme of work. Prisoners are encouraged to develop individual interests in art, sculpting, education, woodwork, physical training or hobbies. The standard rate of prison earnings is paid. Correspondence is censored only during an early supervised period. There is no restriction on the number of visits although visitors must be approved by the community. After the initial supervised period visits may be taken in cells. Visitors are permitted to bring in small amounts of food, tobacco and money.

Any attempt at a self-governing regime, even of a limited nature, within the prison system creates its own pressure. There is continuing tension between self-government and the necessary limitations which exist because of the high degree of perimeter security. Early tensions in the unit were not eased by two serious incidents. In March 1976 one prisoner stabbed another thirteen times and was subsequently sentenced to a further six years' imprisonment. In September 1977 a prisoner was found dead in his cell having consumed a quantity of drugs which had been secretly brought in. The Home and Health Department recorded the dilemma which it faced as being how to cope with 'the rehabilitative elements of a venture originally devised for the more effective *control* of a very limited number of prisoners'.

There are several lessons to be learned from the manner in which the Special Unit has developed since 1973. Despite the radical departure from traditional forms of prison management and frequent description of the regime as experimental no attempt was made to build in a formal assessment and continuing evaluation of the regime. This lack has now been recognised and evaluation is now being attempted (Cooke, 1988).

There has always been an uneasy relationship between the Barlinnie Special Unit and the rest of the Scottish Prison Service. It has appeared at times that the service as a whole has been taken aback by the praise heaped on the unit by external observers, both nationally and internationally. Rather than claim the unit as a significant success the service has tended to hold it at arm's length, more than slightly embarrassed at its perceived success. This ambivalence has resulted in the marginalisation of the unit, leaving it somehow in but not of the prison service. This situation has been encouraged by some of those connected with the unit who wish to retain its 'special' nature as something unique as well as by those elsewhere who are reluctant to examine the implications of the unit for other parts of the service.

As it now operates, the Barlinnie Special Unit is attempting to provide worthwhile support for the rest of the prison system. It has arguably contributed to a reduction of tension in other prisons by isolating some of the system's worst troublemakers. It has allowed many of these difficult prisoners to cope with their long sentences in a positive manner and in several cases has facilitated an earlier return to the outside community than might otherwise have been expected. In a word, it has provided an alternative means of managing prisoners who present difficulties.

The Individual Unit at Peterhead

In 1976 two patients who were detained in the State Hospital at Carstairs carried out an escape from the hospital in the course of which they committed three murders. At their subsequent trial they were found to be sane and both were sentenced to life imprisonment. It was decided that one of them, although requiring conditions of the strictest security, could be located in one of the halls of Perth Prison. The second one, however, was considered to be so dangerous that he required to be located in a specially converted unit in Peterhead Prison. The unit, which has housed this prisoner since that time, includes a cell, work room and ablutions. The prisoner is allowed to circulate within this area during the day. Throughout that period he is supervised by three members of staff.

The Ten Cell Unit at Peterhead

The first of the three conference resolutions which the Scottish Prison Officers' Association had presented to the Under Secretary of State in 1978 had concerned the need for further alternative units and the Minister had agreed to tripartite discussions. When these began among departmental officials, the Prison Governors' Committee and the SPOA in January 1979 the Association pressed the need for a unit in which prisoners would be held under the conditions of Prison (Scotland) Rule 36. Those involved in subsequent discussions concluded that such a unit was necessary. Given that the majority of the prisoners concerned could be expected to be of Peterhead classification, it was decided that the new unit should be built within the confines of that prison so that the prisoners could be dealt with while out of circulation by the same staff who would have to look after them in normal circumstances. It was also agreed that the unit should be under the direct control of the governor of Peterhead Prison and that it should have accommodation for ten prisoners.

Construction work began in June 1982 and at that time it was decided that for presentational purposes it should be described as the Ten Cell Unit rather than the Rule 36 Unit. In that same month the

Under Secretary of State advised the local member of parliament, who had asked for details of the unit:

> The Ten Cell Unit is being built in response to a request from the SPOA – and in recognition of an existing need – to provide alternative facilities to deal with prisoners who require, for whatever reasons, to be removed from normal circulation within our adult penal establishments.

It was later confirmed that the unit was to be simply another facility within the prison of Peterhead which would be available to the governor to assist in managing the numbers of increasingly difficult prisoners held within that prison. The SPOA was unhappy at this development and pressed to have central oversight of movements into and out of the new unit. This difference of opinion was taken up by the press and attracted considerable coverage. On 9 February 1983 *The Scotsman* reported that:

> This equivocation has led to confusion on the part of the SPOA, who are angry at not being consulted; suspicion among Scotland's 4500 inmates, who fear that a new tougher stance is being adopted; and concern by MPs over the possibility that such a policy change is being sneaked through the back door without any attendant political debate.

In March 1984 the *Glasgow Herald* reported that the SPOA considered the unit to be too vulnerable in construction and that it was concerned that its wish to have referrals controlled by the Standing Committee on Difficult Prisoners had not been regarded, thus depriving officers of input into the management of the unit. This latter concern did not appear to take account of the fact that officers at Peterhead were involved in the local working party which was drawing up a regime for the unit. The SPOA continued to urge the Home and Health Department to place control of transfers into and out of the new unit not in the hands of the governor of Peterhead Prison but in those of the Standing Committee on Difficult Prisoners.

In June 1984 the Director of the Scottish Prison Service advised the SPOA that, while the unit would accommodate only prisoners from Peterhead Prison and only the governor of that prison would be able to recommend prisoners for transfer to it, the Secretary of State had decided that for a trial period of one year from the date of opening, the procedures for admission to and transfer from the unit would parallel those for the Inverness Unit. The first prisoner was transferred to the unit in December 1984. The agreed review of procedures never took place and subsequent use of the unit has been influenced largely by events in Peterhead Prison.

The 'B' Hall Unit in Peterhead

Following a serious riot in Peterhead Prison in January 1984, the Governor presented a case to the Scottish Home and Health Department arguing the need for a separate unit and regime which would provide another option in the management of prisoners who were regularly given to offering violence to staff and to damaging the fabric of the prison. After internal discussion and investigation it was decided that such a unit should be provided within B Hall in the prison. The alterations which were subsequently carried out involved blocking off all but the ground floor of the hall, strengthening the security within each cell and providing pens in which prisoners would be allowed to exercise.

In November 1984 the Secretary of State announced that the new unit was ready for use:

> The regime will, of necessity, be strict. It will not, however, be punitive. The main feature will be that at no time will the number of prisoners in association be allowed to exceed the number of staff in attendance. Work (where it can be found), exercise and recreation will normally be in association but it will be in groups of no more than three prisoners. It is recognised, however, that for some prisoners full association will not always be appropriate, in which case permission will be sought in the normal way, in terms of Rule 36 of the Prison (Scotland) Rules, to restrict association.

This hall has been in regular use since it opened, almost exclusively as a unit in which prisoners are held under the conditions of Rule 36, often for very extensive periods of time.

Recent Major Incidents

In the period since 1984 the Scottish Prison Service has had to face an unprecedented series of major incidents. There were two significant features of these incidents. In the first place they were spread across several establishments holding long term prisoners and were not restricted to Peterhead Prison, which traditionally held most if not all prisoners who were actively disruptive within the Scottish prison system. Secondly, most of the more recent incidents involved one or more members of staff being taken hostage.

1984 - Peterhead roof-top hostage incident
1985 - Peterhead tailor's shop hostage incident
1985 - Peterhead separate cells escape attempt
1986 - Edinburgh hostage incident
1987 - Barlinnie, Perth, Shotts, Peterhead and Perth hostage incidents
1988 - Perth and Edinburgh hostage incidents
1988 - Unrest at Glenochil and Shotts
1990 - Shotts hostage incident

Major incidents are not a new phenomenon in Scottish long term prisons although the scale and nature of the latest series of incidents far exceeds anything previously experienced. The two traditional types of incident in prisons have been escape attempts and internal disturbance. Only one of the incidents listed above was a direct escape attempt although others may have included that objective. Previous experience of hostage incidents was limited but they had usually involved a single hostage and one or two perpetrators with the incident taking place in a relatively confined space. In contrast the latest hostage incidents involved the indirect participation of large numbers of prisoners either voluntarily or involuntarily, usually accompanied by considerable destruction to the fabric of the building where the incident had taken place.

Several reasons have been advanced for all or each of these disturbances. What seems most likely is that there has been no one identifiable cause. There have been a series of contributory factors, one or more of which may have applied in each incident. These factors came together at a particular time, either with a degree of pre-planning or with comparatively little organisation. One particular catalyst then sparked off the disturbance.

It has been suggested that the recent practice of courts to pass an increasing number of very long sentences has left some prisoners in a very frustrated frame of mind. It is certainly true that there is a number of young adult prisoners, in their early to mid twenties, who are having great difficulty in coming to terms with the prospect of spending a sizable proportion of their adult lives deprived of liberty.

As an extension of this theory, it has been suggested that the attitude of prisoners has been affected by the statement made by the Secretary of State for Scotland in December 1984 about restrictions on consideration of early release on parole for some prisoners. It has been pointed out in response that the statistics of those released on parole have been little altered by the changed arrangements. However, there was undoubtedly a perception among some prisoners that the likelihood of being granted parole had diminished and this engendered a sense of hopelessness and of having nothing to lose.

The influence of the drug culture is suggested by some as a contributory factor. There has been a significant increase in recent years in the number of long sentences passed on drug offenders. Many prisoners come from an environment in the community in which drugs are an important feature. Some of them maintain their interest in drugs while in prison and the threat or promise of drugs being introduced to prison, given the amount of money which may be involved, may influence the behaviour of some prisoners.

Finally, the balance of stability in any prison regime is always a delicate one. This stability was jeopardised in many establishments in mid 1987 when a significant proportion of the Scottish prison population was re-distributed across several establishments in an exercise which was given the unfortunate title 'Grand Design'. At the time the prison population was unevenly distributed between prisons and young offenders' institutions, with overcrowding in the former and spare capacity in the latter. Shotts Prison also became available for use at that time. The exercise achieved the important objective of giving more even distribution of prisoners but this may have been achieved at the cost of destabilising regimes in several of the establishments involved.

Response to Recent Disturbances

Because of the high public profile in which it was conducted, the incident which brought matters to a head was that which concluded in Peterhead Prison in October 1987. Following this an order went out from the centre that all association among prisoners should cease in every penal establishment. Within a matter of weeks the restriction was relaxed, first in open prisons, then in young offenders' institutions, then in most local prisons. The restriction on association was continued for a much longer period in most long term prisons. This experience has introduced a new American phrase into Scottish penal languages: 'lock down', an unfortunate term which has emotive undertones. Prisoners involved are locked up for long periods of time each day.

In an attempt to restore a degree of normality to the long term prison system it was decided that the sixty prisoners who presented the most serious threat to management should be identified, separated from the mainstream system and located in Peterhead Prison. Although this was done quickly restrictions on association remained in force, particularly in Shotts and Glenochil Prisons, for a considerable period, largely as a result of continuing unrest in those two establishments. The prisoners who were located in Peterhead Prison were, initially at least, held for a long period directly under the provisions of Prison Rule 36 or under broadly equivalent conditions.

This sort of response, while understandable in the short term, is essentially a negative one and cannot be sustained for a lengthy period, let alone indefinitely. We do not know what the psychological effect on prisoners of long term detention in these conditions may be. It certainly increases bitterness and frustration, which are in turn vented on staff. All those directly involved, governors, officers and prisoners, know that it is not practicable to detain a man in such conditions for the duration of, say, a ten or twenty year sentence. Neither is it ethical.

The Scottish Prison Service recognised the fundamental nature of this problem by producing a discussion document *Assessment and Control* in 1988. This document did not meet with universal approval but it underlined that the continuing strategy of the Scottish Prison Service towards the prisoner who has difficulty in coping with his sentence, however that manifests itself, is his location in a small unit where he will be looked after by a specially selected group of staff. A further purpose-built unit with twelve places has been set up at Shotts Prison and opened in April 1990.

The challenge which presents itself at this time is to assess the degree to which positive features and developments can be introduced to the management of these prisoners without threatening good order and control. The essence of this problem was underlined in the report on Marion Penitentiary, Illinois, which was produced by the Committee on the Judiciary of the United States House of Representatives in 1985:

> One of the greatest challenges to penal policy makers is the need
> to control the most violent prisoners in the country while at the

same time exercising creativity in trying to devise and then try,
on an experimental basis, activities that will not contribute to
further deterioration of these inmates – deterioration which can
lead in turn to greater risks of serious injury to staff, other
prisoners, and often to the community upon the inmate's
eventual release.

One is able to conclude from this analysis of how methods of dealing
with difficult prisoners in the Scottish prison system have developed
over the last twenty-five or so years, that the major initiatives have
come from the staff as a body. Most of the units presently in existence
were introduced after approaches made to the Secretary of State by the
Scottish Prison Officers' Association.

The general need for alternative units and for a standing committee
on difficult prisoners have also been pursued by the SPOA with the
Secretary of State at various times. Once agreement on the need of each
of these units was reached the Home and Health Department has
pursued a policy of what might euphemistically be described as
pragmatic regime development. Very few guidelines have been laid
down in the initial stages. When subsequent difficulties have arisen an
attempt has then been made to lay down specific regime regulations.

In the case of the Inverness Unit this attempt appears to have
succeeded. According to official files it is doubtful whether the
attempt at pragmatic regime development has succeeded in the case of
the Barlinnie Special Unit, although in this case one might argue that
the concept of the unit precludes the existence of firm regulations.
Arguably the development of the ten cell unit in Peterhead presents the
best example of how this pragmatic style of management can be
subjected to organised staff pressure. The SPOA pressed initially for
a 'Rule 36' unit and this was agreed by the department. The Association later changed its line of approach to advocate the need for a more
general type of unit which would be subject to oversight by the
Standing Committee on Difficult Prisoners, on which it was represented. In agreeing to this on an experimental basis the Secretary of
State made a significant alteration to the use of the unit, which had been
physically constructed to fulfil another purpose.

It has been rare for the Home and Health Department to take the
initiative. Instead it has followed what has been described as its
traditional management style, based on administrative civil service
culture, of responding to and reaching an accommodation when faced
with persistent pressure.

Stirling Old Tolbooth today - the old local jail. The cells were behind the ground floor windows, hence the ease with which prisoners communicated to those on the outside. *(John Harrison)*

Above: Edinburgh Prison from Calton Hill, 1881 - a place of exile in the midst of the city. Friends were said to gather on Calton Hill to shout to the prisoners. *(Royal Commission on the Ancient & Historical Monuments of Scotland)*

low: Duke Street Prison, Glasgow - the former Bridewell during demolition in 1959. Note how the son blended in with the local tenements. *(Mitchell Library, Glasgow)*

Above: Convict Labour at Peterhead Quarry in the 1950s - prison officers still carried carbine and cutlass. Faces were blacked out to prevent identification of individuals. *(Aberdeen Journals)*

Opposite: Gallery Duty at Saughton Prison, Edinburgh 1991 *(Colin Chalmers)*

Below: 'C' Hall Peterhead in the 1950s *(Aberdeen Journals)*

Above: Peterhead Rooftop Protest 1987 *(Glasgow Herald)*

Below: Passing the Time, Edinburgh Saughton Prison 1991 *(Colin Chalmers)*

ove: Disturbing Times - Scottish Prison Officer 1988 *(BBC Scotland)*

er Page: Protest Outside, Glenochil Prison 1988 *(Glasgow Herald)*

ow: Prisoner's Model, Saughton Edinburgh 1991 *(Colin Chalmers)*

This is not to pass judgement on the correctness of any individual decision. However, administrative responses which seek to accommodate pressure are dangerous in the organisation of a bureaucracy which has operational commitments. The primary concern of the Scottish Prison Officers' Association is the good of its members. In the vast majority of instances this good may well be consonant with the good of the service as a whole but this will not invariably be the case. There will be instances when the good of the service will be distinct from the good of one trade union, even one which represents the greatest percentage of employees. If management adopts a reactive style it will not be an easy task to foresee instances in which this distinction occurs.

One obvious lack in all of the units described has been any real attempt to assess whether they are achieving the purpose for which they were set up or indeed whether that purpose has changed in the course of operation. Such a definition of objective and method of continuous evaluation would be of considerable assistance to the staff who are asked to work in these units.

There are two essential components in the management of the type of prisoner to be found in these units. The first is that they should be identified and separated into small groups apart from the main body of prisoners. It would appear that the Scottish Prison Service is on the way to achieving this objective. The second essential component is that there must be intensive staff involvement with these prisoners. In most of the units there is a massive staff presence. It is arguable in some instances whether or not this presence is translated into involvement. Many of the prisoners concerned are unlikely to welcome initially any attempt by staff to work with them. In such situations staff can be expected to make progress only if they have a clear appreciation of the regime in which they are to operate and of the objectives towards which they are striving. It is a pre-condition that management must in the first instance define the nature of such regimes and objectives.

The development of the system of management of difficult prisoners in the Scottish prison system provides a particularly good example of the dangers of a reactive style of management. Each new departure has come about in response to pressure following particular incidents, pressure often exerted by means of a meeting between the SPOA and the political head of the service. The result has been a piecemeal development based on removing from the system prisoners who, at some point in time, are troublesome.

An alternative strategy would have been to examine the system from which such difficult prisoners come, to consider the need for radical alteration to the strategy for managing *all* prisoners in an attempt to anticipate and prevent management problems. Such an approach might have had considerable implications for the manner in which staff are required to carry out their daily duties and their relationship with prisoners. Such a style of management would have been in contrast to what has actually happened. It would have involved management taking the initiative in developing a continuing strategy. It would have placed the SPOA in a responsive position, obliging it to respond moreover, not simply to the immediate problem, but also to longer term objectives.

This is not to suggest that the staff trade unions should not have the opportunity to contribute to discussion on management policy. However, there is a distinction between consultative management and management which abdicates its responsibility to initiate and develop for the benefit of the whole organisation. In many instances management in the Scottish Prison Service is exercised in a consultative fashion. In this particular instance it may well have gone beyond consultation to participation.

7 The Prison Service as Bureaucracy

Prisons have an abiding fascination, largely because they are outside the acquaintance of the majority of people, unlike other large institutions such as schools and hospitals. The prison as an institution has been the subject of a considerable amount of research by academics who have understood that, despite its aura of secrecy, the prison has much in common with other similar organisations. The majority of this research has been undertaken in North America. The first study in this field in Britain was carried out by Terence and Pauline Morris (1963). They clearly appreciated the comparative nature of their work:

> The maximum security prison, like the mental hospital,
> has been thrown into relief as a challenging area for the study
> of organisational problems, particularly with respect to the
> communication of new ideas about treatment. Data from such
> studies are likely to prove comparable with those derived from
> the studies of other organisational structures such as the office,
> the industrial plant and the military unit.

There have been several subsequent studies in England, including Emery (1970), Cohen and Taylor (1972), Bottoms and McClintock (1973), King and Elliott (1977). These works concentrate on the prisoners in penal establishments either as an autonomous group or as individuals. They do not focus on the staff as a group in their own right. This neglect is not peculiar to English studies:

> For generations, criminologists have entered the prison world to
> study the backgrounds, personalities, attitudes, values and
> criminal careers of the inmates . . . The prison guard, however,

> has rarely been the subject of scholarly research. A student
> interested in the social origins of the guards, their work, and
> their ideology is hard-pressed to find even cursory data. (Jacobs,
> 1983)

In addition, these studies examine the prison as an institution rather than as one element in an organisational structure. Pentonville, Bristol, Durham and Albany Prisons and Dover Borstal are examined in isolation, or at most, with reference to comparable institutions rather than in the context of the prison system as an organisational structure. This method of approach is not unique to prison studies. One useful point of comparison for the prison system, particularly as far as staff are concerned, is the police. There also a microcosmic method of research has predominated (Jones, 1980).

The secrecy surrounding the prison system, which is often encouraged by those who work within it and is accepted by the public at large, comes not least from the notion of the prison as 'a self-sufficient social island' (Korn and McKorkle, 1967) or as a 'total institution' (Goffman, 1957). Some would suggest that because the prison duplicates many of the essential services which are available in the wider community its own isolation from that community is confirmed. Others would suggest that although the isolation of the prison has been modified in recent years the self-sufficiency still remains.

In fact, the myriad links between the prison system, individual prisons and prisoners and the wider society serve to ensure that no establishment functions in total isolation. Even if one was to accept the model of the total institution one could still compare the prison with other similar institutions, with mental hospitals, with old people's homes, with boarding schools (Smith, 1979). One may go much further than that and view not only the prison but also the prison service as a typical bureaucratic organisation.

Two factors, total control by central government and a keen sense of uniqueness, have frequently resulted in the notion that the prison system could not benefit from a comparative understanding of other large organisations since the foundation of the prison system is quite different from that of any other institution. Whereas all other organisations have had to compete for economic resources or to maintain the loyalty of those within them, this has not been true of the prison system with which no other organisation is in direct competition. On the one hand the prison system has not had to reach competitive standards as a profit making organisation and on the other hand it has not required to seek the sympathy and good will of those who funded it, as most non-profit making organisations must do. True, the prison system has to operate within legal limits but the legal requirements, as with other large state institutions, set a minimum standard and not an optimum. This has led to an assumption within the system that it is proper that it should be 'relatively independent of the intensive public scrutiny of success standards that often govern the existence of other institutions' (Grosser, 1960).

Such an assumption has not been discouraged by central government which is ultimately responsible for the administration of the prison system and which therefore arguably has most to gain from absence of public scrutiny.

To these inhibiting factors must be added the traditional reluctance of those within any well-established organisation to lay themselves open to unnecessary examination. Such a reluctance serves to confirm the power which these organisations are able to use to protect what they consider to be their best interests.

> Our social scientists may reasonably complain that while the lives of the less fortunate and less 'efficient' members of society are regarded as appropriate matters for them to explore, the objectives, methods and social ties of those who wield the power are not. The student of British society who entertains such possibilities will find that at best he is invited to admire the cupboard but never to open the door. For it is a simple fact that organisation generates power (this after all is its major purpose); and it is difficult to convince men with power of the necessity for scientific investigation of their behaviour. This is all the more true of a society as respectful as ours is of the established order, to which, as a rule, any organisation surviving early hazards can claim admission; secure in its membership it may well feel entitled to be screened from the prickly gaze of sociologists. (Blau and Scott, 1966)

However, there is little justification for this *sui generis* view of prison organisation. Each bureaucratic organisation requires a special class of administrators who draw up its policy and of executives who put this into practice, as well as a hierarchical system which rewards its members according to their various responsibilities. The notion of the prison existing as an island in isolation from civilian norms and values is inaccurate.

The arguments which are often used in an attempt to demonstrate that the prison service is unique and not similar to other bureaucratic organisations are precisely those which in fact prove that it is bureaucratic. There are clear divisions of labour within the system, each of which is aimed at achieving the primary objective of the system, which is secure custody in one form or another. It has a strongly hierarchical structure. Each member of staff is subject to a particular form of disciplinary control.

There is one other bureaucratic feature which is of particular importance in the prison service, that of institutionalised authority. Such authority, which is confined to relationships taking place within the hierarchical structure, is of prime importance in the prison setting and does not depend on the personality of the individual who exercises it.

While the authority of the governor and of other senior staff within the prison system is exercised only by virtue of the formal legality of their office, and only within the scope of the authority of that office, nonetheless the staff may in individual instances perceive an element of charismatic leadership and obey by virtue of personal trust. This latter feature is seen by many as an integral element in the running of the prison system and there is undoubtedly great personal loyalty from many members of staff. However, this does not detract from the 'legal authority'.

When considering organisation in the context of the prison system particular attention has to be paid to the matter of organisational control. Etzioni (1975) suggests that the three major sources of control, whose allocation and manipulation provide much of the basis for social order, are coercion, economic assets and normative values. He postulates that we should link these three types of control with three types of goal: order, economic and cultural.

The objective of an organisation with an *order* goal is to control those whom society regards as deviant in some way. This is done by segregating such people from society and by preventing them from taking part in further deviant activity. This is essentially a negative goal. These organisations attempt to prevent things happening.

Organisations with *economic* goals produce goods and services for other people. These may be manufacturing industries or service organisations.

An organisation which has a *culture* goal will, according to Etzioni, provide a structure for the preservation of symbolic objects, for their application and creation and for the reinforcement of commitments to such objects.

A coercive organisation is one in which lower levels of participants in the organisation are controlled by coercive means and in which there is a high degree of alienation from the organisation among these lower participants. The use of coercion ensures that the organisation fulfils its primary objective. Typical examples of such organisations are concentration camps, prisoner-of-war camps, prisons, and state mental hospitals. In these cases the primary objective is containment; should the coercion be removed the majority of inmates would leave. The successful accomplishment of all other tasks depends on the effective performance of the custodial task. As the oft-quoted and archetypal Chief Prison Officer was fond of saying, 'We can't reform them if they're not here'.

The task which comes a close second in organisational terms for coercive organisations is the maintenance of internal order. This task is also carried out through the potential or actual use of force. Arguably, the organisation which presents the relationship of power with what McCleery (1957) calls 'naked clarity' is the prison system.

The primary task of prison staff is to detain, against their will, a much larger body of men. Both this and the secondary task of maintaining internal discipline are achieved by organising a detailed regulation of the internal life of the prison. Even in cases where this latter regulation includes a real attempt at reform of the prisoner one may accept that this is not the form of life which individuals would choose voluntarily.

In his Bristol study, Emery (1970) suggests that this form of control, particularly in the manner in which it is imposed on individuals by means of degradations and deprivations creates a 'pervading atmosphere of hatred' between staff and prisoners.

In practice the coercive power is often muted and indirect in its application. There are several reasons for this. Staff cannot supervise every prisoner all of the time. Total surveillance is not physically possible. In addition the punishments as well as the rewards which may be visited on prisoners are severely limited. This means that punitive sanctions on an individual prisoner are frequently one of the least effective forms of sanction. An officer who has to resort to placing a prisoner 'on governor's report', that is, formally charging him with a breach of discipline, may well see this as a failure to exercise proper control on his part. Also, those prisoners who require tightest control are least likely to be overawed by formal punitive action.

What happens in fact is that a high level of discipline is maintained, not with direct sanctions, but with a procedure of regimentation, organised movement, counting and assembly, which imposes a psychology of regimentation and a formal recognition of respect for staff from prisoners.

In addition there is good will and cooperation from some prisoners, who are identified by staff as capable of and willing to, however informally, assist them in maintaining discipline and control. Such prisoners are frequently 'pass men' or hall orderlies. It is in the interests of most prisoners as much as of staff that order be maintained. In quantitative terms staff would be unable to control prisoners if they were a disorganised mass. What McCleery calls 'the custodial goals of peace, order and adjustment' are achieved by formal and informal collusion between staff and prisoners.

Some commentators have taken this argument further and attempt to demonstrate that, while at first sight the prison may appear to be a classic example of an organisation based upon coercive compliance relations, in fact the total power of the staff is an illusion. The power exercised is utilitarian rather than coercive.

It is certainly true that the amount of coercion which any organisation may legitimately use is limited. The state monopolises legitimate use of such power and places strict control on its use (in prisons, for example, punishment by segregation is allowed under set conditions but corporal punishment is not sanctioned). The authority must ensure that not only is the consent to be governed obtained but also that it can be maintained. This means that appropriate measures must be available to control those who indicate by their actions that they have withdrawn consent. However, in applying control the authority must not diminish the degree of consent which remains nor alienate those who have not withdrawn consent.

Official sanctions have to be applied with caution and must be seen to be justly and consistently applied. A failure to exercise this caution can be counter-productive. This was one of the difficulties which faced the Scottish prison administration with regard to the regime in the Inverness Unit in the early 1970s and which continued to be present with regard to regimes elsewhere in the system in the 1980s. This form of restriction on the use of coercive power is particularly relevant in regimes which allow association of prisoners since in these situations staff will normally be out-numbered by prisoners. The use of coercion in such a setting is likely to be ineffective and may well prove dangerous.

This fact is clearly recognised by staff who are required to work in such situations. As a result, recognising the problems of exercising coercion where there is association of prisoners, staff are likely to demand that in extreme cases they will always out-number prisoners, on occasion by a ratio of three to one. In the face of these demands the reaction of management has often been to restrict the association of the prisoners concerned. It might be argued that such a response is in itself utilitarian since what the organisation is doing is simply distributing rewards and sanctions according to the degree in which participants conform to the required norm.

What is being suggested is that even in an organisation such as the prison system, which on the surface appears as a prime example of a coercive organisation, informal structure is significant in an analysis of organisational structure.

> A proper understanding of the organizational process must make it possible to interpret changes in the formal system – new appointments or roles or reorganizations – in their relation to the informal and unallowed ties of friendship, class loyalty, power cliques, or external commitment. This is what it means 'to know the score'. (Selznick, 1948)

Cloward (1960) has suggested that in a prison setting there are three traditional means by which staff make use of informal patterns of social accommodation in order to supplement formal methods of control. The first is by allowing prisoners to have a controlled use of additional goods and services, the second by allowing certain prisoners to have direct informal access to particular senior members of staff and the third by allowing more privileged accommodation to certain prisoners. Variants of these methods are certainly present in Scottish prisons. Every Chief Officer, as he used to be known, had his 'tobacco float' which was used to reward prisoners who provided information. 'Pass men' who assist staff either in the accommodation halls, in the administration area or in the reception and discharge area have a symbiotic relationship with staff.

It would be difficult to argue that the control exercised in a prison system is normative or that all participants in it attempt to reach a common cultural goal. In the high summer of the rehabilitation era some practitioners among the prison governor grades in Britain might have attempted such an argument but the best that can be said of that system was that it was a paternalistic form of utilitarianism. In today's system even the Barlinnie Special Unit is generally regarded as a utilitarian form of control. The individuals concerned, both staff and prisoners, respond in the way they do because of the benefits which result. Early attempts to develop a normative form of control failed primarily because the management of the prison system was unwilling to allow members of staff to ally themselves with prisoners in a manner which would bring staff into conflict with the system as a whole.

This leads us to the question posed by Etzioni (1975). Certain types of goals and certain types of reliance structure tend to be associated with each other.

> Could we go so far as to say that one *cannot* rehabilitate in a traditional prison, produce in a religious order, segregate deviance by normative means? The answer seems to be in one sentence: It is feasible but not effective.

The dividing line between the different forms of control is not an exclusive one. It is true that formal socialisation in a prison setting is likely to be very limited in scope and generally ineffective. But it is also true that much of the control exercised in prison is instrumental and that there is a degree of cooperation between the staff and the prisoner agents of this instrumental control, which ensures good order in the interests of all parties.

The greater this cooperation the less complete will be the segregation of what is described as the inmate social system from the rest of the organisation. Prison officers will never be, nor would they wish to be, regarded by the prisoners as leaders. What may well happen is that in the daily round of activity and interactive dependency between the two groups the starkness of the distinction between 'them and us' will become blurred.

The sources of control being described refer primarily to the relationship which the prison organisation has with prisoners, expressed principally in the relationship between the prison officer and the prisoner. Organisations use different types of power according to the different ranks of the participants controlled. Generally speaking, the higher the rank concerned the less alienating the means of control. Just as prisoners are controlled by a mixture of coercive and utilitarian means, so one would expect prison officers to be controlled by a mixture of utilitarian and normative means.

In practice one can identify similarities in the methods used by management to control both prisoners and staff. In organisational terms there is a division between staff who administer the central prison system and those who administer prison establishments. The latter are career prison employees, the former are generalist administrators. In organisational terms the former are senior to the latter; in terms of knowledge and experience the opposite is the case. This creates an uneasy relationship between these two sections of the organisation. The prison officer is a civil servant and subject to the same organisational controls as all other civil servants. In addition, however, he is subject to a 'Code of Discipline' in which the ultimate sanction is dismissal. This code is an additional restraint and is regarded by staff as such.

Jacobs (1983) found that 'the line officer is often scrutinised as closely as the inmate under his surveillance'. Prison officers may often feel that the organisation is as intent on exercising control over them as in doing so over prisoners. There is a suspicion among them that central administrators make little distinction between staff and prisoners. As a result of his study in Trenton, New Jersey, Sykes (1971) felt able to conclude:

> Guards and prisoners are drawn from the same culture and they
> hold many of the same values and beliefs. They share a common
> language and a common historical experience.

Some officers wonder whether the organisation extends this conclusion to include a value assessment of the two groups.

Getting the Job Done

Machine bureaucracy, of which the prison service is an example, is typified by a proliferation of rules and regulations, formalised procedures for undertaking highly routinised tasks, large sized units which depend on functional grouping, centralised decision making and an elaborate administrative structure. A feature of this type of bureaucracy is that both the functional grouping and the administrative structure are characterised by a sharp division of labour between the line staff and managers. This includes not only job differentiation at local (prison) level between staff (officers) and managers (governors) but also between all staff at local level and those in the central hierarchy. The division is both vertical and horizontal, functional and hierarchical.

The basic purpose of such a tight structure is control. The most important factor is the smooth running of the bureaucratic machine.

All uncertainty is eliminated, hence, the all-pervading rules and regulations. Paradoxically, the existence of such a tight structure leads to a need for control since the divisions of labour which permeate the system carry within themselves the seeds of conflict and require to be contained. In such a bureaucracy senior management is primarily concerned with fine-tuning the machine, not necessarily, for example, with resolving conflict but rather with containing it to ensure that work is carried out. The safe functioning of the machine is more important than flair and initiative. When an organisation requires the precise and consistent performance of a set of repetitive functions, machine bureaucracy is the most efficient method of operation. Mintzberg (1979) sums up the requirement which such a system makes of senior staff:

> The managers of the Machine Bureaucracy are rewarded for
> improving operating efficiency, reducing costs, finding better
> controls and standards; not for taking risks, testing new
> behaviors, encouraging innovation.

Such a description is apposite for what is required of the middle-ranking civil service administrators who are responsible for the central organisation of the prison service. They have been trained in the mainstream civil service, in a stable environment with a carefully coordinated hierarchy. Their traditional sphere of operation is in organising performance rather than in problem solving. The difficulty which faces them in their present area of responsibility is that the prison service, while largely a 'performance organisation', is at times also a 'problem solving' one in so far as it is required to deal directly with people, the prisoners, whose responses cannot always be predicted and whose actions can wreak havoc on a bureaucratic machine which is too finely tuned.

One of the causes of the tensions which exist between career prison officials and those administrative civil servants who staff the central organisation lies in the area of professionalism. Central administrators regard the prison service as simply another arm of the civil service, whose members have to be reminded frequently of their relative position.

Prison officers do not require to have any prior qualifications. In Scotland after recruitment, which is done by a process of interview, medical examination and testing in basic English and arithmetical skills, and a short period of orientation in a penal establishment, the new officer undergoes initial training for seven weeks at the Scottish

Prison Service College where job related skills and knowledge are imparted. This is followed by some nine months probation in a penal establishment when these skills and knowledge are applied under supervision. The period of training is concluded with a further short period at the Prison Service College.

During the course of his career an officer might expect to attend short courses at intermittent intervals. He will also undergo further short development courses if he is promoted. There is no formal examination at the conclusion of any part of the training. This is justified on the basis that there is ongoing assessment and that an individual's aptitude for the work is more relevant than any ability to pass examinations. In practice the failure rate is very low and an officer who is dismissed is likely to have demonstrated unsuitability in a manner other than a simple inability to master necessary skills and knowledge.

Attempts have been made in recent years to increase the standing of the prison officer by developing the role he is expected to carry out and by expanding his area of expertise. However, given the importance which is generally attributed to training in the establishment of professionalism, it is difficult to argue that a system which can recruit its members without prior qualification and provide them with a matter of several weeks' formal training linked to a degree of on-the-job training can properly be described as professional. One might well argue that an increase in the professionalism of the prison officer would be highly desirable; one cannot argue that it is essential.

The only part of a prison officer's training which can be described as essential is that which addresses the primary goal of the prison system, secure containment. Additional qualifications and training relate to the important but nonetheless secondary goals of reform and rehabilitation of prisoners. These are not in themselves essential goals and can therefore be repealed when the climate of management changes. In times of fiscal stringency there is no absolute need to extend the training of staff beyond that which is required to fulfil the primary function.

Leaving aside such groups as teachers and social workers who are professionally trained and who happen to work in the prison service, the other main group of prison service workers who should be considered in this context are members of the governor grades. Since 1987 these individuals have been recruited exclusively from the officer ranks. Until that date they were recruited into the Assistant

Governor grade. In Scotland approximately half of their number were promoted from the ranks of officers and half came from outside the service. No formal qualifications were required. Recruiting literature indicated that a degree was desirable but not essential.

Between 1973 and 1987 all such recruits underwent a sandwich type of training which lasted for two years and consisted of periods spent at the Home Office Prison Service College in Wakefield, and on secondment to other organisations such as mental hospitals and social work departments, as well as a considerable period of on-the-job training in establishments.

In a study of a group of new recruits to the assistant governor grade in the early 1970s Waddington (1983) noted that once selection had been completed there was little subsequent wastage:

> The Staff College had for some years eschewed any secondary
> selection function on the grounds that it was unwise to make
> such a decision without the recruit's performance in the job itself
> having been assessed.

Like the initial training process for prison officers the training of assistant governors does not even in its new format include any examinable element. As with the prison officer grade the justification given is that continuous assessment takes place. Waddington found that as far as the organisation was concerned the status of the assistant governor was as important as his role, that in addition to performing particular tasks he had to be a particular type of person, and that the process of socialisation which went on in a group of assistant governors had a profound influence on recruits and was aimed at giving them particular attitudes and values. This view is confirmed by recruiting advertisements which indicate that attitude and temperament are more important than academic qualifications.

An important factor in the recruitment and training of prison officers and governors is that the decision making body is also the employing agency. The criteria which it applies throughout the probationary period are those which are common to all administrative civil servants and not peculiar to any 'professionalism' in the prison service. The conclusion to be drawn is that as far as personnel are concerned the present organisation of the prison service is not to be regarded as professional in the recognised sense of that word. Whether this should be so is for consideration at a later stage.

A further word should be said about the 'socialisation' which takes place during training. This is one form of the indoctrination which takes place in many large organisations but it is of particular significance in the prison system, which lays such emphasis on authority structures. Authority is that exercise of control which is based on the willingness of subordinates to comply with the directives of a superior. The fact that this compliance is willingly given does not imply absence of social constraint. On the contrary, properly oriented social values play a large part in such a relationship. Members of an organisation voluntarily follow the mandates of their own values, which have been internalised and which are enforced through social sanctions. This process is facilitated in the prison service by the recruitment of people who already have particular attitudes. This was reinforced by the requirement which existed until 1980 or so for staff to stay on prison housing estates, socialising with colleagues and becoming what the May Report in 1979 described as isolated and inward looking.

The prison service is one of the most visible arms of the civil service. It is, therefore, important to remember that several of its best known features are not inevitable elements of the prison system but rather a result of its control by central government bureaucracy. One of these is a tendency towards an excessively centralised structure in which senior members of the organisation seek not only power but also to control the decisions which affect both their own work and that of others. One outcome of this centralised authority and over-emphasis on reporting through a chain of authority is that senior managers, who should be policy decision-makers, become over burdened with decisions on matters of detail which are passed up the hierarchical chain for resolution. As a consequence they are reduced to acting superficially with inadequate abstract information.

Another feature of this structure is that in rational terms organisations do not endlessly search for an optimum model of behaviour or for the best organisational pattern. They seek a working rather than an optimum model. Search behaviour ends when a reasonably good or acceptable pattern has been found and this will be maintained until organisational performance falls below that acceptable level. The outcome of this model is what has been called the non-capitalist state-activity sector. This sector includes the prison system as well as public housing, education and health care. In such a model goods and services are allocated not solely on the basis of a rational interpretation of rules and regulations but at least partly on the ability of interested sectors of wider society to exert pressure and demand a response. As a result state organisations are characterised by 'a reactive avoidance of responsible rational planning in the face of competing contradictory pressure and conflicts' (Clegg and Dunkerley, 1980).

Excessive centralisation also serves to emphasise hierarchical status to such an extent that this attenuates the effectiveness of the organisation itself and can result in dysfunctions such as lower employee morale and lower levels of productivity. The alternative is increased decentralisation. Such an arrangement is likely to lead to a less authoritarian structure, which in turn encourages individuals to play a more active role, to contribute to decision making and to demonstrate an ability to use initiative responsibly. This is a highly functional strategy for both the organisation and the individual. Such an arrangement is of fundamental relevance to the prison system. Despite official policies and directives to the contrary, an officer whose duties are ritualised and routinised is more likely to be punitive and authoritarian towards prisoners and is also more likely to rationalise his attitudes by viewing prisoners through unfavourable stereotypes, which prisoners will in turn reciprocate.

The relationship between a bureaucracy and the people who work within it is of particular interest here. The question as to whether bureaucracies select people with particular personalities is relevant to a consideration of the prison officer as a type. And once recruited, are the personality traits of staff members modified by training and expectation of promotion? Some commentators have suggested that recruitment is particularly important and that a small increase in selectivity will often provide a disproportionately large decrease in the degree of control of staff required by the organisation, with a consequent saving in resource and effort.

Having selected candidates with the approved basic qualities, organisational socialisation subsequently goes to work to adapt these qualities in order to improve organisational performance. The application of these various factors to the prisoner population would be an interesting exercise but the main concern here is with staff. Jacobs (1983) has expressed the opinion that the social origins of staff serve as an indicator of the status of the prison organisation in a particular society; that, where prison administrators are drawn from the same background as other bureaucrats, prisons will be run on the same lines as other major agencies, but that this will not be the case where the administration of prisons is entrusted to members of non-elite groups who cannot get better jobs.

It has been suggested (Emery, 1970) that prison officers and prisoners frequently share a common set of values and that this similarity is enhanced by the fact that typically staff come from the same backgrounds, have attended the same schools and have experienced the same problems of economic insecurity as have prisoners. The traditional responses to this issue have been:

a. Recruitment of staff from parts of society least likely to share the values of those who are to be controlled, for example, from rural areas and from men with long-term service in the armed forces.
b. Segregation of staff from the community at large, for example, by barracks, rotation of duties, uniforms and hours of work.

The adoption of such a pattern by management is likely to influence the expectations they have of staff. It is more likely that work will be highly routine and that there will be little individual choice. Such a dichotomy between choice and structure, between freedom and constraint, is an essential element in the establishment of the theoretical base of any organisation. In practical terms, the situation is rarely so clear cut.

Ambivalence about penal theories has produced penal systems which are inadvertently resistant to change. This has come about for two reasons. Firstly, because a shift in penal objectives requires not only a change in the work habits and attitudes of staff but also a change in the organisation itself. All prisons are structured on a hierarchical line system of custodial ranks and any innovation which cannot be achieved within this hierarchy must either modify or evade this rank structure. The second reason is that in any prison system, unlike industrial or commercial concerns, before any change or innovation can be implemented the participation, or at least the non-opposition, of staff is required.

Bureaucracy within organisations is likely to be more relaxed in situations where a unit is remote from the central organisation or where there is physical danger. The first of these conditions may frequently exist in the relationship between a prison and the headquarters' structure, the second in the particular circumstances within a prison. In both situations the bureaucratic system will be less evident, superiors will become in some sense dependent on their subordinates and this dependence will oblige them to rely on personal, less bureaucratic means of motivating cooperative efforts.

Why the Prison System Exists

Every organisation can be defined as a sub-structure of a more comprehensive social system. The implication of this is that a properly integrated organisation must accept the more generalised value systems of the larger structure. To express this in another way, there must be a close relationship between an organisation and its supporting environment. Without consistent inputs any system will run down.

The larger structure to which the prison system is related is the criminal justice system. Sociologists point out that the definition of crime and the punishment of the criminal as the responsibility of specially constituted organisations such as the police, the courts and the prison system are features of a developed society. Societies with more primitive structures will often exist without these organisations and will rely on the control exercised over a wrong doer by his family or fellow tribesmen. Societies have only gradually developed specialised organisations of control with legislative, judicial and penal functions.

During the course of the last 100 years or so the pace of social change has involved constant alteration to the criminal law. The development of ideas about the treatment of offenders has similarly led to a complex penal system in which, in addition to simple detention, attempts are made to educate, train and employ prisoners and to give them access to religious, medical and welfare services. These changes in emphasis and provision have led to a blurring of the connecting links between the organisation of the prison system and its proper super-ordinate structure, the criminal justice system. Some practitioners and academics have suggested that the home of the prison system lies in a social welfare model rather than in a penal model. This attempt to place the prison system within an improper super-structure has resulted in a confusion as to the proper goals of the prison system.

Historically individuals were held in prison pending trial or, having been found guilty, to await execution of the sentence which the court had passed. It is only in comparatively modern times that imprisonment *per se* has been added to the older punishments of execution and exile, and indeed has come to replace them as the ultimate penal sanction available to the court. Rusche and Kirchheimer (1939) argue that the aim of all punishment is the protection of those social values which the dominant social group regard as good for society. The use of imprisonment as a punishment, they suggest, reflects the prominence of economic and fiscal forces in our society. Be that as it may, the most important factor for the present hypothesis is that imprison-ment is punishment and as such must be integrated, not into a social welfare model, but rather into the criminal justice process.

The nature of this integration became less clear as the organisa-tional structure of the prison system grew. Large institutions are seldom satisfied with merely a primary objective. Secondary and even tertiary ones are frequently developed and expressed. The prison system has been no exception to this norm. The simple notion of punishment as an end in itself might have been acceptable to philoso-phers. It was not sufficient for the legislators and administrators who were responsible for the development of our prison services, particu-larly in Victorian Britain. In their view the punishment of imprison-ment required a justification. Those which were duly advanced came to be regarded as the secondary aims of imprisonment. Subsequently so much emphasis was placed on the secondary aims that the primary aim was all but lost sight of.

This position was taken up as early as 1837 by Frederic Hill, Inspector of Prisons for Scotland, in his annual report:

> ... the legitimate objects of imprisonment are the protection of society and the reform of the offender.

The fact that this rationalisation came to the fore just as the prison system was moving towards centralisation and work related to it was becoming respectable was no coincidence:

> Such a strategy makes life easier for the personnel within these institutions. The hangman's job was never very popular. Those who got a chance slipped into the doctor's role as fast as possible. There are great amounts of ambivalence in having direct responsibility for other people's suffering. There is need for a defence. Major strategies are to claim that what one is doing to other people does not hurt, is intended to help, or actually is very efficient in helping them even though it might hurt a bit in the beginning – just like so many good cures. (Christie, 1978)

This false elevation of secondary aims to a primacy which was not theirs was finally enshrined in the dictum of the Gladstone Report that 'We start from the principle that prison treatment should have as its primary and concurrent objects, deterrence and reformation'. Leaving aside the inconsistency of suggesting that there could be more than one primary aim, the basic error of the report was to suggest that either of these two important but nonetheless secondary objectives of imprisonment was a primary one.

The false elevation of rehabilitation in particular to be the primary purpose of imprisonment has had two major consequences. In the first place it has introduced an element of uncertainty into the length of time which an individual will serve in prison so that the period of punishment is no longer solely determined by the sentence of the court but also by other factors such as his behaviour while undergoing imprisonment or the perceived likelihood of his re-offending. In this connection Rupert Cross (1971) has observed that

> [there] can be no doubt that the increase in the control of the Executive over the offender after he has been sentenced has been one of the major features of twentieth century penal history in this country.

The second consequence is that the various facilities and resources which are necessary for a humane form of containment have been linked to the aim of rehabilitation. As McClintock (1983) has pointed out:

> The merit of Sir Alexander Paterson's campaign in the 1930s – and that of Sir Lionel Fox and other penal reformers later – was to emphasise, in addition to the *right* of the State to punish, the *obligation* of the State to provide facilities for education and treatment on grounds of humanity and social justice. The shortcomings of their aims – and the weakness that lies at the centre of the present debate – is that they coupled the ideas of education and treatment of prisoners with that of crime prevention, in the belief that this would be an important way of reducing individual recidivism.

The difficulty which a separation of these two ideas creates is a modern expression of the principle of less-eligibility. Politicians and the public may reluctantly accept that resources should be channelled towards prisoners, on the grounds that provision of these resources will assist in rehabilitation and, therefore, in reducing the future crime rate. They are not likely to accept this, particularly in an age when resources for the community at large are coming under increasing financial scrutiny, on the grounds that although they may not contribute to crime prevention they should be offered to the prisoner out of respect for him as a person.

From the prisoner's point of view the two consequences described above lay open to question the justice of the main feature of his punishment, which is the length of time he serves in prison. If it is accepted that punishment is the basic tenet which underpins imprisonment there are several far-reaching implications for our penal system, all of them based on the corollary that no person should be sentenced to prison other than primarily for punishment.

In the first place, deprivation of liberty is the most extreme form of punishment in our society and should only be considered when no other disposal is possible.

Secondly, any sentence of imprisonment which is passed should be of the shortest necessary length, even though in some cases this might be a considerable period of time. The average length of sentence for those admitted directly to prisons in Scotland is approximately 220 days. One wonders to how many of these this criterion applies. There should be no question of sentencing an individual to a penal establishment 'for his own good' or 'for training'.

Thirdly, the period of imprisonment should be clearly laid down by the sentencing court and not by any administrative system. Control mechanisms are necessary for the management of our prisons but the length of time to be served in prison should not be one of these mechanisms. One consequence of such an approach would be that the possibility of 'gaining' or 'forfeiting' remission as a result of behaviour during the course of a sentence would no longer be available. Neither would there be any place for a system of early release on parole which was based, even partially, on how a prisoner had 'responded' during his sentence.

The probable result of employing such criteria for the use of imprisonment will be a much smaller prison population which, with the exception of those who require to be detained for very long periods and even for the rest of their natural lives, will be serving much shorter sentences. What kinds of regime will this residue, substantial though it may be as the May Report in 1979 suggested, undergo?

To define the primary purpose of imprisonment as punishment is not to suggest that the only acceptable alternative is that of human warehousing. As the May Report also pointed out, the positive elements which have until now been exercised in the name of treatment and training should not be dismissed, although the rhetoric surrounding them should be. There must be no diminution of resources for those who are necessarily punished in prison, nor any lessening of commitment among staff. What will change, however, is that the use which a prisoner makes or does not make of these facilities will not be used as a measure of the extent of his personal reformation. Instead he will have the opportunity to use the resources which are available either as a means of coping with his own sentence or as an aid to his own reform. We shall move, in the words of one commentator from the arena of 'coerced cure' to that of 'facilitated change' (Morris, 1974).

If one accepts a model of imprisonment which has punishment as its primary aim, the controversies of 'rehabilitation model versus justice model' or 'care versus control' cease to be of major significance. Since neither one nor the other of these models represents the primary purpose of imprisonment they may happily coexist as secondary purposes. The one man in the system who has always been aware of this fact has been the prison officer. Although he might not recognise the descriptions, he frequently makes use of each of these models. In the course of his daily work he constantly exercises both custody and care of prisoners. This is because he is quite clear as to his primary function.

> The officials, in short, know on which side their bread is
> buttered. Their continued employment is tied up with the
> successful performance of custody and if society is not sure of
> the priority to be attached to the tasks assigned the prison, the
> overriding importance of custody is perfectly clear to the official.
> (Sykes, 1971)

This latter is an alternative expression of the argument put forward here. The punishment of imprisonment consists in the deprivation of liberty. Therefore, the primary aim of prison staff is to ensure continuing deprivation of liberty for the duration of a sentence. In the final analysis this fact is recognised by the authorities which employ prison officials. No such official is likely to lose his position because he has not succeeded in reforming a particular prisoner. In recent times, however, prison officials have lost their positions because they have failed to retain prisoners in custody.

It is frequently argued that a clear definition of the purpose of imprisonment is urgently required. What is being suggested here is that such a definition already exists and, furthermore, that it is clearly understood by prison staff if not by administrators and academics. The primary purpose of imprisonment is punishment, a punishment which consists essentially in loss of liberty.

But the truth is that prisons have never *really* been about training at all. They have always *really* been about, and continue to be about captivity, that is, safe custody. There is nothing on earth to be gained from pretending otherwise... what endures and what is common to all is their custodial function for the duration of the sentence of the court; and therein lies the reason for their existence. (King and Elliott, 1977)

The acceptance of such a definition will involve neither a restriction of regime for prisoners nor a diminution in the role of staff for, while the primary purpose of imprisonment is clear, the resources which are necessary for humane containment will provide those prisoners who wish it with the opportunity for 'facilitated change'. Indeed such a clear definition of purpose will result in an increase both in achievement and in job satisfaction for staff. Such a clarity will also be communicated to prisoners, so that they will be given an understanding of why they are imprisoned and what they might individually expect to achieve while so held. Finally, it has to be accepted that

the *criminal justice system* should not, and cannot successfully undertake to deal with fundamental issues relating to questions of *social justice* in the modern state. (McClintock, 1978)

The Introduction of Secondary Goals
The growth of secondary goals is a feature of any large organisation but this development has presented particular difficulties regarding definition of tasks for the prison system, mainly due to a misapprehension of the relationship between primary and secondary goals.

It is difficult to be at one and the same time the punitive arm of the political system and the rehabilitation agency of the educational system. (Katz and Kahn, 1966)

The root of this misunderstanding in the prison system can be traced to the nature of the structure which has been allowed to develop. Large organisations will typically standardise as much as possible, thus reducing the need for direct supervision and enabling relatively junior staff to carry out many of the functions previously exercised by senior management. This also leads frequently to the development of several specialised units which exist to provide support to the organisation but which do so outside the operating work flow.

In the prison system many of these units are staffed by members of what are sometimes described as the proto-professions. In Scottish prisons they are often given the formal title of 'units', for example education and social work units, thus emphasising that they are outside the main work flow. The professional objectives of the members of these units have little in common with the primary goal of the prison service.

As a result of these and other influences the prison service has moved in some respects from being a commonwealth organisation, which exists for the protection of society, to become a service organisation, oriented largely to the needs and the interests of its prisoner 'clients'. Such an emphasis enhances the standing of the proto-professionals but can be a threatening development to the prison officer as he sees himself being excluded from the service function and relegated to a purely custodial position.

This aspect of the prison has been further complicated in recent years by the increasing attention being paid to the rights of prisoners which, in addition to reinforcing the notion of the prison as a service organisation, has contributed significantly to the growth in its bureaucracy, to an increasing dependence on rules and regulations and to administration 'by the book'.

> Until recently, prisons operated as traditional, non-bureaucratic
> institutions. There were no written rules and regulations, and
> daily operating procedures were passed down from one
> generation to the next. Wardens spoke of prison administration
> as an 'art'; they operated by intuition. The ability of the
> administration to act as it pleased reinforced its almost total
> dominance of the inmates. Early law suits revealed the inability
> of prison officials to justify or even to explain their procedure.
> The courts increasingly demanded rational decision making
> processes and written rules and regulations; sometimes they even
> demanded better security procedures. The prisons required more
> support staff to meet the increasing demand for 'documentation'.
> New bureaucratic offices and practices began to appear.
> (Jacobs, 1983)

Traditionally prison staff have not been slow to adopt this service model of imprisonment, not least because it reflects well on their own role. Christie (1978) has pointed out that the protagonists of the 'denial-of-existence' strategy, those who argue for minimal use of the prison sanction, are very often those who are closest to the system, who attempt to improve their own life situations by pointing to similarities between their area of work and other social phenomena; prisons are called institutions, prisoners are called inmates.

Two factors should be borne in mind when considering the assumed growth in professionalism in the prison system which has led to the dominance given to secondary goals. Firstly, the professional status of prison officials is yet to be proved and perhaps cannot be proved. That is true both of those who are career prison officials and those administrators, often in the higher ranks of the British prison services, who are transitory as far as prisons are concerned. This fact is recognised even by prisoners:

> I know that my life for many years may be directed by a
> career civil servant whose next appointment may be with another
> Ministry, for the Chairman of the Prison Commissioners has
> never worked in a prison in any capacity for a single day in his
> life. I know that his first duty is not to initiate anything which
> might prove an embarrassment to the Minister. ('Zeno', 1968)

The second factor to be remembered is that those who come to work in the prison system bringing their own professional skills with them have a somewhat ambiguous relationship with the system. Not infrequently their professional competences will be converted to serve custodial functions. The diagnostic skills of a clinical psychologist, for example, may be used to identify and segregate prisoners who are low custodial risks, or inter-personal skills may be used to produce greater conformity to institutional norms (Vinter and Janowitz, 1959).

One common result of this tension is a high turnover rate among such personnel, which in turn may lead to a reduction in confidence in their position on the part of more permanent staff. This is not to deny the fact that in some parts of an organisation there may be cross-fertilisation between the various professional and non-professional disciplines. The former may take the trouble to learn about the technicalities of work done by the latter; the latter may become familiar with some of the terminology and theoretical background of the former (Weber, 1957).

The relationship between professional skill and organisational loyalty is often in direct proportion to the amount of professional opportunity provided within the organisation in question compared to other similar organisations. If a worker's reference group is his profession rather than the organisation he is more likely to be independent of organisational pressures and to deviate from administrative procedures. Bureaucratic organisations such as the prison service are in a particularly strong position to encourage loyalty and standardisation by means of the carrot and stick of tenure, job security and promotion prospects. A more sophisticated form of this control is the accelerated promotion offered to those who exhibit some form of personal charisma, in order to increase their loyalty to the organisation by means of greater material or symbolic rewards, personal contact with senior personnel and proximity to the informal channels of communication.

At best, administrative and professional authority are uneasy bedfellows, at worst they are incompatible.

> Still the reader is correct in his intuition that there is something fundamentally wrong with the notion of viewing the bureaucracy as a hierarchy in which the more rational rule the less rational. There are two reasons. First, by far most of the trained members of the organization are found not in the highest but in the middle ranks, and not in the regular line of command positions but around them. Depending on the type of organization, they are referred to as experts, staff, professionals, specialists, or by the names of their respective professions. Second, the most basic principle of administrative authority and the most basic principle of authority based on knowledge – or professional authority – not only are not identical but are quite incompatible. (Etzioni, 1964)

Scull (1977) has described at some length the unholy relationship between control organisations such as the prison system and the proto-professions which emerged fortuitously at the same time as these organisations were exchanging their punitive role for an allegedly rehabilitative one. The suggestion that these new professions could cure deviancy was a notion eminently acceptable to the dominant theory of social control in a capitalist economy. The state-supported institutions, such as prisons, provided a guaranteed market for these new experts and also allowed them to develop, in isolation from the community at large, empirically based craft skills in the management of particular forms of deviance.

The most important of the secondary goals of imprisonment, at least in the British prison services of the first half of the twentieth century, was rehabilitation. This is a word with several possible meanings. For William Brebner, Frederic Hill and the first managers of the General Prison at Perth, as well as for the Quaker pioneers in North America, it implied a moral and spiritual regeneration which would break an individual from habits of crime. At the same time it had a distinctly deterrent value, closely related to the Protestant work ethic which equated work with virtue and idleness with vice. The requirement placed on prisoners to complete an allotted scale of work each day both involved a virtuous act on their part and at the same time was intended to be irksome enough to deter them from future crime. This was in keeping with the obligation placed on all working people to accept the duties of their proper station in life. During the golden age of rehabilitation after the First World War the confidence of its proponents was unbounded. Sir Alexander Paterson expressed this simply:

> The Problem of Recidivism is small, diminishing, and not
> incapable of solution. (in Ruck, 1951)

The rehabilitative model espoused by Brebner and others in Scotland in the nineteenth century and developed by Paterson and others in England in the twentieth century was essentially a paternalistic and at times an autocratic one. This form of paternalism was justified on the grounds that the prisoners were in effect wards of the state, which had a consequential responsibility to them that went beyond the simple degree of control necessary to protect society. The modern statement of this position, as advanced by those such as Thomas Murton (1979), is a form of participative management:

> The present system of imprisonment has not worked. Prison
> problems, to a large extent, can be traced to the inequitable,
> arbitrary, unfair, and unjust system of management. To combat
> the traditional negativism of the prison environment, a coalition
> of power between inmates and staff, based on honesty and trust,
> could form a strong power base for change.

Such a strategy, Murton argues, is more likely to help prisoners to reintegrate into society on release; it will require them to accept responsibility for their decisions and for the consequences of their behaviour.

A further factor has been that almost all of those who have promoted the rehabilitative model, in whichever guise, have done so with very little reference to prison staff. Several commentators have remarked on the contrast in the English Prison Commissioners apparently bestowing unearned privileges on an ungrateful body of convicted criminals and at the same time giving nothing to their uniformed staff without a struggle. In North America the involvement of the courts in an assessment of prison decision making has demoralised staff to the extent that Jacobs (1983) contends that prison officers of today are 'more insecure, both morally and legally' than their predecessors.

The development of this model of imprisonment has had specific implications for the role of the prison governor. He is subject to three main pressures:

> As the head of a large bureaucratic apparatus, the warden must
> maintain a balance between the state, which demands
> fulfilment of its regulations at the smallest possible expense or at
> a profit if possible, the staff, which shares the character of every
> bureaucracy in that it tries to increase its power and influence,
> and the prisoners. (Rusche and Kirchheimer, 1939)

In the early nineteenth century the beginning of the elevation of rehabilitation as an illegitimate primary aim of imprisonment led to several difficult situations, the most extreme of which occurred in Millbank Prison in the 1830s when a conflict of authority between the governor and the chaplain led to the replacement of the former by the latter (McConville, 1981). The prison governor, even in his modern bureaucratic role, is a highly visible general manager whose administrative skill reaches out in the first instance to those closest to him but very quickly thereafter to the rest of the prison. Given their perceived exclusion from much of the allegedly rehabilitative work, the relationship between officers and their governors has become subject to change:

> . . . as the reformative movement gathered momentum, so did the
> certainty amongst staff that the bonds between officers and
> governors were being weakened, because of a strengthening
> relationship between governor grades and prisoners.
> (Thomas, 1972)

The Resultant Confusion of Goals

The complex organisation should not be regarded simply as a group of individuals coming together nor as a meeting of friends sharing a common activity. It is rather a coming together of persons and resources in such a manner that their activities constitute the rational pursuit of an agreed set of goals. The concept of 'negotiated order' is important for any analysis of organisational goals. The goals of an organisation are at the same time potent internal symbols of order and also a means of effecting that order. The establishing of a priority of goals is a key element for negotiation within a structure. Smith (1979) describes an organisation as:

> The outcome of the conflicts between different groups, each pursuing somewhat different (and quite rightly conflicting) objectives, yet each attempting to present their own aims as *the* goals of the organisation.

In its initial concept the goal of prison organisation was clear. Some commentators have exaggerated the subsequent confusion of goals, although confusion there undoubtedly has been:

> Correctional institutions can be said to have multiple goals. Their primary functions are to incarcerate – that is, establish custody over – the offender *and* to rehabilitate the delinquent. These goals may be incompatible because maximisation of one may lead to inadequate fulfilment of the other. (Zald, 1960)

This statement is an example of the woolly thinking which has led to this confusion. Cressey (1961) goes so far as to suggest that with all the confusion and conflict among the various groups involved the amazing thing about prisons is that they 'work' at all, that they do not simply disintegrate in organisational terms. Clemmer (1958) points out that there are no communal goals in the inmate world, that their conflict with the staff is only marginally greater than their conflict among themselves:

> There is pain in punishment. Except for the few, there is bewilderment. No one knows, the dogmas and codes notwithstanding, exactly what is important.

Both staff and prisoners are aware that there is frequently a contradictory balance to be maintained between mutually exclusive sets of expectations; but senior staff appear to have ambivalence between justice and leniency, rule enforcement and relaxation, command and cooperation, an ambivalence which presents the individual prison officer with puzzling dilemmas in his daily contacts with prisoners.

How is one to establish what the goals of an organisation are? Is one to accept the view of senior management, of middle-ranking executives or of the bulk of the members? The goals of an organisation partially reflect the views held by all of these groups, but they are more than the sum of the parts. They are that future state of affairs which the organisation is attempting to bring about.

One may expect a major organisation to have a set of manifest goals which provide a legitimation of the system as well as a set of latent goals which relate more directly to the power of the system to survive. One must be aware that elements of an organisation might choose to maintain that certain goals are being sought which in fact are quite different from the ones actually being pursued. This may be because the personnel who state these views are unaware of the discrepancy; more commonly it may be a conscious attempt to obscure the real goal. This is what has happened in the expression of the primary and secondary goals of the prison system.

> The researcher will define as the *real goals* of the organization
> those future states towards which a majority of the
> organization's means and the major organizational commitments
> of the participants are directed, and which, in cases of conflict
> with goals which are *stated* but command few resources, have
> clear priority. (Etzioni, 1964)

This distinction between statement and reality also applies to other areas of organisation and even to the organisation itself. One cannot hope to understand the formally instituted patterns of an organisation without also examining the network of informal relations and official norms. The distinction between the formal and the informal aspects of organisational life is only an analytical one and should not be reified.

In many respects the prison structure typifies an organisation in which these inconsistencies are present. Until recently many practitioners would have stated that the primary goal of the prison is rehabilitation or would at least have described it as a 'concurrent primary objective'. At an informal level first line practitioners, such as prison officers, have always been well aware that the punishment involved in the deprivation of liberty is in fact the primary objective of imprisonment. This confusion extends even to the law. Prison Rule (Scotland) 5 advises that:

> The purposes of training and treatment of convicted prisoners
> shall be to establish in them the will to lead a good and useful
> life on discharge, and to fit them to do so.

In contrast to this the warrant of the court, by force of which a prisoner is legally held, has a much simpler message for the prison governor. The named prisoner is to be held until the expiry of sentence and then to be released without any reference to his social or moral condition when that time comes.

One of the dangers of an expanded bureaucracy is that the original objectives of an organisation may be lost sight of as a result of preoccupation with administrative problems. Survival of the organisation becomes more important than the end for which it was established. Even radical organisations, of which trades unions are a good example, are likely to become increasingly modified and conservative once they develop a bureaucratic hierarchy.

Nor will this displacement occur only at the top of an organisation; it may well extend to its body. It has been suggested that bureaucracy will even affect the personalities of its members, encouraging a tendency to adhere strictly to rules and regulations for their own sake even when a policy of flexibility in the application of rules is officially encouraged. Procedures may become ends in themselves and adherence to the organisational policy becomes the goal of the bureaucrat.

At the same time one has to recognise that the goals of an organisation are not set in a vacuum. As far as the prison system is concerned, a sound theoretical basis and the promise of effective penal intervention are not sufficient. The structure must also be publicly and politically acceptable.

In setting its own goals an organisation takes on itself a particular burden. This was what the prison service did when it attempted to redefine its goals beyond the narrow boundary of punishment. When an attempt to impose a new definition is made from above, the executive is often in fact attempting to retain control and to ensure that alternatives are not pressed from below. In penal terms this increased role of the executive in defining the goals of the prison system has led to that same executive exercising significant control over the sentenced offender in the name of rehabilitation. One disturbing feature of this executive extension of goals is that not only is it unsound in principle – it is also ineffective.

> The depressing finding that has emerged from study after study
> is that, as far as can be determined, not one penal measure
> designed to prevent crime in individual offenders through
> reformation or deterrence is any more effective than any other.
> (Hogarth, 1971)

Occasionally change of heart does occur while an individual is in prison but there is no way of knowing if that would have come about whether or not the person concerned had been in prison. Change of heart is much more likely to occur as a result of external pressures such as accommodation, employment or family support.

The most realistic approach of the executive would be to ensure that the resources which have been provided under the guise of rehabilitation should be deployed in the first instance to prevent deterioration of the individual who has to experience imprisonment.

One must be particularly hesitant about the right of a bureaucracy to set its own additional goals when it is reluctant to accept public accountability. Commentators have contrasted the veil of secrecy which was drawn over the administration of the prison system after centralisation in 1877 with the willingness of government to subject to public scrutiny and independent inspection other large organisations which were not under its direct control.

We are led to the conclusion that, if expressed as primary ends of equal importance, the various goals of the prison system are incompatible. However one might attempt to define the notion of assisting a prisoner to lead a good and useful life on release from prison, it is not possible to define the operative goals of the prison system in that way. The principal reason for this is that the complex operational goals of the prison emerge, in practice, from a direct conflict between the coercive and the treatment models of the organisation which are implicit in the dual primary goals of punishment and reform.

That is not to deny the existence of different goals within the prison system. Cressey (1965) points out that within any prison there is a military system which is designed to keep prisoners within the perimeter, an industrial system which both maintains the prison and produces goods and also service systems which attempt to rehabilitate prisoners. It is wrong to suggest that the primary purpose of the way prisoners are treated is to effect changes in their character, attitudes and behaviour, particularly in circumstances where government officials are able to escape public scrutiny and where the links between repression and therapy become blurred.

To suggest that the contribution of the rehabilitative ideal has been secondary is not to say that it has not been valid at all nor that it will necessarily disappear. The model will remain valid in some cases because, however much we may dislike the proposition, we have to recognise that, while protective paternalism cannot always be justified, equally one cannot always assume the full moral autonomy and responsibility of all convicted offenders. It remains true that the resources channelled into prisons are unlikely to lead to any significant degree of rehabilitation. It is, therefore, necessary to present other justifications of the continuing need for these resources.

Within the prison system 'treatment' goals lead to humanitarian and flexible management practices which generate better relations between staff and prisoners and which are, in short, sound management practice. At a more fundamental level, the state has an obligation to facilitate hope and the opportunity for self-development among those within its custody and care. The incompatibility of goals presents a particular difficulty for prison officers. The Scottish Prison Service has never been subject to the level of para-militarism which was common in England, yet even here the contention expressed by Thomas (1978) that the para-military staff structure, with its overall emphasis on control, was thrown into confusion by the introduction of 'treatment' and 'training', has a certain validity:

> Perhaps it is an adequate summary of the officer level to say that while managers' preferences were also what they were doing, trying to do or thought they *were* doing; officers' behaviour is frequently not a reflection of what they prefer. Compared with any of the other groups, there is tremendous disagreement amongst officers about institutional and personal goals. The condition of anomie is evident. Officers who favour a 'punitive' or 'disciplinarian' stance do not feel supported by their superiors, and officers who favour rehabilitation do not see the opportunity to work for it. (Duffee, 1975)

This confusion has been exacerbated by the introduction of other grades of staff to work as agents of rehabilitation to the exclusion of the officers who are primarily custodians. In some cases senior management is perceived as having aligned itself with the rehabilitators rather than the custodians. Even where this has not happened, custodial and treatment staff may well feel that the other is interfering in their own area of activity. It has been suggested that one of the main reasons for the failure of prison to reform lies in the very nature of its attempt to control and regulate human life. Rehabilitation in these terms means an adaptation to an orderly life with regular work and rests on the false assumption that if this mode of behaviour is learned in prison it will enable a prisoner to re-adjust to life on release. Given this failure, the prison officer has concentrated on the custodial aspect of his task, even to the extent of bureaucratised routines which can express themselves as opposition to progress.

The attitude of the prison officer is of particular significance in any consideration of prison organisation. He falls into that category whose work is uniquely to do with people. It is people-work to the extent that the very objects and products with which staff are required to work are themselves people. This means that, whereas in other organisations such as factories there are separate hierarchies of management and workers, in the prison management extends to the lowest level of employees. The prison officer is at the same time a worker in his relations with management and his response to a system of controls and regulations from above, and also a manager in his interaction with prisoners:

> Guards manage and are managed in organizations where
> management is an end, not a means. (Cressey, 1960)

One of the consequences of this structure is that any attempt to alter or expand the goals of the prison system must be able to count on the tacit support, or at least the non-opposition, of the prison officer. This fact has not always been borne in mind. Indeed, it has been suggested that as the prison system has set itself increasingly reformative goals the prison officer has been excluded from their implementation. His success or failure has continued to be measured by his ability to control prisoners and, if anything, the opportunity afforded him to take on work which is not purely custodial has been restricted. One practical outcome of this arrangement is that it does the standing of the officer no harm at all if occasionally there is a major incident in a prison which allows him to come to the fore. Such irregularities call for action and may well provide officers with opportunities to distinguish themselves, to show that they, rather than the 'specialists', are the most essential members of staff.

The lesson to be learned from these observations is that prison security is likely to be enhanced the more the officers are made to feel an integral rather than a second-rate part of the organisation. This is an expression of the principle that generally speaking the less an organisation alienates its personnel the more efficient it is likely to be, the more job satisfaction employees have the harder they are likely to work.

To a degree, organisational rationality and human happiness go hand-in-hand. But there is a point in every organisation at which job satisfaction and efficiency cease to support each other. Not all work can be well paid and gratifying, not all regulations and orders can be made acceptable. This is a dilemma which faces all organisations. It does so within the prison system because the primary task of the prison officer, that of containment, is basically a monotonous one and also because the other tasks which have been added to it have not been related directly to the officer's role.

The Effect of this Confusion on Junior Staff

In his study of officials in a mid-western American prison camp Grusky (1959) suggests two conditions which can lead to role conflict within an organisation. The first occurs when one or more inconsistent patterns of role expectations and behaviours are attached to a single position in the system; the second, when both of these patterns are defined as legitimate. This conflict occurred in the prison system when one or more of its secondary roles was elevated to primary status. When multiple criteria for worker performance are used, the employee concerned finds it necessary to make a judgement about which of the tasks set him should receive the major part of his attention.

> Somehow he must resolve the claims that the prison should extract vengeance, erect a spectre to terrify the actual or potential deviant, isolate a known offender from the free community, and effect a change in the personality of his captives so that they gladly follow the dictates of the law – and in addition maintain order within his society of prisoners and see that they are employed at useful labor. (Sykes, 1971)

When faced with the need to make that judgement, prison officials have never been in doubt that their primary goal is to retain their prisoners in custody. They have achieved that end by a variety of means. Government of a majority by a minority means that the consent of the former to be governed must in normal circumstances be maintained. Rules cannot be enforced in an arbitrary manner; officials must use discretion and common sense.

The role of the front line prison officer is particularly important since he will often be the most consistent element in the equation. This presents a special difficulty in an organisation in which orders, but not necessarily information, traditionally flow downwards. In any task which has relatively little technical skill or theoretical base one of the substitutes for a body of knowledge is the hoarding of information. It is a feature of the prison system that junior staff constantly have to turn to senior staff for advice and are required to pass upwards immediately any information which they receive from prisoners.

In common with discipline staff, prisoners are clear as to the primary purpose of imprisonment. The traditional contrast between custody and care misses the central reality of the prisoner's life.

> The reality is this: The welfare of the individual inmate, to say nothing of his psychological freedom and dignity, does not depend primarily on how much education, recreation and consultation he receives but rather on how he manages to live and relate with the other inmates who constitute his crucial and meaningful world. It is what he *experiences* in this world: how he attains satisfaction from it, how he avoids its pernicious effects – how, in a word, he survives in it – which determines his adjustment and decides whether he will emerge from prison with intact or shattered integrity. (Korn and McKorkle, 1966)

The same point is made more directly by a former prisoner:

> So don't get the idea that nicks are good places for reforming people, all they are any good for is locking people up in and that's all. So why do they keep on all the time about how good they are. (Norman, 1958)

Prisoners regard prison as part of the hostile criminal justice world. They are being held against their will and that is the basic reason for their opposition to imprisonment. They do not perceive that the rules are for their benefit and, therefore, have no sense of an obligation towards the prison. They cooperate with the prison in order to avoid punishment, to ameliorate their conditions as far as possible and to attempt to secure release as early as possible. Their hostility to the system springs from an understanding that it is essentially custodial and punitive.

It has been suggested that on this basis the fundamental antagonism between staff and prisoners cannot be eliminated. Some commentators have voiced surprise at the relative lack of organised resistance among prisoners and the general degree of order which prevails in penal establishments. By and large the system is in a state of equilibrium, a state which depends on a complex set of checks and balances, both from the prisoners' side and from the staff side. The typical reaction of a prisoner to the system is one of 'dulled acceptance'.

This attitude was voiced by one released life sentence prisoner in a manner which demonstrated that he, having served his sentence throughout the rehabilitative era, had hopes of more than punishment from his period in prison:

> If I am honest, I must admit that on reflection the majority of the governor grades I have come into contact with have been decent men. But something more than decency is required if anything is to be done about the criminal malaise, for the men who have the authority must be something more than decent men, they must be outstanding. Within its present structure, the Prison Department is unlikely to attract these men. All screws are not bastards. But most of them should never be in the Service, unless they are employed solely as custodians, and the Home Office has announced so many times that this is only one part of the prison officer's job. Unfortunately it is the only part most of them are equipped to carry out. ('Zeno', 1968)

This is not to say that even within a penal system which has punishment as its primary goal there is unlikely to be any interaction between staff and prisoners. There may even be friendships on matters of mutual interest such as a common hobby or sporting interest. Attempts to extend this to discussion of primary social attitudes are likely to be much more difficult. Trasler (1972) has suggested that this will only be possible in a setting in which the counselling group is co-extensive with the population of the establishment, that is, including both staff and prisoners, and in which the network of authority and communication is in some way integrated.

Those who raised rehabilitation to the level of a primary goal of the prison system did so without any sound philosophical basis for the theory and their fall has been all the greater for that reason. It is interesting to note that this was not a mistake made by the English Prison Commissioner Sir Alexander Paterson, to whom many practitioners looked as a father of the model:

> It must, however, be clear from the outset to all concerned that it is the sentence of imprisonment, and not the treatment accorded in prison, that constitutes the punishment. Men come to prison as a punishment, not *for* punishment . . . It is the length of the sentence that measures the degree of the punishment and not the conditions under which it is served . . . It is therefore possible to have a considerable variety in prison treatment without disregarding the basic fact that a prison sentence is still used by the Courts as a form of punishment. (in Ruck, 1951)

One study of Albany Prison on the Isle of Wight (King and Elliott, 1977) provides an illuminating description of one attempt, towards the end of the rehabilitative era, to set up just such a regime and to bridge the boundaries between staff and prisoners. In the end, the experiment at Albany failed, largely because of external pressures, but the authors suggest that the prisoners used the experiment to re-draw the boundaries rather than to abolish them.

An immediate consequence of the denial of freedom in prison is the need to control prisoner initiative. Simple physical security is not sufficient, particularly since this was in part compromised by the advent of prison industries which allowed large numbers of prisoners to congregate in workshops. Control means being able to identify potential areas of prisoner unrest before they develop; it means controlling the avenues to such action; it means attempting to control even the will to act.

Any experienced prison officer will acknowledge that the use of punitive action as an exemplary reinforcement of control is a last resort and indeed an admission that the primary means of control has failed. Prison staff are well aware that whatever may be said officially about 'treatment' and 'training' the primary goal of imprisonment is the need to detain the prisoner in custody for the duration of his sentence. Public opinion is much less concerned at the fact that men who leave prison commit further crime than it is at any failure to contain a serving prisoner.

In his study of the regime at Bristol Prison, Emery (1970) concluded that even where there was official encouragement to develop relations between staff and prisoners, the primary task of the prison officer remained undisturbed as the maintenance of security and good order.

If a prison officer finds himself restricted by the role which the organisation expects him to undertake and frustrated by the knowledge that this restricted role differs from the publicly stated goal, he may well seek an outlet for that frustration through informal channels either on an individual basis or, more probably, in some form of association with his colleagues.

In his study of correctional officers in New York, Lombardo (1981) discovered that they did not tend to associate with each other outside the work environment, and that in general they were not proud to be known as correctional officers. They were generally satisfied with relations with other colleagues at work but they did not extend these to personal relationships. Lombardo concluded that one could not safely assume the existence of an officer sub-culture which was capable of influencing the behaviour and attitude of individual officers. Instead of a cohesive group with widely accepted norms and strong sanctions for their breach he found a highly fragmented collection of individuals with a degree of independence from each other and little personal contact off the job.

Lombardo's findings may be true for a particular group of officers in a particular set of circumstances. They are not consonant with other research findings and do not relate to practical experience in Britain. Until recently the vast majority of prison officers in Scotland stayed in accommodation which was provided by the prison authorities, normally close to the prison, often in a relatively remote location. A social club would be provided. The social life of the whole family, not only of the officer himself, revolved around the prison environment. In that set of circumstances peer influence played an important role in developing group attitudes.

> A fundamental characteristic of authority, therefore, is that the willingness of subordinates to suspend their own judgement in advance and follow the directives of the superior results largely from social constraints exerted by the collectivity of subordinates and not primarily from the influences the superior himself can bring to bear upon them. (Blau and Scott, 1966)

The integration of social life and work experience is a two edged sword. On the one hand, it can lead to isolation from the world at large and to insulation from a need to come to grips with the image which the general public has of the work of the prison officer. This was a criticism levelled against prison staff, including members of the governor grades, by the May Report in 1979. On the other hand, when co-workers know each other off the job they are more likely to derive deeper social satisfaction on the job. In such a world the position which one has at work may well become an important measure of individual status and prestige.

However, it should be pointed out that since 1980 staff in the Scottish Prison Service have not been obliged to live in prison quarters. There has been a financial incentive for the officer first to purchase his quarters and then on transfer to move to his own accommodation. The majority of staff have taken advantage of this facility and will identify this as having led to a significant improvement in their quality of life.

If peer group influence does exist among staff to any degree it is likely to be reflected in relations with management. The significant influence which prison officers as a group have had on the development of policy in the Scottish Prison Service will be discussed in chapter nine. It is quite normal that staff who are able to wield some degree of affiliated strength will use this in an attempt to reduce the threat inherent in management's power over how they go about their daily activities. Junior staff in an organisation may well seek to reduce the rights, prerogatives or sphere of latitude of superiors by means of legislation, collective bargaining or any other method which allows a redefinition of the superior's ability to act legitimately. This activity can have many aims.

In the early part of the twentieth century trades unions used much of their new found power to oppose scientific management, which they saw leading to a decline in the need for their craft skills and the control which they had over their own work. The roots of trade unionism in the prison system can be traced to the clandestine National Union of Police and Prison Officers which was established in 1914. It is sufficient at this point to note that trade unionism has been and continues to be a significant influence on the evolution of the prison service. In 1963 the first major sociological study of an English prison (Morris and Morris, 1963) painted a somewhat negative picture of what had by then become the Prison Officers' Association.

> The characteristics of the POA at national level are such as to create for prison administrators a stereotype of conservatism. The Association tends to be exceptionally suspicious of change, authoritarian in its penal views and given to tenacious bargaining over comparatively small details. Above all, it is a militant association.

This view is confirmed by later commentators (King and Morgan, 1980) who found the POA to be disillusioned with the attempt to forge a more constructive role for its members and unable to comprehend the logistics of a prison policy dictated by a distant headquarters' organisation. As a result the POA focussed its attention on the traditional trade union concerns of pay and conditions of service. This stereotype does not fit the Scottish Prison Officers' Association, at least at national level. However, it has to be recognised that pay and conditions of service are determined at a British level and, while the representative of the Scottish POA takes an active part in these negotiations, the running is made by the POA. Also, a distinction has to be made between the Scottish POA at national level and at local level; the extent to which the national body reflects local sentiment in respect of some of its more progressive positions is at least open to question.

Associations formed by workers are primarily designed to enhance the social and economic welfare of their members. They achieve their tasks by use of a set of internal and external relations. Internally they must work in a democratic manner through the 'supreme authority' of the membership. Some unions fall short of the democratic ideal but all adhere at least to the form if not the practice. Externally, a union relates to the organisation in which its members are employed and it cannot exist without it. This means that implicitly the organisation defines the membership of the union, sustains it and provides the benefits which the members need.

Traditionally one of the main tasks of the union is to extract the best possible package of benefits from an unwilling organisation. So, the union is at the same time dependant on and in conflict with the organisation. The relationship between management and staff in the Scottish Prison Service is particularly symbiotic. Given the transient nature of the administrative members of senior management, the SPOA is placed in a particularly strong position with respect to experience of the service. Given also that the primary role of senior management is to service the political master, the Secretary of State, and to ensure that he is not embarrassed, not least by internal wrangling, there is a tradition of minimal confrontation and maximum accommodation. This is not an unusual bureaucratic response and in the next chapter the influence which this style of management has had on the development of the service is examined.

8 'The Justice of Administration'

The form of management adopted for the Scottish prison system in 1877, with the establishment of the Prison Commission, was typical of the period in which *ad hoc* boards abounded: the Local Government Board, the Board of Commissioners in Lunacy, the Fishery Board, the Board of Agriculture and so on. Gordon Donaldson (1974) has described how this tradition developed in Scotland:

> The general concept lying behind the earlier boards was that
> administration should be directed by bodies composed partly of
> specialist and professional members who were usually paid –
> for example, medical or legal practitioners or individuals with
> knowledge of fisheries – and partly of eminent laymen
> representing the public, for example, Lord Provosts or Sheriffs,
> who were unpaid.

In 1885 the newly appointed Secretary for Scotland took over parliamentary responsibility for all of these boards, including the Prison Commission, and their independent character grew less obvious. In the early years of the twentieth century there was considerable debate about the wisdom of continuing with this arrangement. The nature of the debate remains topical today.

There was concern, on the one hand, that the concentration of these responsibilities in the hands of the Secretary for Scotland merely increased the power of permanent officials, who were neither adequately supervised nor properly accountable. As a consequence public administration in Scotland was more bureaucratic than in England and Wales. The various boards, it was suggested, allowed for control by people with a combination of technical knowledge and experience of public affairs.

The contrary argument was that the boards were not responsible to Parliament, that they blurred the necessary distinction between political and permanent appointments and that they were filled through patronage. In 1914 the Royal Commission on the Civil Service expressed opposition to the board system.

The debate was concluded in favour of the Secretary for Scotland in 1926, when his post was upgraded to Secretary of State. Consequent to the enactment of the Reorganisation of Offices (Scotland) Act of 1928 the Prison Commissioners ceased to hold office and on 1 April 1929 they were replaced by the Prisons Department which, along with the Departments of Agriculture, Education and Health, came under the control and direction of the Secretary of State for Scotland.

Each of the new departments of the Scottish Office had its own Permanent Secretary. Lieutenant Colonel R E W Baird, OBE, until then Governor of Barlinnie Prison, was appointed to the post of Secretary of the Prisons Department. His deputy was John Fulton, who had previously been Chief Clerk in the Commission. When Baird died in 1935 he was succeeded by Lieutenant Colonel W Leith-Ross, MC, who had previously been Inspector of Prisons.

A further Reorganisation of Offices (Scotland) Act was passed in 1939 and on 4 September that year the Prisons Department was assimilated into the new Scottish Home Department, later to become the Scottish Home and Health Department, where it now remains. Leith-Ross was given the title of Director of Prison and Borstal Services. The final absorption of the management of the prison system into the administrative civil service came in 1950 when K M Hancock, a career civil servant, was appointed Director on the retiral of Leith-Ross. This arrangement remains in force today. The Director of the Scottish Prison Service is in the Administrative Unified Grade 3 (Under Secretary) and reports directly to the Secretary of the Scottish Home and Health Department.

Historical analysis provides a major source of understanding of how prison policies, regimes and practices have evolved. Such an analysis suggests that the administration of prisons has not developed in a reasoned evolutionary manner but rather in a series of fits and starts, of turning back on itself and of response to crisis.

> In the first place, rather than emphasise the 'inevitability' of the last one hundred years or so of 'prison reform', it seems to me important in 1974 to recognise that they were very largely (though not entirely) a mistake, a blind alley into which the

> British Government wandered as much through short-sighted
> financial and political expediency as through any considered
> penal philosophy. (McLachlan, 1974)

Few commentators have shown any interest in the development of
Scottish prison administration, either contemporaneously or in an
historical context. We have seen that the establishment of a Scottish
Prison Commission in 1877 was a logical conclusion to the process of
centralisation which had begun forty years earlier. The Commission
itself represented, in the Scottish tradition, a combination of legal
experience and public interest. The former in particular, not least
through the two *ex officio* members, served to place the prison system
firmly within the criminal justice process. The abolition of the Commission in 1929 was not a logical step, it was one of McLachlan's
'blind alleys'. The subsequent absorption of the Prisons Department
into the Scottish Home and Health Department was thoroughly understandable in administrative terms but quite illogical in terms of
penological development. These two administrative changes were
achieved with very little public or parliamentary comment.

This was not the case when the Prison Commission for England and
Wales was abolished. It had originally been intended that this would
follow shortly after the earlier abolition in Scotland but action in
England had been shelved at the outbreak of the Second World War.
It was quietly resurrected in a section tucked away in the Criminal
Justice Act 1961. The proposal attracted fierce opposition in the House
of Commons, in the press and in other informed circles. The government stood alone in supporting the proposal, enthusiastically backed
by its officials. The scale of the problems which have faced the English
prison system over the years since then has caused many people to look
back with nostalgia to the good old days of the Commission, forgetting
that it too came in for more than its share of criticism. Nonetheless,
much of the present argument has been measured. The difference in
emphasis was summed up by a retired prison governor:

> Once the Service became an integral part of the Home Office
> there was always a feeling that everyone was looking over his
> shoulder, anxious about big brother in the background.
> (Evans, 1980)

This uncertainty, it has been argued, was in the first instance deliber-
ately fostered by the officials in Whitehall who objected to the

autonomy of the prison service and sought successfully to bring it within the control of traditional bureaucracy.

> The confusion and loss of morale which have helped to bring the Prison Service to the brink of disaster were predicted as long ago as 1963 by opponents of Whitehall's successful attempts, made then and subsequently, to gain greater bureaucratic power over the prison system . . . The growth of bureaucracy followed moves by Whitehall Mandarins and Ministers, introduced with some deviousness against fierce criticism in and out of Parliament. Their purpose was the absorption of the old Prison Commission, set up in 1877 to be responsible for prisons, within the control of the Home Secretary. (Evans, 1980)

The purpose of the exercise was not so much to bring prisons within the control of the Home Secretary, since he had always held parliamentary accountability for them, but rather within the control of the Home Office itself, to make the prison service part of the mainstream civil service.

It would be wrong to argue that the organisational problems which have plagued the Home Office Prison Department since 1963 have existed to a similar degree in Scotland. That they have not done so is mainly a result of the comparatively small size of the Scottish service which precludes the anonymity which has at times existed in England and Wales.

The prison service is unique in that it is the only large organisation in our society, apart from the armed forces, which is directly under the control of central government. All others, including education, the health service and the police, have a combination of local management and central oversight.

Leaving aside the question of whether or not this is a good arrangement, it means that the management role of the seven divisions within the Scottish Home and Health Department which make up the Scottish Prison Service Headquarters, and which are properly known as the Prisons Group, is significantly different to that of the other divisions within the department. Until 1982 the headquarters of the Scottish Prison Service was technically merely a division within the Scottish Home and Health Department. Its head, although carrying the title of Director of the Scottish Prison Service and graded at Middle Executive Directing Band, slightly above Assistant Secretary, reported, as does any other head of division in the Scottish Office, to an Under Secretary, who in turn reported to the Secretary of the Scottish

Home and Health Department. In management terms the responsibility of the then Prisons Division was considered to be little different to that of, say, Police Division which monitors but does not manage the work of the police in Scotland. This was despite the fact that the Director of the Prison Service had day-to-day responsibility for in excess of 5,000 prisoners, of 3,000 staff in twenty penal establishments, of some 150 staff in headquarters and of an annual budget of some £60 million.

Since 1982 the Director has reported immediately to the Secretary of the Home and Health Department, like himself a permanent official. He now has seven full blown divisions within his group and in 1989 was given the grade of Under Secretary (Administrative Unified Grade 3).

Strict central control of any large organisation has several results. One of the most common of these is the tightening of communication flow and a consequent increase in secretiveness. This aversion to publicity is more a feature of direct central government control than of the prison system itself. The best example of this is probably the role which inspectors of prisons have been called on to undertake under successive forms of management, and in this respect one has to note the failings of the Prison Commission for Scotland. Prior to 1877 the form of inspection and annual reporting carried out by inspectors such as Hill and Kincaid contributed significantly to the development of penal policy and practice. Their comments, both critical and constructive, were made public.

> However scathingly the Inspectors criticised the prison governor,
> or the prison administration generally, the Home Office of 1835–
> 1877 did not find that it was destructive of discipline or inimical
> to good administration to issue these reports to the world.
> (Webbs, 1922)

This changed after 1878 when the inspectors became 'assistants' to the commissioners and by 1900 the inspector's position had become so debased that the Elgin Committee recommended that the post be abolished. The opposite view was taken by the May Committee in 1979, which recommended the establishment of an inspectorate 'distanced from the prison service'. We have seen that this new inspectorate was established in 1981. There was a great outcry from prison governors that the person appointed to fill the post had no experience of working within the prison service. This argument deflected attention from a much more fundamental flaw in the arrangements.

May had recommended 'a system of inspection of the Prison Service' (paragraph 5.61). What was set up was a system of inspection of prisons. The new inspector was given no authority to inspect either the organisation of prison service headquarters or the way in which policy decisions were made within the Scottish Home and Health Department. Furthermore, he reported to the Secretary of State, not directly, but through the Secretary of the Scottish Home and Health Department who in policy terms might be adjudged to be more in charge of the prison service than the Director. So, on these two counts, the distancing and the extent of inspection recommended by May were quietly misinterpreted by senior officials in a manner which removed any danger that the spotlight of publicity might be turned on them.

The last thirty years have witnessed a more dangerous feature of extended centralisation and growing bureaucratic power, that of the increased power of the executive over the sentenced offender. The most obvious example of this is the extent to which the executive, rather than the judiciary, exerts control over the actual length of time spent by an offender in prison, irrespective of the sentence passed by the court, by means of the parole system.

Garland (1983) lays the blame for some of this extended statism at the feet of a criminology which has extended the power of prison administrators, forensic scientists and psychiatrists into what was previously an exclusively judicial domain, and which has sought to effect a shift of power away from the judiciary and towards a non-legal executive staff.

Justice is a delicate flower; justice for those in prison is the most delicate flower of all. One of the basic criteria for justice is that it should not be arbitrary, that it should be based on premises which are open to scrutiny. We face a real danger that many of the processes in our penal system are not open to that scrutiny. In the case of parole, the Parole Board for Scotland argues that the very fact that the justice meted out is executive rather than legal implies that it should not be open to scrutiny. But,

> The spectre of executive justice . . . casts deep shadows across the light of freedom under the law. When decisions are made in committee rooms even the minutes do not necessarily tell the story of what has happened. The delegation of powers by Ministers must inevitably enhance the labyrinthine processes of bureaucracy that are imperfectly understood, not least by those whose interests and liberties may be at stake. (Morris, 1976)

Jacobs (1983) has suggested that the trend towards increasing bureaucracy and professionalism in prisons in both Great Britain and the United States has been strong since at least the 1950s. It has been suggested in these pages that the trend towards increasing bureaucracy in the central administration considerably pre-dates that period. With increasing centralism came growing control from the centre. Duffee (1975) suggests that there will be inevitable conflict between local and central management since the main concern of the former will be with daily management and individual prisoners while the latter will be more interested in organisational development:

> Central Office personnel will probably view institution managers
> as short-sighted and crisis-oriented, since they are 'over-
> interested' in the fate of individuals . . . Institutional managers
> are likely to perceive the Central Office as naive meddlers,
> unfamiliar with institutional problems and continually forcing on
> institutions programs or activities that seem only tangentially
> related to treatment and custody concerns.

One suggested reason for this different approach is that institutional managers are generally people who have risen through the ranks rather than professional managers and that their behaviour is therefore more likely to relate to previous experience rather than to management as such. The growth of a centralised bureaucracy requires central administrators who are responsible for policy. Traditionally they will be graded in a strict hierarchy with clearly assigned duties and responsibilities. There will be formalities symbolising the various pecking orders. There will be specific procedural devices which are intended to foster objectivity and are specifically meant to restrain the 'quick passage of impulse into action' (Merton, 1957).

The bureaucrat's official life stretches out in front of him as a graded career and he is tacitly expected to adapt his professional work to the prospect of this career. Inevitably this will lead the central organisation to an over-concern with adherence to rules and regulations. In a word, the great symbolic importance of the means leads to a situation in which they become more important than the end. Nowhere is this more likely than in the organisation of the prison system.

There are two main reasons for this. In the first place ambivalence and conflict as to the value of particular theories have produced prison systems which are inadvertently designed to resist change. Secondly, management in the prison system is an end in itself rather than a means to an end. The most junior prison officer can rightly be described as a manager in his dealings with prisoners, despite his lack of status with senior management, and the latter will do well to remember this.

The difficulty which the prison service faces in this respect is what Mintzberg (1979) has described as 'centralisation of decision making in the face of cognitive limitations'. This means that senior management prefers to concentrate on detailed decision making, which should be delegated, rather than taking an overview and concentrating on broad strategies.

There can be several reasons for this. It may be that management does not trust its subordinates to do the job; it may be that it genuinely believes that it can take wiser decisions even in minor matters than its subordinates; or it may be that immersion in the fine print of decision making is thought to absolve senior management from the need to concern itself with wider policy matters. The May Report noted this tendency in the senior ranks of prison administration:

> Management has become preoccupied with fighting the daily tactical battle. We hope that the general effect of what we recommend will lift some of that load and allow management to resume more creative roles. (paragraph 5.88)

This had been recognised in 1978 in Scotland in a review of the management in the Prisons Division.

> Among the shortcomings we have noted in the recent management of Prisons Division is an undue, though natural, preoccupation with the short-term problem and the *ad hoc* solution.

This involvement in detail to the detriment of wider concerns is not merely a failure of the present management structure but rather an inherent failure in what is described as the machine bureaucracy. A considerable amount of the energy of senior management goes into maintaining the structure of the organisation, into fine-tuning the bureaucratic machine. The daily running of the prison system requires the precise and consistent performance of an integrated set of simple repetitive tasks. Strategic diagnosis is simply not a part of standard operating procedures.

This preoccupation with immediate problems and short-term solutions is not peculiar to the Scottish prison administration. In the United States a Task Force of the President's Commission on Law Enforcement and Administration of Justice reported in 1967. One of its conclusions was:

> The most conspicuous problems in corrections today are lack of knowledge and an unsystematic approach to the development of programs and techniques. Changes in correctional treatment have been guided primarily by what Wright calls 'intuitive opportunism', a kind of goal orientated guessing.
>
> If the range of alternatives for solving correctional problems were narrow, well-organised, and familiar, the best approach might be this intuitive and pragmatic one. But this is not the case. Failure to attempt really systematic research and evaluation of various operational programs has led to repetitive error. Even more, it has made it impossible to pin-point the reasons for success when successes did occur.

A fundamental weakness of a system based on 'goal orientated guessing' is that it is likely to lead not only to 'repetitive error' but also to injustice. A combination of low visibility and high discretion will eventually lead to corruption; not necessarily material corruption, but the more insidious corruption of power.

> It is evident that correctional administrators have for too long operated with practical immunity in the back-washes of administrative law. They have been unmindful that the processes of justice more strictly observed by the visible police and courts in relation to rights due to the accused before and through adjudication must not stop when the convicted person is sentenced. The justice perspective demands accountability from all processors even the 'pure of heart'. *Properly understood, the justice perspective is not so much concerned with the administration of justice as it is with the justice of administration.*
> (Fogel, 1975)

In other words the basic feature of the justice model of imprisonment is that it requires the administration to treat prisoners with justice. A system of administration which allows prisoners to be treated unfairly cannot be justified by a process of moralising. But a system which has justice and fairness as its 'bottom line' is far removed from the traditional Scottish system of pragmatic prison administration. It is in this context that one can interpret the statement of a senior administrator that the justice model is 'burdensome on staff and headquarters and very time-consuming'.

The optimum system of organisation for the prison service remains open to debate. It is generally accepted that the present arrangement of total absorption into a larger central government department is far from ideal.

It has already been indicated that the basic grade prison officer is a manager in his own right. This management does not consist of making policy decisions nor of dealing with grand strategy. It consists of controlling the daily lives of a sizeable group of other human beings. The control may sometimes be positive but it is frequently negative; it involves limiting the freedom of other people in a very direct and observable way. The prison officer on the gallery is continually asked by those whom he manages why he is exercising his control in a specific manner. It is satisfying to neither the prisoner nor the prison officer if the response is that an administrator somewhere has for some reason decided that it should be so.

In England and Wales dissatisfaction with the present organisation often takes the form of nostalgia for the days of the Prison Commission. Whether a return to the Commission is feasible or not is in a way unimportant; what is important is a recognition of the roots from which this nostalgia springs. Thomas (1980) draws attention to this feature.

> The May Committee took the view that a resurrection of the
> Prison Commission is not desirable. Although this must remain
> questionable it is vital to acknowledge what it was about the
> Commission which prison staff seem to miss, namely the ability
> to associate decision and action with personality: to know
> precisely who is making a decision which affects people.

Within the Scottish Office there is a number of departments, including the Scottish Home and Health Department, each of which is subdivided into various divisions. Seven divisions within the Home and Health Department are grouped together into what is known as the Scottish Prison Service Headquarters. The heads of these divisions, led by the Director of the Scottish Prison Service, collectively make up the Prison Service Management Group.

In strategic planning terms there is another administrative tier above 'headquarters', the Secretariat of the Scottish Home and Health

Department. The Director of the Prison Service reports to the Secretary of the Department. This is a structure which is not easily comprehended by prison staff, by prisoners, by the public and perhaps most important of all in organisational terms by many of those who work within what is formally described as Prisons Group.

It should be borne in mind that the civil servants who work in the Prisons Group are not members of the prison service. They are generalist administrators, many of whom spend a few years in 'Prisons' on their way from 'Education' before going on to 'Agriculture'. In other words, they have no career commitment to decisions which they make concerning the prison service. There is a danger that such a bureaucracy will feed off itself, that it will create a *raison d' etre* of its own, divorced from the structure which it was set up to serve.

The prison service exists because there are prisoners; prisoners are held in prisons by prison staff. These are the only essential elements in the system. All other elements, including the headquarters' structure, are useful but have no separate right of existence. The *Report of the Advisory Committee on the Management of Correctional Institutions in Canada,* which was published in November 1984, recognised this fact:

> The Institution is the most important organizational component
> of Correctional Services. All components of National
> Headquarters and Regional Headquarters must be, and be seen to
> be, in existence to serve the Institution.

Given the tendency of the administrative machine to deal with short term solutions to immediate problems the organisational style which has developed within the Scottish Prison Service has been one of control. Prisons have come under the scrutiny of a 'distanced' inspectorate, so headquarters has responded by setting up its own 'operational assessments' of establishments, a kind of pre-emptive strike force. Headquarters has set up a system of staff inspection, so the trades unions have set up a watchdog staff inspection committee. A great round of *'quis custodiet?'* has developed and the system spends so much time in reactive response that there is little opportunity for pro-active planning. This reactive style of management is an understandable method of coping with the learning curve which is bound to exist where there is a changing headquarters' staff who have little or no knowledge of the three basic elements of the system: prisoners, prisons and prison staff.

An essential feature of the present form of central machine bureaucracy in the prison service is that it encourages principles of management and discourages notions of leadership. Its method of achieving a controlled style of management in the 1980s was by a system of 'accountable regimes' and of 'financial management initiative'. It has already been suggested that in England the bureaucratic wish to rein in any tendency to charismatic leadership was behind the move to abolish the Prison Commission. The lack of identifiable leadership was recognised in the Mountbatten Report which attempted to reverse this bureaucratic trend by recommending the appointment of an Inspector General who would be the recognisable professional head of the service. The fate of this recommendation has been described as 'the most instructive episode in recent British history'. The attempt to provide a leader for the service failed precisely because the first and only individual appointed to the post attempted to take on just such a role. The bureaucratic machine was inevitably able to neutralise him and he resigned from office before completing his second two year term.

Leadership and management are not by definition exclusive of each other; nor is the absence of leadership inherent in the nature of a bureaucratic system. Leadership can be used to describe an attribute of personality, it can be seen as characteristic of a particular position or it can be an attribute of behaviour. In the latter context it has been described as 'any act of influence on a matter of organisational relevance'. Such a definition will include routine acts of supervision. Essentially, however, it has to do with that influence which goes beyond routine and which makes use of elements of power beyond those which are organisationally decreed.

Organisational powers include reward, punishment and legitimate authority. Leadership powers are either referent, that is to say, dependant on an attachment between leader and follower, or expert in that they depend on the knowledge and ability of the leader. Some commentators view executive leadership as the key function of management; necessary for making critical as opposed to routine decisions, decisions which constitute commitments which shape the essential character of an organisation. Such managerial leadership will defend the integrity of an organisation in the face of development and will maintain order and control in the event of internal conflict.

It is common, however, for power in a machine bureaucracy, such as the administration of the prison service, to be restricted to a formal, institutionalised or legitimated level. This use of power is restricted to the formal structure of the organisation and it is to be distinguished from the exercise of leadership. At the same time, it should be recognised that legitimate authority cannot be divorced from the dynamics of persuasion in an efficient management structure. The leadership inherent in efficient management is a form of education.

> In short, it is recognised that control and consent cannot be
> divorced even within formally authoritarian structures.
> (Selznick, 1948)

The notion that leadership and the authority of legitimate management are at the same time distinct yet interrelated is of particular interest when examining the personal traits and backgrounds of public servants and observing the exercise of authority and leadership in public bureaucratic settings. The expression of leadership as well as legitimate authority is necessary in the efficient management of penal establishments. No prison governor can be effective in either control or direction unless he can inspire his staff to respond in a manner which is more than routine and beyond what is organisationally decreed.

A problem arises when governors and staff look for a similar form of leadership in the central organisation. This part of the service is staffed mainly by generalist civil servants of the administrative class. The ethos in which these individuals have been trained is one which does not relate primarily to the management of people. They have been schooled, one might argue, in the antithesis of leadership, in the need to be anonymous, to have no public face.

The senior administrators who form the Prison Service Management Group bring this tradition of management with them from previous experience. Their point of reference continues to be upwards to more senior officials and Ministers rather than the leadership which is expected of them by those whom they are called on to manage. The fact that this is so, but that it need not be so, is confirmed when on occasion a senior administrator emerges who breaks the mould, who does provide recognisable leadership and who in consequence attracts a support from prison staff far in excess of what he might expect on the basis of his legitimate authority alone.

In her history of the Home Office between 1848 and 1914, Pellew (1982) refers to a feature of its management which is as relevant to other government departments, including the Scottish Prison Service, today.

One characteristic in particular strikes the historian of the late nineteenth century Home Office: its frequent inability to bring about desirable change – in prison administration, factory inspection, the management of statistics – without the impetus of public criticism. Was this due to its hard-pressed, sometimes incompetent officials at the upper division level? Was it an inherent aspect of a naturally conservative department? Or was it an inevitable feature of bureaucracy?

The answer is, certainly in today's terms, that it is none of these. It is a feature of the form of central government administration which we have in this country, a form of administration which operates on the basis of responding to and interpreting pressure.

Pressure from staff has led to significant change in the prison service. This was discussed in the previous chapter in relation to the management in recent years of 'difficult' prisoners in Scotland. Other examples of external pressure recently have been the changes in channels of communication and of complaint allowed to prisoners, which have been brought about by pressure from the European Commission on Human Rights. There have been changes in internal disciplinary procedures against prisoners as a result of judicial appeal. The period for parole eligibility in England and Wales was reduced as a result of pressure on overcrowded accommodation.

Before 1877, and under direct government control until 1929, the Scottish system had been located firmly within the criminal justice process. The prison service is primarily the servant of the court and its goals are part of the wider goals of its super-ordinate criminal justice system; the former are an integrated part of the latter.

Despite the administrative arrangement since 1929 the prison service remains part, not of the administrative civil service, but of the criminal justice system. Prison affairs are part of the political process and cannot be divorced from theories of the state. More particularly, they can only be considered within the context of the criminal justice system as a whole.

This is not a peculiarly Scottish phenomenon. In 1969 the *Report of the Canadian Commission on Corrections* listed what it considered to be basic principles and purposes of criminal justice. It considered one of these to be that the 'law enforcement, judicial and correctional processes should form an inter-related sequence'.

This principle was confirmed by the 1984 Carson Report in Canada. This report indicated that in addition to providing leadership to the prison service the Commissioner of Corrections had an important responsibility for articulating and communicating 'corporate correctional policy as it relates to the overall Criminal Justice system'. As a result of the 1969 report the Correctional Service of Canada has been made responsible for all convicted offenders whether serving their sentences in an institution or in the community. The Commissioner reports to his political head, the Solicitor General.

In other countries the chief executive of the prison service reports commonly to a Minister of Justice. The possibility of such a development in the United Kingdom has been raised from time to time. In the parliamentary debate following publication of the Mountbatten Report in 1966 one speaker advocated:

> The structure of the Service must be considered much more
> carefully than Lord Mountbatten had time to do. I am not sure
> that in the long-term the aim should not be an inter-related
> Service – I do not say integrated – through the whole field of
> what the United States calls corrections – in other words,
> breaking down to a degree the present water-tight compartments
> between Prison Officers, Probation Officers, Parole Officers and
> the kindred services. These bodies will have to be extended and
> expanded. Why should not Prison Officers be eligible to transfer
> to these services more freely? This would widen the scope of
> promotion, encourage men of quality who have an inclination for
> the public service and prevent the institutionalisation of Prison
> Officers. I hope that thought will be given to the matter.
> (Deedes, Hansard, 16.2.1967)

This was precisely the arrangement which the Ouimet Report was to recommend two years later for Canada and which was subsequently implemented in that country.

The matter of coordination between the prison services and other related departments was frequently raised in the United Kingdom in the late 1960s. The Chairman of the Prison Officers' Association addressing the association's annual conference in 1968 had this to say:

> The ideal would be a Department of Correction, in which all the
> present differing sections of the public service which are
> nowadays concerned with the problems of social criminal
> behaviour could be embodied and co-ordinated in one cohesive
> department, with free and complete interchange ability to all.
> Probation, imprisonment, parole, after-care; all are facets of the

same problem and all should be dealt with by a comprehensive correctional service, in which Prison Officers should certainly have an important role to play. Such a service will surely come into effect some day, just as surely as tomorrow's sun will rise; but it will not be in my day and perhaps not in yours either.

Nor was this a newly perceived problem. The Scottish Prison Commissioners, a recognised part of the criminal justice system, had pleaded in their annual report for the year 1912 for 'a much closer coordination between the various Courts and Departments responsible for the administration of justice in the country'.

There is a growing appreciation that the fundamental problem which faces the prison system in Scotland today is not one of shortage of resources or of external pressure but rather one of organisational structure. The present political climate accepts the need for, indeed encourages, organisational change in public institutions. There are several examples of large public institutions which have undergone radical change to a degree which until recently would have been thought impossible.

The first real possibility of change in the management of the prison services in the United Kingdom was signalled with the publication in 1988 of the 'Next Steps' Report. This document, prepared by the Prime Minister's Efficiency Unit under the chairmanship of Sir Robin Ibbs, recommended a radical restructuring of the conduct of the business of government:

> The central Civil Service should consist of a relatively small core engaged in the function of servicing Ministers and managing departments, who will be 'sponsors' of particular government policies and services. Responding to these departments will be a range of agencies employing their own staff, who may or may not have the status of Crown servants, and concentrating on the delivery of their particular service, with clearly defined responsibilities between the Secretary of State and the Permanent Secretary on the one hand and the Chairmen or Chief Executives of the agencies on the other.

The distinction between a small central government department which would be responsible for policy making and a separate executive agency which would carry out that policy could obviously be applied in the case of the prison service and might well be attractive to a government which had set itself the objective of reducing the overall number of direct government employees. The Scottish Office employs less than 10,000 civil servants; of these some 4,000 are members of the Scottish Prison Service.

In 1988 the Home Office Prison Department embarked on a review of the organisation of the prison service in England and Wales above establishment level. This review was completed in 1990 and included reference to the possibility of agency status for the prison service, commenting that this notion 'has a particular resonance for the Prison Service because of its Prison Commission history'. The review concluded that there would be no advantage in creating a number of small agencies to carry out the ancillary functions of the prison service and significant disadvantages in separating the operational arm of the service from its policy one:

> The choice is between turning the entire Service into an agency and maintaining the status quo. A Prison Service agency would entail some adaptation of the Next Steps concept to fit its unusual circumstances.
>
> There would be a number of advantages for the Service in becoming an agency including a stronger sense of corporate identity and the scope for more visible leadership from the director general. But there could also be disadvantages if the links between the Service and the rest of the Home Office and ministers were loosened.
>
> The key question in practice is how far the Home Secretary would be able to stand back from the day to day business of the Service given the strong Parliamentary interest in prisons and prisoners.

Some commentators might argue that discussion about giving the prison service agency status is merely the shallow end of the debate about whether the service should be placed in private hands, particularly in view of proposals being considered in England and Wales to do just that with the remand sector of the service. Privatisation of prisons, although not of prison systems, is already relatively common in some parts of North America. Several of the private companies involved have shown an interest in extending their business to the United Kingdom. So far there has been little encouragement.

> There has always been, and indeed still is, a strong tendency among certain academics and practitioners to play down the

politics of privatisation, to narrow it to an argument about
measurable performance or efficiency . . . While we accept that
such a separation does have some analytical value, it should be
equally obvious that the two issues are intimately connected.
After all, the fact that the 'productive efficiency' of the private
sector is being discussed at all is a reflection of changing
political and moral perceptions and in any case it is difficult to
believe that the 'productive efficiency' of any social institution
or service can be sensibly measured by using criteria which are
'largely' divorced from political and moral values. (Ryan and
Ward, 1989)

Open debate on the future organisation of the prison system in
Scotland has not yet been entered, although the ground is being
cleared. In 1989 the Scottish Prison Service produced its first 'Business Plan' and attempts are now being made to define the 'customers'
of the prison service. The next stage is likely to be a review of the
management structure. There are several possible alternatives to the
present arrangement, ranging from the separation of the prison service
into a new department in the Scottish Office, for which the Secretary
of State would still retain direct accountability, to full agency status,
akin to the system that existed under the Scottish Prison Commission,
in which a chief executive would have full responsibility for running
the prison service, reporting to the Secretary of State who would retain
parliamentary accountability.

What is fundamental is that the prison system should return to a
penal model which would place it firmly within the criminal justice
system, as was the case before 1929. A radical alternative would be to
seize the opportunity to bring the various forms of community sentencing under the same umbrella not, as some of those quoted above
have suggested, in a social welfare model, but within the same penal
model. Community sentences, like custodial alternatives, should be
recognised as primarily punitive. To go down this path would be to
move towards the example, followed in several other jurisdictions, of
a ministry of justice.

One of the most consistent cries to be heard from those who work in
and around the prison system concerns the need for more and better
resources. It is wrong to talk about the failure of the rehabilitative
model, argue these protagonists, when it has never been given sufficient resources to be properly tested. If only overcrowding were

abolished and adequate facilities provided, the prison system could become a positive vehicle for social reform. There is a shortage of resources in the prison system, resources which are necessary to maintain a penal model in which prisoners could be humanely dealt with, but even if the prison system had all of these resources and more it could never become a vehicle for social reform because that is not its primary function.

The courts which the system exists to serve do not send criminals to prison to be reformed. For the same reason a dramatic increase in the quality of personnel who staff the prison system would not result in any greater degree of success in attempting to impose the regime of the custodians on the prisoner population. The reason for this is quite simply that the lack of a sense of 'duty' among the prisoners, the failure of coercive methods, and the inadequate system of rewards and punishments which are used to induce compliance, are the result not of limited resources nor of staff inadequacies but rather of structural defects in the system.

One of the principal defects arises from the continuing attempt to justify the humane handling of prisoners on the grounds that such humanitarianism is 'treatment'. Prison staff are being asked increasingly to explain why recidivism rates remain so high, why 'training' is not more effective in reducing future offending by former prisoners. Faced with these impossible questions staff have become confused as to their function, they have not been precise enough about the nature of their role to respond that the 'caring' element of their work is exercised not in the name of rehabilitation but in the name of humanity. All that need be said in addition is that if a prisoner is to succeed in rehabilitating himself, that is, in restoring himself to his former condition, he is more likely to do so in humane conditions of containment than in inhumane ones.

It may be as well at this stage to point out that the disturbances which occur within prisons from time to time do not necessarily indicate confusion within the system. The prison, particularly the maximum security one, is not a self-regulating mechanism in which disturbances to the equilibrium bring about changes which act towards a restoration of the original state of affairs. The concept of crisis is not necessarily the antithesis of the concept of organisation. To an extent the organisation within a maximum security prison may be a series of disorders which are not allowed to become too disorderly, a series of crises tied together in a recognisable continuity.

This truth, however, should not be used as an excuse to avoid developing a recognised pattern of organisational behaviour. It was demonstrated in a previous chapter that the organisation of the prison service has been largely reactive in its management style, and it was further argued that this is principally a consequence of its position within the mainstream of the administrative civil service. Policy in this environment is likely to be retrospective rather than prospective; it is largely a policy of recognition, of acknowledging what already exists. Policy making, properly understood, should include a category of forward decision making which can effect the structure of the organisation. Management of the prison service has until now been characterised by a lack of any attempt at self-assessment or review of how policy is made. Referring to the only attempt made in recent years by the Home Office to review policy, King and Elliott (1977) make a significant comment:

> But in retrospect, and perhaps to a few observers at the time, the truly remarkable thing about 'Penal Practice in a Changing Society' was that it expected that its aims could be achieved by new building and staff training, and without major overhaul of the creaking administrative structure and unwieldy procedures which had grown up over three-quarters of a century. Its concern for science and professionalism was directed solely to understanding the causes of crime and finding better ways of treating it, not at all with the management of the prison system itself and the control of the establishments which make it up.

Much of the confusion surrounding the goals of the prison system can be analysed in terms of poor managerial practices. The significant factor is often not the impossibility of achieving the goals if set at their proper levels but their inaccurate implementation, consequent in part at least on poor techniques of evaluation.

One model (Duffee, 1975) suggests that there are three possible frameworks within which to fit the behaviour of prison management and its consequences. It can attempt to be a closed, self-contained organisation with unchanging parameters. It can be an open system with boundaries which change as its operation develops. Or it can be a learning system; that is, an open system which is capable of changing its own internal structure in order to improve production or goal achievement. In order to meet the last set of criteria a prison system would require goals which were clearly stated, the ability to measure significant deviation from these goals, and a strategy to deal with any deviation. The crucial element in such a system, concludes Duffee, is management:

> Essentially, it is on the ability of correctional management to adapt and improve that the evolutionary fate of correctional organisation depends.

An obvious but nonetheless fundamental factor in achieving such a system is a clearly understood method of internal communication. The prison grapevine can only flourish where there is a lack of information. Research shows that the more communication of a formal type which exists, the less informal communication there will be. This is particularly so where information comes through democratic decision rather than by being handed down. The normal organisational pattern shows a positive correlation between the amount of activity in formal and informal networks.

Foucault (1975) has described how pressure from penal reformers in the eighteenth century led to demands that power be exercised in a legitimate rather than an indiscriminate manner and that criminal justice should not exact revenge but should punish the wrongdoer. The art of this new punishment was to find a sufficient level of disadvantage to rob crime of its attractions. This led in due course to a more general use of imprisonment whereby the seriousness of crime was to be reflected only in the length of the period of imprisonment. Prison was now to be used *ad puniendos* not solely *ad continendos homines,* to punish and not merely to contain.

From the earliest days of nineteenth century reform, the punishment of imprisonment was linked to a technique of disciplining prisoners in such a manner as to ensure docility and utility. In due course this notion was further developed into that of reform or rehabilitation. The penal machine concentrated not primarily on the offence, nor even on the offender, but rather on the 'delinquent'. It was no coincidence that many of those most closely involved in the development of the prison system have been (and often still are) closely affiliated to recognised religious bodies. There is a highly moral element in the modern notion of imprisonment, based as it is on a criminal justice process which is concerned with assigning guilt to individuals in a manner which denotes the process as a secularisation of the older ecclesiastical system of identifying the wrongdoer and exacting punishment in expiation of guilt.

This development took the prison system beyond its criminal justice roots into the arena of social welfare, to the suggestion that it was sometimes appropriate to send individuals to prison 'for their own good' or 'for training'. What we now have to recognise is that the only proper way to consider the prison system is within the context of a criminal justice system. One of the first consequences of such a model would be seen in the courts where sentencing would be based on principles of justice rather than the intention of controlling crime. In other words, not only the prison but the whole criminal justice system would be drawn back into a penal model.

As far as the prison system itself is concerned it would be underpinned by the notion of 'justice-as-fairness' (Fogel, 1975). Only those individuals for whom there was no alternative disposition would go to prison and then for the shortest necessary time. While in prison they would be able to take advantage of opportunities for self-development, although these would not be a condition of eventual release. This would be more in keeping with the view which prisoners have long held of so-called rehabilitative tools; they dismiss them in that guise but welcome them as a means of ameliorating the bleak conditions of imprisonment. Humane treatment of prisoners would be acceptable simply for what it was. There would be no need to cloak it in rehabilitative jargon. Such a definition of purpose would make the task of the prison officer much more precise.

> The amount of 'training' in which officers can become involved in respect of prisoners is slight, because of the reality of the conflict in a modern prison system between control and reformation. This is not to be confused with a more modest goal which would be that officers should treat prisoners decently and humanely. But the vague aim of making officers quasi-social workers had an especially dysfunctional effect. (Thomas, 1980)

It has already been suggested that the difficulties which face the prison system are structural in nature rather than related to the quality of personnel. At the same time, we assume the integrity of the prison staff, an integrity which will allow them to exercise humanity in the inhumane world of the prison.

Keeping fellow human beings confined is a complex and difficult task. In order to fulfil it properly an officer must gain the legitimacy needed to exercise his authority effectively. The method of achieving this legitimacy is consistency in the handling of prisoners, a consistency which will allow the officer to shift from reliance on formal authority to a more personal type of authority. This development is more likely to occur if the officer is quite clear as to the primary purpose of imprisonment and, by extension, of his own principal role.

If we allow this model of imprisonment to flower we shall sound the death knell of the spectre of executive justice which 'casts deep shadows across the light of freedom under the law' (Morris, 1976) and which has been described as one of the major features of penal history in the twentieth century.

9 From Turnkey to Prison Officer

> It is in fact remarkable how little serious attention has been paid
> to prison officers in the quite extensive literature on prisons and
> imprisonment. It is almost as though they were, like the postman
> in G K Chesterton's celebrated detective story, so commonplace
> and routine a feature of the scene as to be invisible. Yet their role
> is clearly of critical importance. (Hawkins, 1976)

The central position occupied by the prison officer has not gone
entirely unrecognised in British penal literature. The more discerning
have recognised that in staff terms the number and influence of the
prison officer group is so overwhelming as to be pivotal in any scheme
which attempts to influence either the administration of the prison
system or regimes for prisons.

Even today one is quite likely to discover a polarisation of attitude
within society at large towards the prison officer to the extent that
many prison staff are reluctant to disclose the nature of their occupation to social acquaintances. John Maclean's biographer and daughter,
Nan Milton (1973), described prison staff as being 'specially chosen
from the army, the police force and from mental hospitals, for their
hardness and brutality'. Sir Evelyn Ruggles-Brise (1921), writing of
the same period, was of the opinion that 'discipline with kindness is the
watchword of our Prison Staff'.

Society has always been somewhat ambivalent about the reality of
imprisonment. On the one hand, it welcomes the sentences passed on
serious criminals and the fact that they will be removed from its midst.
On the other hand, it is uneasy about the environment and conditions
within the prison. This ambivalence is often transferred on to the
prison officer. On the one hand it is recognised that he carries out a
thankless task on behalf of society. On the other hand, there is often a

feeling that there must be something brutish about an individual who would choose a job which involves keeping other human beings in captivity. As a consequence of this public doubt, prison staff have developed an uncertainty about their own status. Until recently the majority of them stayed in a ghetto of official houses around the prison and lived an insular social life. It was almost as though the walls of the prison continued in an imaginary line to include the lives of the staff.

In earlier chapters the organisational development of the Scottish prison system was traced in order to demonstrate the particular influence which prison staff have had on the service. This emphasis was traced back to William Brebner, who had already trained a cadre of efficient staff at Glasgow by the time Frederic Hill, the first Inspector of Prisons for Scotland, came on the scene in 1835. Hill took up this theme and devoted considerable space in his early annual reports to the need for recruitment and training of suitable staff. The Prison Commission for Scotland and its successor the Prisons Department continued management's recognition of the central role played by staff, a feature emphasised much more in Scotland than in England.

This management style was certainly assisted by the relatively short lines of communication in such a compact service in Scotland, but it was also the result of a deliberate policy of involving staff at lower levels in duties which were much more than custodial. Since 1929, with central direction of the prison service located firmly within the mainstream of the administrative civil service, management has dealt with staff by reacting to the pressure which they have been able to bring to bear. In practical terms this has given staff, particularly as represented by their trade union, a significant say in the management of the service.

An important operational distinction between the Scottish Prison Officers' Association (SPOA) and the Prison Officers' Association (POA) is the way in which the national executive committee of the Scottish body has been able to retain tight control over its members to a degree which has been impossible in England and Wales, where a significant level of decision making has been delegated to local branch committees. An important outcome of this centralisation in Scotland has been the opportunity which it has afforded the trade union to push on a national basis for a more participative form of management structure for the Scottish Prison Service.

In view of the way in which the prison officer has been able to influence the findings of various departmental enquiries and the management practices in the service in Scotland, it is pertinent to ask whether his role has changed fundamentally since the mid nineteenth century. Has the change of title from turnkey, to keeper, to warder and finally to prison officer, denoted any change in basic task? There are one or two key areas in which a pragmatic form of participative management is most obvious.

In chapter six it was shown how the method adopted within the Scottish Prison Service for managing difficult prisoners who require particular forms of control has been greatly influenced by pressure from the SPOA. This method has involved an attempt at what one might describe as cure rather than prevention. That is to say, having discovered *post factum* that some prisoners are difficult to control within the system, a strategy for segregating them into groups has been developed.

This removes their influence from the mainstream of the prison population, labelling them as control problems who require to be managed in a distinctive fashion. This response has been developed in a cumulative manner, each developmental step being to a considerable extent a response to pressure from the SPOA, often as a result of individual incidents, a response which has been hammered out in a participative forum, normally expressed through a departmental working party. The primary objective of the trade union in influencing the development of these responses has been the physical protection of its members, and the system introduced has been largely successful in achieving this objective.

In responding so directly to pressure from staff, management has until recently neglected the opportunity to embark on a more radical reassessment which might have investigated the possibility that some conditions within the system create, or at least encourage, the extreme behaviour of some of these difficult prisoners and that in these instances prevention before the disorder rather than cure after it had occurred might have been a better option. Such a reassessment of regimes would inevitably have involved a re-evaluation of the role of the prison officer. The fact that this has not taken place leads one to conclude that the basic task of the prison officer has not changed fundamentally in the last 150 years; it remains that of the secure custody of the prisoner, a task which is best carried out in conditions in which good order can be maintained.

Prison Officer Pay and Conditions: An Historical Summary

The newly appointed General Board of Directors turned its attention in 1839 to the recruitment and training of staff at an early stage in its proceedings. Within a few months of entering office it asked the Inspector, Frederic Hill, to report on the subject. He responded that the recruitment of competent staff was more important than prison architecture, finance or discipline. He warned the Directors that if they wished to obtain good staff they would have to be clear in their own minds as to the necessary qualifications. Staff had to be 'superior in habits to the ordinary run of the working classes', of sterling honesty, sober and industrious, intelligent, kind and even-tempered but also firm, able to read and write and interested in their work. He was realistic enough to point out that if men with such qualifications were to be recruited an attractive salary would have to be offered.

In 1841 the newly appointed Governor of the General Prison at Perth discovered that policemen in Glasgow earned between 13s. and 20s. a week while their counterparts in the prison earned 18s. Police in the city of Perth were the lowest paid in the country at 10s.6d. a week. Officers in Perth County Prison earned 14s. a week. At a higher level, the Superintendent of Police for Glasgow, the most senior officer in the city, found it worthwhile to transfer to the post of governor of the city prison in 1845.

The Glasgow Committee (1891)

Prior to the final centralisation of the prison system in 1877 the pay of warders in Scotland was lower than the average paid in England; a fact which reflected a more general lower level of pay in Scotland in comparison to England. This differential continued after the Prisons Acts of 1877 when the Scottish Commissioners decided that their warder staff should be paid at the equivalent of the English assistant warder. The annual report of the Prison Commissioners for Scotland in 1889 noted that in the twelve years since the Commission had been set up the average rate of pay to warders had increased from £61.18s.4d. to £72.5s.10d., an increase of 16.8 per cent.

In 1891 the warders at Peterhead submitted a petition 'praying that they may be placed on the same scale as Warders in the same position in England'. The Prison Commissioners supported this petition, pointing out to the Secretary for Scotland that this had already happened in the case of other public servants such as policemen and postmen. They suggested that a committee should be set up to enquire into the pay and hours of duty of subordinate staff. The Secretary responded on 7 August 1891 by appointing the Earl of Glasgow to chair a committee 'to consider some questions which have been raised by the subordinate staff regarding pay, hours of duty, etc'.

The Board of Trade gave evidence to the Glasgow Committee that average wages in Scotland were 5 to 10 per cent lower than in England except in the 'well-organised' industries such as mining, ship building and engineering, where they were almost equal. It was reported that the maximum annual pay of a second class warder was £75, compared to the maximum of £72.16s. for a police constable in Edinburgh. First class warders received a maximum of £90, compared to £88 for a police sergeant, and head warders £135, compared to £120 for inspectors of police. The Governor of Edinburgh Prison at the time was still paid on the old County Board scale at a level of £850 while the comparable new scale was £500; the Chief Constable of Edinburgh was paid £700 per year.

Recruits to the prison service had to be between twenty-two and forty years of age (members of the armed forces were eligible until they were forty-five) and at least five feet seven inches in height. Candidates were required to pass examinations in arithmetic, handwriting and spelling and had to be of 'unexceptionable moral character, and of undoubted sobriety'.

Warders worked an average of nine and a half or ten hours each day, commencing at six o'clock in the morning and working, with breaks of two hours for meals, until five or seven o'clock in the evening. They had alternate Sundays off as well as a half holiday on alternate Saturdays. Ordinary warders were entitled to two weeks' leave each year.

The Committee's recommendations, which were duly accepted by the Treasury, were that the maximum pay of head warders should be increased to £150 per year but that those of first and second class warders should remain at £90 and £75 respectively. There was, however, one significant concession, for which staff representatives had argued strongly in their evidence: that of free quarters or rent allowance in lieu thereof. In addition, warders at Peterhead Convict Prison were to receive an inconvenience of locality allowance of £8 yearly.

One of the main features of the Glasgow Committee was the precedent which it set. Pressure from a group of staff, in this case at Peterhead, had resulted in the establishment of a committee of inquiry.

The evidence taken by the committee allowed staff to establish their point of comparison.

> (Chairman) 'Do you think the work of a Warder compares with work in the Army? Sentry-go, for example?'
> (George Smith, First Class Warder, Barlinnie) 'It is a great deal harder than Sentry-go. It is harder than the work of a police constable also. I have tried them both.'
> 'Take a railway porter, he is paid much less than you are?'
> 'But a railway porter does not compare with a Prison Warder at all. He is not locked up in prison. He is out in the centre of life. There is a great difference between them, I think.'

This was the point of comparison which was to be stressed consistently by staff to subsequent committees of inquiry. Like the police the basic task of the prison officer was to control the criminal element in society, and prison staff argued that they were entitled to the same conditions of service as the police.

The Stanhope Committee (1923)

The next significant alteration to pay took place in 1910 when staff in Scottish prisons were brought on to the same scales as their English counterparts. Another pay rise was awarded in 1913 and in 1919 a 'substantial' increase was awarded.

In 1923 a committee was set up under the chairmanship of Earl Stanhope

> to Inquire into the Pay and Conditions of Service at the Prisons
> and Borstal Institutions in England and Scotland and at
> Broadmoor Criminal Lunatic Asylum.

For the first time evidence was taken from representatives of the staff boards which had recently been set up within the services, the Superior Officers' Representative Board and the Prison Officers' Representative Boards for England and for Scotland. The last named body was represented by its chairman, a guard sergeant at Peterhead, and by the Head Warder of Aberdeen Prison.

The report of the Stanhope Committee opened with a testimony to the high morale which it found throughout the services and to the mutual good feeling which existed between the higher ranks and their subordinates. What the report went on to recommend did nothing to maintain either of these features. The Chairman of the Superior Officers' Representative Board at the time subsequently wrote in his memoirs that the Stanhope Committee . . .

> produced some lukewarm recommendations which improved the pay a little for the superior officers and a very little for everybody else. The long-awaited report, in fact, gave a slight measure of satisfaction and caused infinite disappointment. (Rich, 1932)

With respect to pay the main thrust of the prison officers' argument had again been for parity with the police on the grounds of equivalent responsibility. Stanhope was quite unequivocal in its refusal of this claim, finding the responsibilities of the police and the quality of initiative and resources required of them to be 'definitely superior' to those required of members of the prison services. The report insisted that it did not wish to underrate the qualities required of the prison officer but paid him the doubtful compliment of being 'especially impressed with the monotony of his life'.

The committee found that officers were recruited from the skilled artisan class and concluded from available figures that their pay compared favourably with that in the better-paid occupations of this class. As a result of these findings the committee concluded that existing pay scales were adequate both in relation to the character of the work and the type of man they were meant to attract. It did recommend limited increases for principal and chief officers. The report noted that the pay of governors had remained largely unaltered since 1878 but that the character of their work and the type of man required for its proper performance had changed almost completely. For these reasons substantial pay increases were recommended for prison governors in England.

In a separate chapter dealing with Scotland the report recommended that its comments on prison officer grades should apply equally to the English and Scottish services. As regards governors, however, the committee commented on the fact that establishments in Scotland were generally much smaller than English prisons and that, in a more centralised service, less was left to the initiative of individual governors. It did note that governors in Scotland had an additional responsibility to find work for prisoners. The report concluded that governors in Scotland should be paid on a scale one below the equivalent rank in England with the proviso that the Governor of Barlinnie Prison should receive an additional pensionable allowance of £100 yearly.

The Stanhope Report was dismissed by officers as a farce and a 'class' report and it did much to harm the credibility of the infant Prison Officers' Representative Board. Staff continued to press regularly for pay increases, frequently arguing the comparison with the police. In 1937 they won the right to take their case to arbitration and in the following year a tribunal made a substantial award, although still without reference to police rates of pay. In 1939 improved rates for overtime pay were introduced, several of the allowances for which staff were eligible were made pensionable, and the hours of duty were reduced from ninety-six to eighty-eight per two weeks.

In 1946 the Prison Officers' Association submitted a further claim arguing once again for parity with the police who had recently been granted a pay increase. The claim was substantially conceded by the Prison Commissioners for England and Wales in January 1947. In 1948 the Oaksey Committee awarded pay increases to the police. The Prison Officers' Association followed this with a similar claim which, although rejected by the Commissioners, was subsequently conceded by an arbitration tribunal in 1950. The success of these two claims for parity with police pay scales was regarded by the POA as an important milestone in their struggle for improved conditions. In evidence to a 1954 arbitration tribunal they quoted Sir Alexander Paterson as their authority:

> To ensure the services of a grade of men worthy of this career
> and capable of meeting its demands, the penal administration
> must offer pay at least the equivalent of the Country's Police.

The Wynn Parry Committee (1957)
The steady stream of recourse to arbitration on pay matters and continuing dissatisfaction with conditions of service led to the establishment in 1957 of a committee under the chairmanship of Mr Justice Wynn Parry to enquire into the remuneration and conditions of service of both officer and governor grades in the English and Scottish services.

The Wynn Parry Report, which was published in 1958, was to stand as the seminal document on the pay and conditions of service for prison staff for twenty years. It enunciated the principle, frequently referred to by staff in succeeding years with reference both to other parts of the civil service and to outside agencies, that the prison service was *sui generis*, unique unto itself. During the 1960s and early 1970s this Latin tag became the motto of governors in the English Prison Service and was used as a motif on their service tie.

Wynn Parry dismissed demands made by the POA that all promotions to the governor grades should be made from within the service, while at the same time concluding that because of the general problems of undermanning it would be inappropriate to raise entry standards in any significant way. The POA had complained at the slow rate of promotion for officers. The committee recognised this problem but saw little alternative in view of the fact that there was so much routine work to be done, which was a way of restating the observation made by the Stanhope Committee on the monotony of the work of the prison officer. The only suggestion which Wynn Parry had to make in this area was that a vocational examination should be introduced, success at which would entitle an officer with at least ten years' service to be paid at the minimum of the Principal Officer scale.

The committee compared unfavourably the treatment meted out to staff as opposed to that enjoyed by prisoners:

> In short we saw living and working conditions which can only be
> described as Dickensian. Substantial improvements have been
> made for the prison population with the emphasis now on training
> and rehabilitation, but in our view parallel improvements have not
> been made for the staff.

As far as prison governors were concerned the report ruled against their claim that they should have the same entitlement, which had been given to officers by the Elliott Committee in 1919, to two years' pension for every year worked in excess of twenty. They did, however, recommend that Scottish governors should be given equal rates of pay to their English colleagues.

With respect to salaries in general the committee recommended that entry pay should remain virtually unaltered but that there should be an 11 per cent increase at the maximum of the officer scale. The Principal Officer scale was to be raised by a full 30 per cent and chief officers were to maintain their existing differential with junior grades. There were to be consequential increases for senior grades in order to maintain internal relativities. With regard to future pay movements the committee recommended that governors should be linked broadly to the executive class of the civil service. The majority of the committee recommended that there should be a link between the pay of prison officers and that of agreed ranges of civil service pay.

The general terms of the Wynn Parry Report were highly satisfactory to staff. A leading article in the magazine of the Prison Officers' Association of December 1958 commented:

> The Report of the Wynn Parry Committee marks a stage of the greatest importance in the development of conditions of employment in the Prison Service. The recommendations deserve whole-hearted support not only from those employed in the Service but from all concerned with its well-being and with modern penal methods . . . The Report is indeed a great contrast with the perfunctory and unsatisfactory report of the Stanhope Committee of 1923, whose conclusions gave such little comfort to Prison Officers and have, until now, bedevilled persistent efforts to improve conditions.

Notwithstanding the fact that the Wynn Parry Report was so well received by staff and that it was consistently quoted in succeeding pay negotiations, it in fact finally established the principle that the point of pay comparison for prison staff should be, not the police as staff argued, but rather the administrative civil service. This fact went virtually without notice in the general euphoria over the level of pay increases awarded. Confirmation of this point of comparison was welcomed by the official side in its continuing effort to bring the prison service within the mainstream civil service.

The May Committee (1978)

The most recent enquiry into the pay and conditions of staff in the United Kingdom prison services was carried out by the May Committee which reported in October 1979. The background to its establishment has already been described in chapter five. Although it was set up as a result of continuing poor industrial relations in the prison services, the immediate impetus for its appointment was a long-standing demand by the POA in England and Wales for payment for meal breaks taken within duty hours, a claim for what was described technically as continuous duty credits. These did not apply in Scotland and consequently need not be of interest here other than as a reminder that, not only was the May Committee set up primarily to deal with matters relating to pay and conditions of service for staff, it was to deal principally with a very precise element in this field.

The first conclusion drawn by the committee in the chapter of its report which deals with pay is a critical one:

> Prison Service grades are to some extent an isolated and inward-looking group who may not always appreciate the true value of the pay and other benefits, for example housing and superannuation.

Prison staff had been looking to the May Committee to produce a pay formula which would once again relate to police scales of pay, particularly in the light of the Committee of Inquiry on the Police in 1978, which had recommended a significant increase in police rates of pay. May recognised that this comparison was being asked for but reached no explicit conclusion on the matter, although by implication it had been rejected in the recommendation which advised that the Wynn Parry formula should continue to apply.

The May Committee went to some trouble to establish outside comparisons for the earnings of prison staff. As a result, it concluded that junior prison staff stood well in relation to national average gross earnings, and even better if free housing, free uniform and non-contributory pension were added, but that they had to work nearly nine hours more each week on average than manual workers to do so. The committee further concluded that officers' earnings with or without overtime had not lost any real ground since 1958. The consequent recommendation was that a large increase in basic pay could not be justified but that there should be increases to reflect more difficult control problems in prisons and the need to recruit more staff.

There was general discontent both outside and inside the prison services at the failure of the May Committee to undertake a radical re-appraisal of the role of staff in the prison services, although given the initial narrow justification for the establishment of the committee this was not surprising. It was more unfortunate that the report failed to take the opportunity to grasp the nettle of the labyrinthine prison officer pay structure. It noted that overtime payments for officers amounted on average to almost 60 per cent of basic pay. The May Committee argued on the one hand that the various allowances and overtime payments should be consolidated into basic pay, while on the other concluding that basic pay could not be significantly increased because of the amount of the other elements of pay.

There are two principal conclusions to be drawn from this analysis of how the pay structure of prison officers has developed. The first is that from the staff point of view the foundation of all pay claims this century has been parity with the police. The basis of this comparison has been that the main function of both occupations is the control of offenders. This is hardly surprising when one considers that prior to the establishment of a separate prison staff in the nineteenth century the two offices were frequently interchangeable and often carried out by the same individual. When levels of pay for prison staff were set in Scotland in the mid nineteenth century the point of comparison used by management was the police. Furthermore, in the early years of the twentieth century the first attempts at forming a staff association were undertaken jointly by police and prison officers.

The first official refusal to treat the two services on a basis of parity came from the Stanhope Committee in 1923. This, linked with the fact that this committee refused to concede virtually any increase in pay for prison officers, has guaranteed staff opinion that this was the most unsatisfactory report to come out of any committee of inquiry into the prison service. In the 1930s and 1940s prison officers were able, by skilful use of the newly opened access to industrial tribunals, to gain and maintain virtual parity with police rates of pay.

Prison staff today still speak enthusiastically of the Wynn Parry Report of 1958 which granted substantial increases, although as far as governors were concerned it sounded the death knell of any realistic hope of achieving the 'two for one' superannuation provisions to which officers were entitled; that is, the award of two years' superannuation for each year worked in excess of twenty. In the long term, however, Wynn Parry did not help the case of prison staff since it established that the broad base of comparison for prison staff pay should be not police but the rest of the civil service. The May Report confirmed this arrangement and this fact, coupled with the separate arrangements made for police following the Edmund-Davies Report of 1978, has left prison staff well adrift of police to the extent that it is hard to envisage that they will ever regain parity of pay. This is an important conclusion in so far as it affects the status of the prison officer and the role which society expects of him as one element in the 'law and order' process.

The second conclusion to be drawn from this analysis is that no committee of inquiry was able to unravel the arcane combination of basic pay, some dozen or so allowances, substitution and overtime payments which over succeeding pay settlements went to make up the take-home pay of the prison officer. The May Committee was driven to comment

that in a number of cases officers cannot fully understand of
what their pay is composed.

There were several reasons why this complicated system of pay
developed. One typical example relates to the various housing allowances. In the middle of the nineteenth century most staff were accommodated within the prison perimeter. This arrangement compromised
security and as an alternative, separate staff quarters were built outside
the prison but within the immediate vicinity so that off-duty officers
would be available in the event of an emergency. Staff were charged
a rent for this accommodation but in 1891 the Glasgow Committee
recommended not only that quarters should be free but also that a rent
allowance should be paid to staff for whom accommodation was not
available.

Until 1980 the vast majority of prison staff stayed in quarters. In that
year, as a consequence of general housing legislation, staff were given
the entitlement to purchase quarters at discounted prices. Many of
them took this opportunity and on subsequent transfer moved to
private housing. This allowed them to take advantage, not only of their
entitlement to allowances as prison officers, but also of the allowances
available to all civil servants. This change had a significant fiscal effect
on personnel management. Instead of being able to transfer an officer
from one prison to another at minimal public expense a substantial cost
was now likely to be incurred.

In addition to the many allowances, the system of prison officer pay
had become increasingly complex. Each officer received a 12.6 per
cent increase in basic pay as a 'shift disturbance allowance'. This was
paid even to officers who were not required to undertake shift work.
Officers were conditioned to working any five days out of seven but
received additional payments for working at weekends and on public
holidays. This complicated pay structure developed partly as a means
of avoiding substantial increases in basic pay and through the mechanism of making some allowances non-pensionable.

A major factor in this piecemeal development has been the absence
of clear consensus as to the context within which the prison officer
should operate. The officer wished to place himself alongside the
police as belonging to a major 'law and order' occupation. Prison
service management, on the other hand, wished to place him within the
mainstream of the civil service. However, in order to accommodate the
ten grades between the most junior officer and the most senior
governor within a structure comparable to the administrative class,

basic pay in the prison service was artificially compressed but compensated for by a plethora of other payments.

This complex system of payments had wider implications in that staff had an incentive to pursue methods of working which were likely to increase their levels of gross pay without having regard to whether or not all of these methods were of benefit to the service. Equally they were likely to be opposed to any changes in working patterns or regimes for prisoners which threatened any of these payments. The working day in a prison extends for twenty-four hours and covers seven days in each week. The system of staff payment allowed premium rates of pay for any period outwith a Monday to Friday. In addition, shift patterns in England and Wales often involved overtime rates of pay for any time worked outwith eight o'clock in the morning and five o'clock in the evening. Such an arrangement provided a 'dripping roast' for staff in terms of additional payments.

Thus was the scene set in the mid 1980s for the introduction of the radical restructuring which was known as 'Fresh Start'. Before describing this in detail we have to turn our attention to the important issue of how staff were promoted and how management posts were filled, since this matter was also dealt with in the 'Fresh Start' arrangements.

Promotion opportunities

A useful field of study in respect of any organisation is the type of promotion opportunity which it can offer to staff and the method which it follows for appointing staff to promoted posts. When setting pay scales for the General Prison at Perth in 1862, the Managers advised the Secretary of State that they did not see the necessity in Scotland of having three grades of warder and accordingly proposed that the general body of warders should be paid on the same scale as that of the lowest grade, the assistant warder, in England. They confirmed this in 1873, stating that their principle was

> to avoid any accumulation of discipline officers between the
> Governor and the Warders in actual charge of prisoners.

This restriction in the number of grades was continued in Scotland after 1877. The only two grades in Scotland were Chief Warder and Warder, whereas in England there were two intermediate grades. The Prison Commissioners for Scotland at first retained the limited number of grades but within a dozen or so years had recognised the need for an additional grade, giving its incumbents the title of First Class Warder while the most junior grade was known as Second Class Warder. In due course the English title of Principal Warder was introduced.

Promotion beyond warder grade was based almost entirely on seniority. The Stanhope Report recommended that more weight should be attached to individual merit. It suggested that a qualifying examination should be introduced, containing both educational and practical elements, before an officer would be eligible for promotion to Principal Officer and that subsequent promotion to Chief Officer should be entirely on merit. In its evidence to the 1938 arbitration tribunal the Prison Officers' Representative Board stated that fewer than 7 per cent of officers could hope for promotion to the grade of Principal Officer and only 1 per cent had any reasonable expectation of going beyond the prison officer class. The Prison Officers' Association claimed in evidence to the Wynn Parry Committee in 1958 that promotion in England and Wales from officer to Principal Officer took nineteen years, from Principal Officer to Chief Officer Class II a further eight years and that it took an individual twenty-nine years from his date of joining the service to reach the rank of Chief Officer Class I. The Prison Commissioners agreed with this evidence and, almost proudly, confirmed that if an officer was considered to be qualified for promotion he stood in

> no danger of being jumped by a junior officer regarded as better qualified.

The Scottish Home Department pointed out in evidence to the same committee that the promotion procedure was different in Scotland. All officers were called by seniority to a testing panel 'which assessed their potential character'. They then appeared before a selection board consisting of three officials from headquarters and three governors.

> This board awards to each candidate a numerical marking, and the names of the candidates are sorted out into an existing list in numerical order. The candidate at the top of the list being the first choice for promotion subject to weight given for seniority. Special reports are obtained from the governors and senior officers for all candidates near the top of the list, and, if favourable, these men (according to the number of vacancies) are recommended for promotion. The names of successful

> candidates are circulated to all establishments by means of a
> circular which also invites appeals from any officer who may be
> senior to any officer nominated for promotion.

Unfortunately in the evidence there is no indication of the average length of time for promotion under these arrangements in Scotland.

The Wynn Parry Report noted that there was a difficulty with promotion but made no recommendation other than that a vocational examination should be introduced and that any officer who passed it should be paid on the minimum scale of the Principal Officer grade. Such an examination was introduced in 1959 as a prerequisite for attendance at a subsequent promotion board. Officers with a minimum of ten years' service who passed the examination received a pensionable allowance of £1 per week until such time as they were promoted. The Prisons in Scotland Report for 1961 notes that of the 108 officers who sat the examination that year 58 reached the qualifying standard.

The matter of the grading of staff was next taken up by the Mountbatten Report in 1966 which concluded that the proportion of promoted ranks was not sufficiently high to supervise the basic grade officers. Rather than simply increasing the number of higher ranks Mountbatten recommended the introduction of a new grade between those of officer and Principal Officer. This recommendation was accepted by the Home Office and the Scottish Home and Health Department.

It was decided that members of the new grade would undertake a range of duties stretching into the Principal Officer field, thereby enabling the latter to concentrate on more responsible managerial duties, even extending into those of the Chief Officer grade. The new grade of Senior Officer was also to participate in the more responsible duties of the basic grade officer. Success at the vocational examination was to be a normal requirement for promotion to the new grade. In Scotland this meant a reduction in the qualifying length of service for eligibility for the examination from ten years to seven in 1968, to six years in 1969, to five years in 1970 and to four years thereafter.

The title of Senior Officer given to the new grade by Mountbatten was unfortunate as the public did not immediately appreciate that 'a senior prison officer' was in fact only once removed from the most junior grade. In 1971 the Scottish Prison Officers' Association asked that the title be changed to Principal Officer Class II, which it suggested would bring it into line with the designations for Chief

Officer and Steward. The Scottish Home and Health Department was sympathetic to the request but was unable to adopt it in the face of strong opposition from the Home Office.

Promotion to Governor Grades

During the formative years of the Scottish prison system in the middle of the nineteenth century, it was quite common for junior staff to be appointed as governors of prisons. A capable former warder might well progress from the charge of a small prison to that of a larger one. On the other hand, there was no question of filling all senior posts from within the service. Brebner's successor in Glasgow, for example, had previously been Superintendent of Police in that city, while the second governor of the General Prison at Perth had held a similar post in Edinburgh. This dual pattern of recruitment to the grade of governor continued throughout the nineteenth century.

In England in contrast there was a tradition, particularly in the convict prison system, of recruiting staff at all grades from the armed services:

> It is not surprising that the Directors, with their military
> background, sought to resolve some of the problems of staff
> selection by taking into employment a large proportion of men
> with army and navy backgrounds. So consistent was this policy
> that by 1876 over two-thirds of subordinate officers had been in
> the army, marines or navy, a pattern which appears to have been
> repeated among Governors and Deputy Governors.
> (McConville, 1981)

This pattern was formalised to the extent that the Home Office pursued a policy whenever possible of filling senior posts in the prison service with former Army and Naval officers 'with a view to facilitating retirement and promotion in those services'. While Scotland always had a proportion of former military men among its senior ranks, particularly in the periods following major wars, there was never such a high proportion as there was in England and Wales.

In the wake of the Gladstone Report of 1895 there was a significant change of emphasis in the English Prison Service, particularly in the Borstal system. This was achieved partly by the direct recruitment to junior governor posts, known at the time as 'house masters' in the public school tradition, of men who were in tune with the new principles and who

> by leadership and understanding were to help strengthen a boy's
> character, to encourage loyalty, trust and an *esprit de corps,* and
> to develop any latent ability for leadership. (Grew, 1958)

The English Prison Commissioner who is most closely identified with this period of prison development is Alexander Paterson. He has also suffered from being selectively quoted by those of his successors who have particular hobby horses to ride. One rarely hears, for example, of his views on recruitment to the governor grades:

> If great care is exercised in the choice of junior officers, and if a
> comparatively high standard of merit and education is insisted
> upon, it is probable that a large number of these officers will be
> destined for promotion to senior positions. The ideal
> combination in a penal system would be to place half its
> establishments under the direction of men who have acquired
> their experience of the service in the lower ranks, and the other
> half under the direction of men formerly in other professions,
> who bring to their new career new ideas, a fresh inspiration and
> different viewpoints. (in Ruck, 1951)

This ideal was never achieved in England. In evidence to a board of arbitration in 1938 the POA pointed out that only 1 per cent of officers had any reasonable expectation of promotion to the governor grades. Two years later they made great play of the fact that two Chief Officers had been promoted to the grade of Governor Class IV. Demands that posts in the governor grades should be filled exclusively or at least predominantly from the ranks of the officers appear repeatedly in the columns of *Prison Officers' Magazine*. The response from the Home Office was invariably negative.

The picture in Scotland after the Second World War was much closer to Paterson's ideal of a fifty/fifty recruitment pattern. The first three governor appointments in Scotland in the post-war period came from inside the service and the POA recorded its gratitude to the departmental officials who were prepared to recommend such appointments. In succeeding years individuals from outside the service were appointed as governors and this matter was taken up at the departmental Whitley Council. The departmental response was a moderate one:

The Official Side were not in favour of making the Prison
Service an entirely 'closed shop'.

In 1949 the POA appeared to have won the Secretary of State for
Scotland round to their view. In his address to the Scottish conference
of the association the Right Hon Walter Elliot had this to say:

> The responsibility of administering our prisons from the inside
> should be left exclusively to the Prison Officer. His right of
> promotion to the higher posts is indisputable, for it is only by
> practical experience that one can gain a thorough knowledge of
> the job, and such knowledge is necessary to the administration.

The majority of appointments to the governor grades in Scotland
continued to be made from within the service but this was not done
exclusively and at Polmont Borstal Institution in particular several
individuals were recruited at Assistant Governor level. In September
1955 representatives of the Scottish POA met with the Parliamentary
Under Secretary of State to urge that the 'back door', as it was
colloquially known, should be closed once and for all. In his response
the Minister summed up the existing position:

> Whenever a vacancy occurred in the higher posts and the
> Secretary of State was satisfied that it could be filled from the
> existing staff, this was done. It was only in the rare cases of
> doubt that the post was filled by open competition. Even in
> such cases existing staff were always invited to apply for
> consideration. Since the end of the war there had been thirty-nine
> appointments to senior posts on the discipline side. In only nine
> cases had the posts been filled by open competition, and of these
> nine, four were filled by candidates from the Prison Service (one
> of them from the English Service). Outside appointments were
> thus exceptional; and he hoped that in time it would become
> possible to agree that all appointments should be made from
> candidates with experience of the Prison Service. (Quoted in
> *Prison Officers' Magazine*, January 1956)

The Scottish service continued its practice of recruiting the majority of
its junior governors from the ranks of prison officers and in 1957 the
Assistant General Secretary of the POA, speaking at the Scottish
annual conference of the Association, held the Scottish Home Department up as an example to the Home Office in this respect. One

interesting feature of this period in Scotland was the number of office bearers of the Scottish Executive of the POA who were promoted to the rank of Assistant Governor; these included three consecutive chairmen.

Pressure for exclusive recruitment from the ranks to the governor grades continued and in 1969 the Home Secretary set up a working party to examine the matter in respect of England and Wales. Its first term of reference was:

> To recommend what changes are necessary to secure that over a period a one-tier system is introduced into the Prison Service in England and Wales and that meanwhile an increasing proportion of the vacancies in the Governor class is filled from within the Prison Service.

This working party reported in 1972. While it made several recommendations as to how greater numbers of eligible prison officers might be identified, encouraged and trained to become governors, it came firmly to the conclusion that exclusive promotion from the ranks was not an option:

> However, no matter how much may be done in this respect, it is unlikely that sufficient officers of the requisite quality will be found to meet the needs of the service by this means alone.

In 1973 the Scottish Office set up a working party on recruitment to the governor grades. This working party did not directly address the issue of exclusive promotion from the ranks but concentrated on methods of identifying potential assistant governors at an early stage and developing their potential. The working party noted that in January 1974 the various governor grades included thirty-four former officers and thirty who had been recruited into the service as assistant governors.

An examination of the minutes of the annual conferences of the Prison Officers' Association both in England and in Scotland, of the columns of *Prison Officers' Magazine* and of correspondence between the association and the respective departments shows that consistently the issue which stimulated greatest debate was that of promotion to the governor grades. The position adopted by the POA was simple: there should be no direct recruitment; all promotions should come through the ranks. The departmental response was agreement in principle but an insistence that it was impossible to achieve this aim in practice while maintaining the necessary standards. This debate was ultimately settled in the light of changes introduced under the banner of Fresh Start.

The Growth of Trade Union Activity in the Prison Service

Frequent reference has been made to the role of the Prison Officers' Association in dealing with management on major issues affecting the service in general and conditions of service for staff in particular. As a prelude to discussion on the most recent changes introduced as a consequence of Fresh Start it will be useful to chart the development of the Association.

The major function of any trade union lies in the relationship which it has with management. This relationship is normally expressed in a dual manner, by dependency and conflict. The latter is often the more obvious aspect, both in terms of attracting public attention and as the inevitable result of the different interests which management and union represent. But dependency is also a key element of the relationship; it is management which recruits the future members of the union and both management and union have a common vested interest in the continuing welfare of the organisation.

At the same time some of the activities of a trade union may be construed as an intrusion into areas which management regards as its province. In its concern for the welfare and security of staff the union may well find itself expressing an interest in the central operating system of the organisation. How, when and in what manner workers carry out their work are such central issues. Attempts by a trade union to control these areas may represent a more serious threat of conflict as far as management is concerned than will an issue which relates purely to pay and conditions.

Such control is traditionally a management prerogative and any infiltration into this area by a trade union is likely to represent an organisational and perhaps even a personal threat to the managers concerned. One has, therefore, to be aware of the possibility of a struggle for power which goes beyond economic considerations. A further possible source of conflict may arise from the fact that unions, which are at least in principle democratically organised, have to justify the need for their continued existence to members and on occasion are likely to feel a necessity to adopt a publicly belligerent posture. This may result in a form of conflictual behaviour which is not obviously justified by the economic issue at stake.

Some managers may take the view that their job would be easier without the presence of trades unions but in the long run the relationship between management and union may have a beneficial effect on the way the organisation is run. The union, for example, is a source of pressure for management to keep on its toes. It may represent an important incentive to improve techniques of operation. In such a setting management may invite the union to help in formulating policies for the organisation and may be prepared to accept and act on criticisms levelled against it by the union. This implies an increased union influence or control but it does not necessarily mean less control by management. On the contrary, it may make the union more receptive to management's point of view. One outcome of this development will be that the active union member may well have a higher degree of job satisfaction than those who are not active.

All of these features of management/union relationships can be traced within the prison system through the historical analysis of the growth of trade union activity. It may be argued that this is particularly true of the Scottish model, which has developed in a distinctive way to the extent that it might almost be described in practice as participative management.

One other important influencing factor should be mentioned. Research has shown that union participation is likely to be high in situations where there is an 'occupational community' in which workers have social as well as organisational contact and in which their families participate. Mining and shipping communities are obvious examples of this phenomenon; so also are prison staff communities.

The continuing effort by prison staff to maintain parity of conditions of employment with the police can be traced partly to early attempts at joint union activity. These were based on an understanding of common responsibility to society for control of the criminal and a consequent similar status in the eyes of society. In his study of police unionism Robert Reiner (1978) suggests that the origins of this 'right to confer' go back to the last three decades of the nineteenth century. There is no evidence of such joint prison/police staff involvement at that time in Scotland but we have already seen how the Glasgow Committee of Inquiry into pay of 1891 was set up in response to staff pressure.

In 1913 the Metropolitan Police Union was founded in London. It soon established a provincial branch and the following year became the National Union of Police and Prison Officers. Membership was illegal and its members were forced to hold clandestine meetings because of the vigour of official opposition. The union did not make much headway among prison staff although two warders were appointed to its executive committee. Home Office officials at the time told the Home Secretary that prison officers formed an insignificant element of the union but they expressed concern that, if the warders appointed the union to act on their behalf in connection with a pending pay claim, the union would have to be recognised. In the event the case was not handled by the union (Reynolds & Judge, 1968).

On 8 July 1918 a Police Bill was introduced to parliament which among other things proposed the establishment of a Police Federation, prohibited police officers from becoming members of any trade union and made it an offence for anyone to induce a police officer to withhold his services. Union activists described the proposed federation as 'the goose club' to emphasise its inability to do anything other than march in step with the authorities.

On 31 July 1918, in protest at these elements in the Bill, the National Union of Police and Prison Officers attempted to call a strike of all its members. Response was very limited among the police. As regards prison officers, sixty-eight at Wormwood Scrubs and six at Birmingham Prison struck without previous notice. In common with the police they had received prior warning that any man who refused duty would be dismissed and under no circumstances be re-employed. All strikers were duly dismissed. No policeman or prison officer in Scotland was involved in the strike. The cases of those men dismissed were subsequently considered by a committee of inquiry, chaired by Sir William MacKenzie, which confirmed the dismissals.

However, following a widespread and relatively successful strike by London police in August 1918 it was agreed that representative boards for the staff of the various police forces and for prison officers should be set up. The Prison Officers' Representative Boards, both in Scotland and in England, were in-house bodies which were prohibited from having any connections with an outside body. The MacKenzie Committee felt able to conclude:

> In the case of the prison officers the Representative Board
> worked very satisfactorily.

That may have been the official view at the time. It was certainly not the view of staff, nor was it the eventual view of the official side. In November 1950, addressing the annual conference of the Scottish Prison Officers' Association, the Establishment Officer of the Scottish Prison Service observed:

> Rightly or wrongly, the staff were never satisfied with the
> working of this arrangement and a feeling of frustration
> continued to grow among them.

In 1937 the Prison Officers' Representative Board was given the right to external arbitration and to outside assistance in the preparation and presentation of its case. This was a gradual and grudging recognition by the government of the validity of the staff argument that, as civil servants, they could not be legally subject to any restriction other than that contained in the existing trade union legislation. In the longer term this facility confirmed a distinction which the staff did not wish to make between themselves and the police, who did not have the right of access to outside arbitration. Management was logically able to argue that prison staff had implicitly accepted that they were primarily civil servants rather than an essential element of the structure of law and order like the police.

In April 1940 the Prison Commissioners and the Scottish Home Department finally recognised the Prison Officers' Association. In Scotland a semi-autonomous branch with direct access to the Scottish Home Department through the machinery of the Whitley Council was established. The view of the Scottish prison officers was expressed by an entry in the April 1940 edition of *Prison Officers' Magazine,* which had been operating for several years as the clandestine voice of staff:

> The Scottish Prison Service has cast the nightmare of the
> Representative Board into the realm of forgotten things.

The final seal of government approval for the properly constituted staff trade union came in 1946 and was described by the chairman of the Scottish branch of the association in his address to annual conference in September of that year:

> This is a historic Conference for it is the first that you have had
> the honour of listening to an address from the Secretary of State
> for Scotland. This address, following as it does the attendance of
> Mr Chuter Ede at the English Conference in May, is indicative
> of two very important things. First, it shows the Scottish
> Department recognises completely the Association as a partner
> in the work before us. Secondly, it proves that the Association
> has, by its tolerance and understanding of the Official Side's

position, earned for itself a name as a body which has accepted
its obligations with a sober understanding of all that implies.

One may wonder what might have been the reaction of officials to the
patronising and ironic description of the association's 'tolerance and
understanding' of their position.

The final recognition of trade union status came with affiliation to
the Trades Union Congress and the Scottish Trades Union Congress.
The lead in this matter was taken in Scotland. A motion that the Prison
Officers' Association should affiliate to the TUC was presented to the
1966 Scottish annual conference and in November of that year the
Scottish office-bearers met with the General Secretary of the Scottish
TUC to discuss affiliation. In the spring of 1967 the POA duly
affiliated to the TUC and the SPOA to the STUC. In organisational
terms this could be described as the final break from any attempt at
comparison with the police as a body. The Police Federation is
explicitly prohibited from affiliation with the TUC or from any form
of industrial action.

The office bearers of the association in Scotland were all serving
officers who undertook their trade union activities in a part-time
capacity. Their professional credibility did not suffer since a steady
stream of them in the 1950s and 1960s were promoted to the Assistant
Governor grade. In 1963 a motion was presented to the annual conference that a full-time officer should be appointed in Scotland. On this
occasion the motion was remitted but two years later it was successfully moved

> that a Secretary from outside the Service would in the long run
> prove more beneficial to members

and a committee was set up to investigate the possibility. This
committee duly reported that this was not a practical proposition. In
time the matter was reconsidered and the post of full-time secretary
was advertised in November 1970. At the following annual conference
the appointment of John Renton, until then a Principal Clerk Officer
at Perth Prison, was ratified. In October 1977 the Scottish POA began
publication of *The Link,* its own magazine.

Neither the government nor prison management took easily to the
notion of trade union activity within the prison service. Prison staff had
to fight every inch of the way for recognition and this memory in
England and Wales has influenced subsequent staff attitudes to man-

agement. Thomas (1972) describes the early situation in England:

> And gradually there came to fruition that incipient feeling which had been noted in the period up to 1921, that all the organisational resources at a time of great stringency, all the articulated sympathy of the community, were addressed to the prisoner. This feeling on the part of officers is clearly justified by the evidence . . . In these years of the boldest reforms the English system had ever seen, the officer was excluded from the socially approved work of rehabilitation. The controlling task, with its coercive overtones, was depressed and the status of its agent, the uniformed officer, was depressed with it.

During this period staff experienced the frustration often felt by prisoners at the inconsistency of the application of rules. They were being told in response to pay claims that they did not merit parity with the police because they were civil servants. They knew what the rights of civil servants were in respect of trade union activity and asked that these be applied to them but then had to listen to the Home Secretary in 1944 announce to parliament:

> I cannot accept the suggestion that rules applicable to the Civil Service generally are necessarily appropriate to discipline services, such as the Prison Service.
> (Quoted in *Prison Officers' Magazine,* July 1944)

One American commentator (James Jacobs, 1983) has described how prison administrations in the United States continue to see staff unions as 'a mortal enemy', intent on usurping their legitimate authority. This accusation could be levelled against prison management in England and Wales in the early part of this century and its existence goes some considerable way to explaining the attitude adopted by staff.

Terence and Pauline Morris in their classic study of Pentonville Prison (1963) describe the Prison Officers' Association as being above all a militant organisation. This cannot be said of the Scottish POA. It has never organised a full-scale strike, confining itself to threats of 'work to rule', which were carried out in January 1973 at Longriggend Remand Unit in pursuit of a staff social club and later that same year in a matter affecting allocation of staff quarters at Barlinnie Prison. There have been subsequent isolated incidents. In using its craft to recognise and reach an accommodation with pressure which is not transitory, management has learned the necessity of working alongside one of the most significant permanent pressures, that of the staff as a body.

It should be noted that the task of management in this respect has been made considerably easier by the fact that the national executive committee of the SPOA has been able to maintain close links with its grass-roots membership in a manner which has allowed it to retain firm central control of branches in a way which has eluded the POA in England and Wales. While the management of the Scottish Prison Service would reject any suggestion of participative management, its style of accommodation with the SPOA in practice has come very close to this. All trades unions which have members working in the Scottish Prison Service are members of the Whitley Council of the service and are frequently consulted by management in this forum on issues of policy.

In 1963 the POA issued a memorandum on the Role of the Modern Prison Officer which described in detail how the association wished to see the role of the prison officer developed. This subject has been pursued with unfailing regularity at the annual conference of the SPOA and the present management support for the development of the role of the officer has undoubtedly been influenced by this pressure. The politically sensitive area of the management of difficult prisoners has been another clear example of how staff have been able to influence and at times direct the pragmatic style of management in the Scottish Prison Service.

The Training of Prison Staff

Professional training plays a central role in establishing the status of any group of workers. It was suggested in an earlier chapter that, while training of prison service staff could be described as highly desirable, it was hardly possible on the basis of past evidence to describe it as essential. Staff have always been recruited by a selection panel on the basis of a set of indefinable 'attitudes' rather than against a set of objectively evaluated criteria.

One recommendation made by the Gladstone Report in 1895 which was explicitly rejected by the Prison Commissioners for Scotland was that two or more prisons should be selected as training schools for all ranks of prison staff and should be placed under the charge of the most experienced officers, thus allowing probationary officers to be trained while in a supernumerary capacity. Opposition in Scotland was based on the argument that duties for a junior officer in a large prison were not so varied as in a small one. They did not consider it desirable that one prison should be taken as a model for others nor that its officers should be seen as model staff. They preferred rather that all staff should be equally efficient. This was a luxury which the first Inspector of Prisons had not had in 1836 when he had in effect used one prison, supervised by William Brebner at Glasgow Bridewell, as a training school for the whole country.

The first modern reference to the training of Scottish prison staff occurs in the annual report of the Prisons Department for 1937, which notes the approval of both the Secretary of State and of the Treasury to a proposal that probationary officers should be sent for a period of two months' testing and training to the Imperial Training School for Warders at Wakefield Prison. This was to be followed by one month's training at a Scottish prison. In 1937 the course at Wakefield was extended to nine weeks. Training of Scottish recruits at Wakefield came to an end in August 1938. It was proposed at that time that a course lasting nine weeks should be established at Barlinnie Prison but it was not until July 1946 that these classes began, each lasting only three weeks.

In 1950 the department indicated to the Scottish Prison Officers' Association that recruitment had recently reached a sufficient level to consider the introduction of a system of only two intakes of new staff each year, who would undergo three weeks' training at a local prison before attending the Barlinnie class for nine weeks. This extended course did not materialise and at the annual conference of the SPOA in 1954 its chairman made a plea to the department to reintroduce training for recruits instead of allowing them to be 'pitch-forked into the job'. The SPOA apparently took the view that the three weeks' course at Barlinnie, organised by a principal officer, could not be regarded genuinely as training. Their view may well have been justified since, as was pointed out in evidence to the Wynn Parry Committee in 1958, officers under training were part of the agreed staff complement rather than supernumerary.

By 1966 initial training of prison officers had been extended to five weeks, with an additional two weeks for Civil Defence training. In November of that year the Governor of Barlinnie Prison, who had nominal oversight of the training, wrote to advise the department that the instructors involved were working excessive hours during courses in order to complete the curriculum. He suggested that the course should be lengthened by one week. The department responded by forwarding an amended syllabus which provided 'for the omission of certain items and the telescoping of certain talks' so that the necessary material could be covered in the allotted five weeks.

The staff association continued to press the department to develop more fully what came to be described as 'the modern role of the prison officer', by which was meant an extension of tasks beyond the purely custodial. As a prerequisite of this the SPOA sought a more professional form of training. At its annual conference in May 1963 the Chairman of the SPOA called on the department to establish a proper training school which would cater for all the needs of prison staff. The department responded to this request and in November of that same year obtained the use of facilities at the Civil Defence Training Centre at Bishopbriggs near Glasgow. Intermittent use was made of this facility as a back-up to the provision at Barlinnie until 1967 when all training was transferred to Bishopbriggs.

On 27 July 1970 a purpose-built Officers' Training School was opened on a site adjacent to Polmont Borstal Institution. The Prisons in Scotland Report for 1970 described the new development in the following terms:

> The school's main function must meantime be the training of
> new recruits to the Service in a course which lasts six weeks.
> At the end of this initial course the recruits are posted to penal
> establishments and are on probation for a further period of
> twelve months, on completion of which they return to the school
> for a further week's training. All other grades of prison staff now
> have an opportunity of attending refresher courses whose
> purpose is to ensure that staff are kept abreast of new
> developments and able to meet the challenge of a changing
> penological situation.

During the succeeding eighteen years the training of prison officers changed little. The name of the establishment at Polmont was altered to the Prison Service College and it began to offer a wider range of development courses but its basic function remained the initial training of officers. That training, at six weeks, remained at the same length as it had been when centralised training was introduced to the newly opened General Prison at Perth in 1842.

The May Report in 1979 regretted that it had not been able to examine staff training in as much detail as it would have wished. It did, however, feel able to make a conclusive observation:

> Throughout our visits to establishments, and in our examination
> of the evidence submitted to us, we have reached a clear

conclusion that training, at all levels, is neither as effective nor as comprehensive as we think it should be and that it is not given sufficient priority at all levels in the service. We accordingly recommend that, as a matter of urgency, steps should be taken to carry out a searching review of all training facilities and programmes in order to ensure that the best possible provision is being made in this matter.

Following publication of the May Report, the Prison Service Management Group set up an internal working group on training. This group met regularly for some three years until its role was taken over by a sub-committee of the departmental Whitley Council. Although a great deal of effort went into the meetings of these respective groups there was little practical outcome other than the appointment of full-time staff training officers at all large establishments. The individuals appointed were all experienced prison officers but were given virtually no training in their new role; nor were any arrangements made to release staff for training.

From the middle of the 1980s a set of circumstances combined to set the pace for a new training initiative. In the subsequent analysis of the series of traumatic incidents which swept through several major Scottish prisons during this period, several commentators both inside and outside the service drew attention to the urgent need to develop training in a manner which would prepare staff to deal more confidently and positively with the demanding situations in which they frequently found themselves. Also during this period the series of initiatives which went under the generic name of 'Fresh Start' radically altered the promotion and management structures in the service and underlined the urgent need for a new strategy for staff training.

In early 1987 a planning group was set up within the Scottish Prison Service to develop a training strategy. This group reported some six months later. It suggested that a new training initiative should be based on the concepts

- that staff should acquire the skills and knowledge to carry out the tasks in their existing grade efficiently;
- that they should be prepared for the work of the next grade;
- that courses should be provided within a modular structure.

And recommended that:

– a Directorate of Training should be set up;

– a Training Planning Development Unit should be established;

– local training should be developed within a national framework;

– trainers at both local and national levels should be adequately trained.

These recommendations were all subsequently implemented and financial provision for training was significantly increased. The business plan for the Scottish Prison Service covering the years 1989 to 1992 laid out an action plan for training which addressed two main areas:

> Further improvements will be made to recruitment procedures for and to the initial training of new entrant prison officers; steps will be taken to maintain the momentum in the development and implementation of a national programme of operational and management development training, with the modular structure which will allow training to be pursued, so far as possible, according to individual needs.

The prison service has now reached a recognition that if staff are to be expected to carry out their duties in a professional manner they will have to be professionally trained. This recognition is being translated into practice both in terms of internal training and through initiatives such as the Higher National Certificate in Prison Studies. It is premature at this stage to pass judgement on whether in due course it will be possible to describe the professional training of prison staff as essential rather than merely highly desirable.

Fresh Start

There was widespread dissatisfaction within the prison services at what was seen as the failure of the May Committee to come to grips with the underlying problem of the pay structure of prison officers. Staff were discontented that they had to work so many hours overtime to earn what they considered to be a decent wage. Management was frustrated that the 'demand led' nature of the prison service and rigid staffing levels provided staff with a set of arcane working practices which guaranteed virtually unlimited overtime. The May Committee had identified the problem but had been unwilling or unable to provide a solution. It had recognised the need for a significant increase in basic pay for prison officers in order to decrease their dependence on overtime payments but had felt unable to recommend such an increase before the level of overtime was reduced.

Over a period of time there had been a growing perception that the staff structure in the prison services encompassed too many ranks. Specifically, there was an overlap in functional responsibility between the junior grades of governor and the chief officer grades. The former were technically senior to the latter but had markedly less experience and in many instances had less credibility with junior staff. The problem was compounded by the salary structure. Governor grades were not eligible for overtime payments while chief officers were, leading to disparities in actual earnings. One of several consequences of this was a reluctance among suitable prison officers to come forward for promotion to the governor grades.

During the course of the mid-1980s the Home Office Prison Department concluded that this combination of problems would have to be addressed by a set of radical proposals. This was designated 'Fresh Start', and consisted of new working arrangements for staff, a reorganised management structure in establishments and a unification of the governor and prison officer grades. These changes were linked to a new system covering pay and conditions of service.

The Home Office described the aim of the Fresh Start proposals in the following terms :

> The general aim is to replace existing management structures, systems and methods with working arrangements that:
>
> i.   match more closely the work requirements of the establishment;
> ii.   are responsive to changing pressures and demands;
> iii. enable managers to manage more effectively;
> iv. promote the unification of governor and prison officer grades and a sense of purpose, ownership and responsibility at all levels;
> v.   improve the efficiency, effectiveness and economy with which the Prison service discharges its public service;
> vi. provide the basis for the enhanced delivery of regimes;
> vii. bring increased job satisfaction to prison officers through a reduction in hours of attendance and a closer identification and involvement with their work by increased continuity;

    viii. provide greater predictability of attendance;
    ix. provide clearer lines of operational accountability;
    x. provide clear definition of roles and responsibilities.
        (*Fresh Start Bulletin No 7,* 1987)

Former chief officers joined governor grades in working uncondi-
tioned hours. For the remaining officer grades overtime payments
were abolished. Individuals were given the option of working an
average of thirty-nine hours or forty-eight hours each week. Those
who chose the latter option were paid an additional allowance. The
number of additional hours which staff contracted to work were to be
reduced each year so that by 1992 all staff would be working an
average of thirty-nine hours each week. In each of the years in question
a proportionate amount of the additional allowance was to be transferred to salary. In order to offset the gradual reduction in hours
worked by each officer a proportionate number of new staff was to be
recruited.

The result of this reorganisation was a unified structure which went
from Grade I, the most senior governor, to Grade VIII, the discipline
officer. The two grades of chief officer amalgamated with the two
junior grades of governor. Promotion was to be exclusively through
the ranks. All staff were in future to be recruited at officer level and
arrangements were to be put in hand for selecting appropriate individuals for accelerated promotion to more senior posts. Thus, at long last,
the Prison Officers' Association won the argument about promotion
exclusively from within the service which they had waged for so many
years.

The staff structure in each establishment was based on functional
groupings which were intended at the same time to be more efficient
and to encourage a sense of group identity among staff. At management levels these new groupings were meant to reflect, and to enable
the effective discharge of, the functions of each establishment and to
provide clear lines of accountability. It was also argued that these
changes would enhance regimes for prisoners by ensuring greater
continuity of staff and encouraging development of positive regimes.

The Fresh Start plans were initially exclusively a Home Office
initiative for England and Wales. There was no great enthusiasm
among management in the Scottish Prison Service to follow the lead
from south of the border. Average overtime in Scotland was at the time
about eight hours per officer per week, in contrast to England where it
was about twelve hours. There was, therefore, little incentive for the

Scottish service to adopt a system which would allow staff to work and be paid for an additional nine hours each week. Division of responsibility between the junior governor grades and chief officers in Scotland did not present the problems which existed in England. The significant salary increases which were part of the package, together with the requirement to recruit a large number of new staff, posed unwelcome budgetary problems for the Scottish service.

Despite these factors it was clear from the outset that the final settlement which was reached in respect of the Fresh Start package would apply to both prison services, given that staff in both enjoyed equal pay and conditions of service. A rolling programme of introduction for staff in England and Wales began on 1 July 1987. All grades in Scotland were finally incorporated by 1 November 1987.

Fresh Start will not be fully implemented until 1 April 1992 when all staff will be contracted to work an average of thirty-nine hours each week. There were significant teething problems in the first years of the scheme. There was an inevitable hiatus while new staff, who were required to make up the shortfall which had previously been covered by overtime working, were recruited and trained. The reorganisation of management structures was particularly painful for an organisation which operated on the basis of well-established tradition. For many individuals the difficulties presented by by these changes were epitomised in the perceived removal of the man who had previously been head of the discipline staff, the chief officer.

The changes are now generally accepted in Scotland as having led to significant improvements in both conditions of service for staff and in management structures. The high level of recruitment in recent years has meant that a large percentage of staff have no knowledge of what went before Fresh Start and have no prejudice against the new arrangements. The changes have been coupled to a considerable development in staff training and this has also helped to create a climate in which the new arrangements have been seen positively.

This chapter began with the suggestion that the basic task of the prison officer has not changed in 150 years. It remains that of the secure custody of the prisoner and this is inevitably so. Society, and on its behalf, the Secretary of State, to whom prison staff are accountable, expect that prisoners will be detained in custody until the expiry of their sentence of imprisonment. Prison officers are employed to ensure that this is the case.

We may now be at the beginning of a fundamental reassessment of how the prison officer carries out this task. We are not yet at a position where we have enough evidence to describe the prison officer as a professional worker in the traditional terms described earlier. If present trends and initiatives with regard to recruitment, training and the way in which the officer is required to carry out his or her responsibilities can be maintained, in the not too distant future the prison officer might properly be described as a professional worker within the strict definition of that term.

10 Signal to the Future
Custody, Order and Opportunity

Attention is frequently drawn to the proportionately high rate of imprisonment in Scotland, a rate which in terms of people held in custody is one of the highest in Europe and which in terms of the number of people admitted to prison is twice as high as that in England and Wales. Realisation of these facts has led to an increased intensity of debate about the purpose of imprisonment as a sentence of the court. Is it meant to achieve rehabilitation or retribution, reformation or deterrence?

A dictionary definition of prison is 'a building to which a person is legally committed while awaiting trial or for punishment'. The key word in this definition is 'punishment'. 'Penal' and 'penitentiary' are derived from the Latin *poena,* which means quite simply and unashamedly a punishment. Indeed the word is personified by both Cicero and Horace as the goddess of punishment. There can be no argument that the judicial disposal of imprisonment is intended primarily as a punishment.

The classical definition of legitimate punishment given by philosophers includes five main elements:

1. The person who undergoes it must experience suffering.
2. The individual concerned must have committed an offence and his guilt must have been established.
3. The punishment must be inflicted on an identified individual.
4. The punishment must be imposed by human agencies and not be a natural consequence of the action of the offender.
5. Those who impose the punishment must have the authority to do so.

This means that the suffering involved in punishment is directly inflicted on one person by an individual or agency who claims to have the authority to do so. Such an act requires justification and philosophers have not been slow to attempt to provide this. There are those who follow Plato in describing the punishment of 'wicked acts' as some kind of moral medicine as a result of which the person who is punished is made whole again and *rehabilitated*. Others, following Hegel, suggest that punishment is inflicted so that the offender may repent of his offence and as a consequence will be *reformed*. The utilitarian argument, as advanced by Bentham and others, is that if the prospect of the pain of punishment is greater than the pleasure of the offence people will be *deterred* from committing offences. A fourth proposition, coming from Kantian philosophical principles, is that since man is a free agent who is both responsible and accountable for his actions then both logically and morally he expects to face *retribution* in punishment for any offence which he has committed.

In reality life is not a neat set of philosophical principles and it is not possible to identify one justification for punishment which can be universally applied. All or part of each of the above justifications for punishment may well be applicable in individual cases. For example, in sentencing a high financier who has been convicted of corporate fraud to a period of imprisonment, the judge probably intends to inflict retribution for harm done and will certainly wish to deter others from pursuing a similar course of action. He probably has little thought of reforming the offender as a person. On the other hand, in sentencing a young man who is a drug abuser to prison, the judge may well have some hope that the offender will be weaned from his habit while in prison.

Rehabilitation might well involve a degree of paternalism which comes close to arrogance in assuming that behaviour in another which is considered to be unacceptable will invariably be the result of moral weakness. The offender may well consider that what he has done requires neither repentance nor reformation. The deterrence of punishment assumes that the offender knows that he will invariably be caught and subsequently convicted if he commits an offence. Yet it is statistically unlikely in most cases that this will happen.

The principle of retribution assumes a degree of individual responsibility for each of our actions which may not always be present. The high financier referred to above is more likely to have fully considered the consequences of his actions than did the drug abuser. The man who stabs another to death in a drunken brawl must accept some responsibility for his action, but is his circumstance the same as the man who kills in a calculating manner in the course of an armed robbery?

This dilemma is particularly sharp when one comes to apply the principles of punishment to the reality of imprisonment. During the first half of the twentieth century the rehabilitative element of imprisonment found almost universal favour. It was subsequently replaced by the notion of retribution expressed through what became known as the justice model of imprisonment. The weakness of both these paradigms of imprisonment was that they were presented as being exclusive whereas in reality neither they nor any other models are sole and sufficient justifications for imprisonment. What is required is a model which will incorporate responses to criminality which are both acceptable in principle and defensible in practice. Before attempting to present such a model it may be useful to review some of the main characteristics of these two key rationales of imprisonment.

The Rehabilitative Ideal

In discussing the prison system as a bureaucratic organisation it was suggested that its primary aim is the punishment of the individual prisoner, a punishment which should consist solely of the deprivation of liberty. Some confusion has been caused among those concerned with prisons by the attempt which has been made to present rehabilitation as their primary aim. This emphasis on the so-called rehabilitative aspect of imprisonment did not come about by accident. It was a reinforcement of the concept of the use of prison as a vehicle of social control.

> One may begin by saying that the rehabilitative ideal is the notion that a primary purpose of penal treatment is to effect changes in the characters, attitudes, and behaviour of convicted offenders, so as to strengthen the social defence against unwanted behaviour . . . (Allen, 1981)

This notion of the power which is exerted by one sector of society over another has been central to the development of imprisonment as a punishment, however one prefers to present it. For sociologists, such as Emile Durkheim and Michel Foucault, it is closely linked to the development of industrial society. The prison presented an opportunity for the coercion of individuals by the use of secret administrative power in a disciplined manner. For Marxists, such as Rusche and Kirchheimer (1939), the expansion of the punishment of direct imprisonment can be traced to the capitalist mode of production:

> Rehabilitation means adaptation to an orderly life with
> regular work, and rests on the assumption that the mode of
> behaviour learned in prison will enable the convict to readjust
> himself to the outside world after release.

David Garland (1985) has argued that what can best be described as a system of 'penal-welfare' has its roots in the twenty years between 1895 and 1914. Other penologists place the high summer of the rehabilitative era, the stage at which an organised structure was provided for the earlier paternalism, immediately after the Second World War:

> The introduction of social scientists into the penal system, as
> practitioners and academics, has helped produce that optimism
> which has led magistrates and judges to believe there are
> answers to all problems. (Bean,1981)

More recently commentators such as Scull (1983) and Cohen (1983) have pointed out how, under the guise of community alternatives, the power of social control has been extended beyond the walls of the prison to the community.

The notion of rehabilitation of deviant members of society within the coercive environment of the prison has its foundation fairly and squarely within the context of power, although for a variety of reasons great efforts have gone into denying or at least ignoring this fact. The most common form of denial has been the concealment of this exercise of power under the guise of paternalism. A standard of individual and general behaviour has to be set. The standard set is invariably that which is recognised by those who are in a position to exercise power. The rehabilitation of an offender is measured by the degree to which he conforms the imposed standard.

The best known example of this paternalistic imposition of what were often alien standards of behaviour was the Borstal system, introduced in the early years of the twentieth century when there was a comparative certainty about what was acceptable and what was necessary to achieve acceptability. The key to conforming behaviour was to be found in the discipline of education, epitomised by the public school system. If only this could be made available to the offending classes a mortal blow might be struck against recurring criminality.

The Borstal system was unashamedly a pale reflection of the public school system, to the extent that the first and major such institution in Scotland, at Polmont, had previously been a public school 'for gentlemen's sons'. Borstals were organised on the 'house' model, each of them under the charge, not of an assistant governor, but of a housemaster.

The introduction of the parole system in 1968 provided an important additional means of influencing the behaviour of offenders while in prison and of subsequently exercising power over them once they had been released. In an attempt to set some objective standards by which to measure the extent to which a prisoner could be adjudged suitable for the 'privilege' of release before expiry of sentence, great store was set by the degree to which any such prisoner made use of education, vocational training and other facilities within the establishment and above all by the extent to which he conformed to the rules and regulations imposed. An assessment was also made of the likelihood that he would continue to conform with supervision requirements after release.

There was much to commend many of these initiatives in themselves, particularly those developed within the prison setting. Education, social work support, interesting and useful work all helped to relieve the monotony of imprisonment and opened up the possibility that the experience of imprisonment in itself need not be completely negative. What was unsound both in principle and in practice was the attempt to use the extent to which any one prisoner made use of these resources as a measure of his 'rehabilitation'; that is, the likelihood that he would offend again after release.

There is considerable vagueness as to how 'rehabilitation' should be defined or measured. In reality it is closely linked to the notion of conformity with agreed standards of behaviour and is measured by the rate or seriousness of future offending. There is no evidence to suggest that the behaviour of a prisoner during the course of imprisonment, nor the level of his involvement in the facilities made available in prison, is a worthwhile measure of the likelihood that he will re-offend or not after release. Future behaviour will more probably be influenced by the environment to which the offender returns after release, by his prospects of employment and by the support which he can expect from family and friends.

This is not to suggest that the experience of imprisonment is irrelevant and what happens during its course unimportant. Deprivation of liberty is the most extreme sanction available in our society. Its use places on the community the obligation to ensure that its debilitating consequences are not extended beyond those which are inevitable. Society has a duty in terms of simple humanity to provide resources such as work, education and recreation to those of its citizens who have been deprived of their liberty.

Such a stance, however, makes the argument for increasing or even maintaining resources for the prison system much more difficult. It is one thing to argue, however tenuously, that increased resources for the prison system may eventually lead to the rehabilitation of prisoners and a consequent reduction in the crime rate. It is quite another, particularly in a period when provision for other public sector organisations such as hospitals and schools is being restricted, to argue that these resources should be made available in prisons out of considerations of humanity and with no reference to future rates of recidivism. Those responsible for administering the finances of the prison system were well aware of the benefits of continuing to pursue the rehabilitative ideal as long as was possible.

If rehabilitation within the prison system is measured by the number of prisoners who lead a law-abiding life after release, it is little more than an illusion. This fact has been recognised, at least by academics, for some considerable time. Administrators and practitioners within the system have been more reluctant to admit the reality. Among the former this unwillingness may well have sprung from a desire to press for increased resources. For many of the latter such an admission would have put into question much of their lives' work. A frequent rationalisation was that rehabilitation had never been properly tried due to a lack of general commitment or insufficient resources.

The truth of the matter was that the seeds of the failure of the so-called rehabilitative theory lay in the definition which had been given to it. Brebner and his contemporaries in Scotland in the middle of the nineteenth century had recognised that if prisoners were to be encouraged away from a life of crime the experience of imprisonment could only be the first stage in the process. Contact with friends and relations had to be maintained during the course of sentence and support had to be provided on release. However, this attitude was criticised by those who were closest to the Home Office, who were more in touch with the notion of the prison as a place where both body and mind were to be disciplined by external means in order that obedience would result.

The proper definition of rehabilitation involves the notion of restitution or reinstatement from within rather than imposed change from without. The notion that personal change can be forced on an individual is at best patronising and at worst arrogant. 'Re-habilis' implies placing on again the garb of citizenship. This can only be done freely by the individual concerned. The garb of citizenship is not a straitjacket into which one can be forced.

If this definition is understood and accepted, the principle of rehabilitation from within is sound enough. The difficulty was that the incorrect notion of rehabilitation as something which could be imposed from without had become so much part of the accepted rhetoric that it was virtually impossible to separate it from the underlying concept. The word rehabilitation had fallen into such disrepute that it had become necessary to find a different form of words to present the essential notion of the possibility of change coming from within an individual.

The Justice Model

> By the seventies, everyone seemed agreed that the 'treatment model of corrections' was dead and buried. In its place were coming restricted horizons and less ambitious goals, a return to justice, neo-classicism or (in more conservative terms) deterrence, incapacitation, law and order and a new version of social defence. Of course, treatment personnel fought back, tried to retain parts of their empire or colonize new territories, even claimed that their methods were, after all, effective and that they only needed better resources to get on with the job. But everyone sensed that an era was over. (Cohen, 1985)

What was shortly to become known as the justice model of imprisonment was a result of the coming together of a discrete and at times unrelated set of circumstances. There was in the first instance a growing appreciation that the resources which were often available in prisons, such as education, vocational training and social work support, had been wrongly linked with crime prevention. That is, the extent to which any one prisoner made use of these facilities in prison was not necessarily an appropriate measure of whether he was likely to offend again after release from prison. The state did have an obligation to make these and other facilities available in prison, not as an aid to rehabilitation but in simple humanity and out of respect to prisoners as people. The fact that a prisoner chose to make use of such resources should not in any way accelerate the date of his release from prison, nor should his failure to do so lengthen the period of his imprisonment. This change of emphasis was encapsulated in what Norval Morris (1974) described as 'the substitution of facilitated change for coerced cure'. There was also growing concern in the United Kingdom at the discrepancy between the length of sentence passed by the court and the actual length of time which the offender spent in prison. A prisoner, for example, who was sentenced to three years in prison could expect to be released after two years with full remission and, if he managed to convince the parole authorities that he 'deserved' parole, might be released after one year. Decisions as to whether the prisoner should be released after one year or three were made not by the judiciary in open court but by executive authority behind closed doors. Any suggestion that the judiciary took account of this discrepancy in their sentencing policy was strenuously denied but public credibility in the way in which the process operated was at times stretched.

Closely linked to concern about the notion of executive justice with regard to time spent in prison was the debate about the exercise of administrative justice within the prison system. Given the assertion that the punishment contained in the sentence of imprisonment should consist exclusively of the deprivation of liberty, commentators expressed increasing concern about how to justify the additional elements of punishment which were invariably included in a sentence of imprisonment. Why, for example, if imprisonment itself is the punishment, is there a need for restrictions on all forms of communication and contact with family and friends, an obligation to work for the benefit of the state or the prohibition on any form of business? This concern was often focused on the perceived exercise of unaccountable power by prison administrators.

A fundamental tenet of prison administration is that it must be seen, not least by the prisoners, to be treating law-breakers in a law-abiding fashion. This, according to Fogel (1975), is what the justice model is all about.

> When men are confined against their will in this country, the bottom line of the arrangement of life for both the keeper and the kept should be *justice-as-fairness*. Opportunities for self-improvement should be offered but not made a condition of freedom.

During this period in which the prison population increased significantly and there was considerable concern at overcrowding in prisons, there was a strong body of informed opinion that fine-defaulters and others should be dealt with by penal sanctions other than imprisonment. This was a view which united those who looked for better value for money from the prison system and those who wished to see the prison population reduced.

Perhaps as a consequence of the efforts of those who pursued the justice model, the courts began to take an increasing interest in the administration of prisons and the extent to which the rights of individual prisoners were observed or ignored. This trend began in the United States in the 1960s but within ten years there was an increasing number of precedents in the United Kingdom. In Scotland public awareness of the issue was heightened in the 1970s and 1980s by several cases, relating to such matters as freedom of correspondence, which were pursued by the Scottish Council for Civil Liberties, in some instances as far as the European Court.

The separate but related responses to these several issues were collectively described as the justice model of imprisonment. In the first instance it was suggested that sentencing policy should be based on principles of justice rather than on any notion of crime control. Offenders were to be sent to prison solely on the basis that their offence merited such a punishment. There was to be no question of sending offenders to prison with the primary intention of turning them into law-abiding citizens. That objective could best be achieved by some form of community penalty. It would not be acceptable for a judge to send a man to prison 'for his own good' or 'for training'. The punishment of imprisonment was to be proportionate to the crime which had been committed and not to any future social gain. Imprisonment would therefore be reserved for only the most serious offenders and for them it would be without argument a punishment.

Since imprisonment was to consist fundamentally of the deprivation of liberty, all other rights of the prisoner, with the exception of those forfeited as a direct consequence of the loss of liberty, were to remain intact. The actions of all who lived and worked in prisons, administrators, staff and prisoners, were to be subject to scrutiny by the court.

The influence of the justice model has done much to extend a structure of legitimate and accountable administration into the darker recesses of the prison system. The reality of prison governors facing personal civil law suits amounting to several million dollars for alleged maladministration, which is not uncommon in the United States, is not yet known in this country. However, governors are now well versed in explaining their decisions on an almost daily basis to solicitors representing their prisoners and the Secretary of State has become used to replying to applications made to the courts for judicial review of administrative decisions.

The consequences of these developments have not all been positive. To some extent considerations of personal and individual circumstances have been ignored as concerns for legalism have increased.

> The indirect effects of the prisoners' rights movement are difficult to identify and difficult to evaluate. Is it better or worse that today's prison is more fully bureaucratised than the prison of a decade ago? Some of the autocratic wardens may have been rooted out of corrections, but excessive bureaucratisation has its own dysfunctions. Prisoners may find something insensitive and inhuman about administration by the book. While bureaucratisation was a response to an earlier form of organisation which could not justify its decisions or focus responsibility, excessive bureaucratisation may lead to the same result: a mass of offices and office holders insulated from effective outside scrutiny. (Allen, 1971)

It is important to recognise that, rather than being an expression of new thinking, the concepts behind the justice model represent a retreat from the determinism of rehabilitation and a return to the earlier theory of individual responsibility for one's actions. Its theoretical foundation lies in the moral philosophy of Immanuel Kant.

> It is a return to old ideas, old values and old philosophies, and marks a loss of faith in 'new fangled rehabilitative criminology', a loss of faith in the idea first of all that the causes of crime can be diagnosed, treated and cured, and secondly, a loss of faith in the expansionist state as benevolent provider of caring, curing services. Return to justice is a retreatist position based on hopelessness and disillusion: the criminal justice system cannot take upon itself the task of curing the ills of society, not even the ills of the hapless individuals who come within its ambit. The principles upon which the criminal justice system operates should be principles which set limits on its powers over citizens, rather than principles which facilitate unfettered intervention in people's lives. (Hudson, 1987)

Towards a New Ideal

The point has now been reached at which we can recognise that neither the rehabilitative ideal nor the justice model is an exclusively sufficient description of the reality of imprisonment. The rehabilitative argument, at least as traditionally presented, is unsound in principle and in practice. In principle it assumes with a degree of arrogance that one human being or group of human beings can take on the responsibility for enforcing change on another human being. It cannot deliver in practice because the experience of imprisonment, no matter what resources and facilities are provided, is less important to the prospect of future offending than external influences. The justice model on the other hand fails to take sufficient account of the human factor in respect both of the keeper and the kept. Imprisonment cannot be defined merely in terms of either law and order or facts and figures.

We have to find a vocabulary, a set of principles which will extract the positive elements from each of these paradigms and combine them into a new presentation. The ideal of rehabilitation must be combined with the safeguards of justice.

> Neither as individuals nor as a society are we able to escape the question of whether persons who come within our influence or control are better served by a posture of protective paternalism emphasising educative and socialising influences or one that assumes the full moral autonomy and responsibility of such persons. The issue is inescapable because, however distasteful to modern sensibilities the fact may be, neither posture is valid in all cases and each in varying degrees is appropriate in some cases. (Allen, 1981)

There can be no argument that in some instances the court has no alternative but to send an offender to prison. But in such cases the perceived need to punish must be exercised within narrow limits and has to be balanced by the obligation to help. Considerations of public morality cannot be avoided. We must recognise that what we now have to term facilitative regimes may not result in either extensive individual rehabilitation or in a widespread reduction in crime. But we must also be careful not to remove from prisoners the possibility of self development and hope for the future.

Any new statement about the principles of imprisonment must take account of the realities which are experienced by those who undergo imprisonment and by those who enforce it. The first of these realities is that the punishment of imprisonment and its genuine pain consists of the deprivation of liberty. That it is a punishment cannot be doubted. Despite what the tabloid press may suggest from time to time, no prison is a holiday camp. This is particularly true of the local and remand prisons in which petty offenders are held. No prisoner, whatever the circumstances to which he may be returning, asks to be allowed to remain in prison once his sentence is complete. The first question which any prisoner will ask when he passes through the gate of the prison will be about the date of his release.

Acceptance of the primacy of punishment in the prison sentence has two main implications for sentencers. In the first place only those for whom there is no reasonable alternative should be sent to prison. This message has recently been underlined by the Secretary of State for Scotland:

> The Government's penal policy is that the prison sentence
> should be imposed upon those, and only those, for whom an
> alternative disposal is not appropriate.
> (*Opportunity and Responsibility*, 1990)

The second implication is that those who have to be sent to prison should go there for the shortest necessary time compatible with justice. In some instances this may be a very long time but the period of imprisonment should never be lengthened on social or other rehabilitative grounds. The main consequence if these two considerations were to be consistently applied would be a significant reduction in the present levels of imprisonment. The number held on remand would be reduced as would be the number of those sentenced for minor offences. These are the two groups most responsible for the high level of imprisonment in this country.

These two considerations are based on an appreciation that in essence the act of imprisonment is always negative. While positive benefits, such as presenting a criminal with the opportunity to consider his behaviour or to come to terms with, say, drug or alcohol addiction, may in some instances result from a period in prison, these will come about as an indirect consequence. It is important to underline the essentially negative purpose of imprisonment in an unequivocal manner which leaves no room for doubt in the minds of those who have the responsibility for sending offenders to prison. However, when an individual has been sentenced to imprisonment one may then proceed to a consideration of the essential features of that imprisonment and how they might be applied in a constructive and positive manner.

Custody

After an offender has been admitted to prison the first responsibility of the prison system and of its staff is to ensure that the punishment of deprivation of liberty which has been passed by the court is duly observed and that no prisoner is released before the expiry of his sentence or until release is otherwise legitimately authorised; in short that no prisoner escapes. Security is without question the first task of the prison system. If we reach a position at which only those for whom there is no reasonable alternative are sent to prison, the importance of security will be reinforced, not least to ensure that the public is protected from those who might present a threat to its safety.

The paramount importance of this proposition has always been recognised by the two groups of people most closely involved with the prison system, prisoners and prison staff. Prisoners live day after day with bars on their cell windows, faced by a door with no handle on the inside. They are left in no doubt that whatever academic discussion may take place about the justification for, or objectives of, imprisonment the most pressing reality is that they are deprived of liberty. They may not leave prison.

Prison staff are well aware that while they will not be taken to task for failing to rehabilitate a prisoner they undoubtedly will be if he is allowed to escape. The priority to be given to this feature of imprisonment was underlined by the findings of the Mountbatten Report on prison escapes and security in 1966 which was referred to in chapter five.

In Scotland there has been an uneasy balance between the security categorisation of individual prisoners, which was adopted following the Mountbatten Report, and the security rating of prison establishments. Prisoners are given a personal security rating in descending order of A, B, C or D, which determines the degree of supervision to be imposed on them. A prisoner given an 'A' security rating will have his movement personally supervised by a nominated officer at all times. One in category 'D' will require no direct supervision. These categories should relate only to the degree of risk which would be presented to the public if a prisoner were to escape: a category 'A' prisoner should be prevented from escaping in any circumstance because of the threat which he poses; a category 'D' prisoner will present no threat at all.

In practice there is likely to be a close correlation between the degree of supervision to which a prisoner is subjected on security grounds and the 'privileges' which he is accorded, given that many of these will imply a reduction in supervision. These range from the possibility of more enjoyable work within the prison to eligibility for activities outside the prison, including the option of visits home. The decision to enhance a prisoner's treatment in this way is based not only on his security status but on his behaviour and response to the conditions of imprisonment.

An inevitable consequence of this confusion is that both staff and prisoners have come to link security category with behaviour. If a prisoner conforms to the requirements of prison life he is more likely to be recommended for, and himself to expect, a reduction in his security status so that he can qualify for additional 'privileges'. But these two considerations should be quite distinct. In principle, a prisoner may be at the same time one of the most obstructive of individuals and a low security risk or conversely a model prisoner and a high security risk. In reality, the former will be much less likely than the latter, but both equations are possible. The position is further complicated by the fact that many of the prisons which hold prisoners in lower security categories have more facilities to offer than those which hold prisoners of higher security status. In consequence prisoners who have spent some time in prison and been of good behaviour may come to expect the reward of reduction in security status in order to enjoy the advantages of a less restrictive environment.

The threat posed by this confusion on the part of both staff and prisoners has now been recognised. Attempts are being made in Scotland to confirm the distinction which has to be recognised between the security category of a prisoner and his behaviour while in prison. One way of doing this is by having two distinct rating systems, one to measure the degree of security to which a prisoner should be subjected, the other to measure the amount of control which must be imposed on him. If these criteria are applied in an appropriate manner regimes can be tailored to meet the needs of groups of individuals. There will be a range of regimes which cater for prisoners who present a high security risk but who require varying degrees of control. At one end of the spectrum these are likely to be restrictive, at the other they will allow a considerable facility for internal freedom of movement within a secure perimeter. A parallel set of regimes will be provided within environments with lower security. A prisoner who presents a high risk to security but who does not present a threat to internal order will progress to a secure regime which offers a high quality of life. However, he will only progress to a less secure regime when the risk which he poses to the public is lessened. In some cases, despite continuing good behaviour in prison, this may never happen since the high-quality regime in less secure establishments will include the possibility of activities outwith the prison.

The recognition of the priority to be given to the dictates of custody does not, despite what some critics may say, imply the introduction of a *new* negative element to the concept of imprisonment. It does imply a new honesty in recognising the essentially negative foundation on which imprisonment has always been based, the deprivation of liberty.

Good Order

The opposite of order is disorder. Prison systems across the world have in recent years experienced the anarchy and chaos of disorder, none more so than those in the United Kingdom. The problem of maintaining order in prison is not a new one but the consequences of disorder are now universally and immediately observed by the world's media, and disorder in prison is likely to be demonstrated in spectacular fashion which lends itself to sensational reporting, be it from New Mexico, Peterhead or Strangeways.

An environment which has its reason for existence in the fact that one group of people deprives another group of their liberty is in essence unnatural and liable to be subject to considerable tension. The fact that the prison system is neither a normative nor a utilitarian but a coercive organisation was discussed in chapter seven. The basis of such an organisation is the exercise of power. In some circumstances this is achieved in such an indirect manner that its existence is hardly acknowledged; in others it is exercised in a stark fashion. This is the difference between the minimum and the maximum security prison. Nonetheless, the exercise of power is no less real in the former than in the latter.

A major expressed justification for the exercise of power in prison is the need to ensure that there is good order within the establishment. This means that the prison should be a safe living environment for prisoners and a safe working environment for staff. A society which commits offenders to prison does so on the understanding that prisoners will not be placed in physical danger by the very fact of their imprisonment. This safety has not always been guaranteed. The notion that prisons may not be safe places underlies their depiction as 'schools of crime'. The introduction of central inspection to local prisons in the early and mid nineteenth century was due in no small extent to concern at the disorder in so many jails at the time. Nor is this merely of historical interest. Prisoners themselves are often the first to suffer when good order is lost in prison.

The breakdown of good order implies that staff have ceded control of the prison to prisoners; but it will not be to the prisoners as a body. Rather it is likely to be to a small number of prisoners and that fact will not be welcomed by the majority, for the control exercised by this group over the majority will be much less even-handed and disciplined than that of the staff. It should not be forgotten that prisoners are rarely a homogeneous group. They have little in common other than the fact that they have each been convicted by a court and sentenced to a period of imprisonment. They would not often choose to associate with their fellow prisoners and may well be apprehensive of doing so too closely.

Prison officers carry out their duties on behalf of society. They do not choose which offenders should be locked up in prison, nor how long they should spend there. They are required to exercise their duties in accordance with the prison rules which have been agreed by parliament. In return they are entitled to expect that they can carry out the task which society has set them without fear for their personal safety. If on occasion their personal safety is threatened, for example, by physical assault, they are entitled to the full protection of the law. Physical violence is no more acceptable from any quarter in our prisons than in our town centres. 'Rough justice' on the part of prison officers is never to be tolerated nor condoned. In return they have to be assured that an assault on them in the course of their duties will be regarded just as seriously by the court as if it had occurred in the high street.

The use of the description 'good order' rather than the more commonly used one 'control' underlines the shared need for this feature. It is not merely a question of staff having control for its own sake over prisoners. Good order is in the interest of all parties. Furthermore, the two concepts do not in themselves equate. The good order of the prison implies a degree of control but it is more than that. It implies an acceptance on the part of the majority of prisoners of the need for order and a willingness to cooperate with it. That is why prisons can usually function with large numbers of prisoners being supervised by small numbers of staff in worksheds and in recreation areas. This is what is entailed in the statement that prisons run only with the consent of prisoners.

If consent is withdrawn then staff will have to resort to control and that can only be achieved with very significant restriction to the regime. Under such circumstances staff will only be able to guarantee control if they outnumber the prisoners at any one time. This in turn means that the movement and activities of prisoners will have to be severely curtailed. The majority of prisoners recognise the need for good order in prisons. There is joint agreement in practice if not in principle that this can only be maintained by cooperation between the keepers and the kept.

Opportunity

The argument that the main purpose of imprisonment is to punish an offender by depriving him of his liberty has already been presented. In order to achieve that objective, the first function of the prison is to ensure an appropriate level of security. There is also a need to ensure the physical safety of those who live or work within the prison.

So far so good. But this is not sufficient. If the court has decided that, because of the offence he has committed, a man must be deprived of his liberty for twenty years, or ten years, or two years, or even two months, society cannot be content merely that he is held securely in a prison for that period and that he is physically safe. So, what else should we look for?

The concept of individual repentance for sin and of consequent cleansing of guilt looms large in the Christian ethic. It was no accident that organised religion, particularly of the reformed tradition, played such an important role in the development of the prison as a punishment. The Quakers in Pennsylvania were at the forefront of prison expansion in the United States in the early nineteenth century and many of the penal reformers in the United Kingdom at the same time had strong church connections. It is worthy of note that this tradition has by no means disappeared and is continued by many individuals who work in or about the prison system today.

It was no great intellectual feat to translate the concept of individual repentance and consequent divine forgiveness for acts which were morally wrong to that of repentance and consequent social forgiveness for acts which were legally wrong. It was no coincidence that this notion began to take root and to develop just at the time that the prison system was becoming better organised and being taken under central supervision. There was an emphasis on the need to recruit and to train a better standard of prison governor and keeper than the blind jailer whom the House of Commons Committee found at Linlithgow at the beginning of the nineteenth century, or the keeper who doubled as a chimney sweep in Alloa.

The senior staff who were recruited to administer individual prisons and the prison system were not content to take on a purely custodial role and many of them were only too happy to translate concepts of personal repentance and forgiveness to the new work. These principles were also applied to the architecture of the new prisons which were built at that time and subsequently. Prisoners were to be kept apart from the bad influence which they might exert on each other. This notion of solitude was one of the reasons why the separate system of imprisonment was preferred to the silent system. The solitude of the individual prisoner was broken by frequent visits from those who were likely to bring good influence to bear, the chaplain and the governor. The repetitive work which he was given to do would not distract his thoughts from repentance.

It has been argued in the early chapters of this book that, in so far as this model applied to Scotland in the early and mid nineteenth century, there was a significant difference in its application from that in England. It was recognised that change could not be forced on an individual and that the circumstances to which a prisoner returned on release were quite likely to have a greater influence on his future behaviour than any experience which he underwent in the course of imprisonment.

Be that as it may, the Scottish administrators found it impossible to resist the tide of enthusiasm which swept over the prison systems in the wake of the Gladstone Report of 1895, setting an impossible agenda from which we are only now breaking free; impossible since it set unrealistic goals which, because they were unattainable, sowed the seed of later disenchantment.

The notion that the experience of imprisonment might in some instances have a positive effect on individual prisoners was encouraged by senior prison administrators. Even today the prison governor who responds to a query as to what his job entails with the statement 'I lock people up' is likely to evoke a less positive reaction than the one who replies 'I rehabilitate people'. The move from the correct understanding of rehabilitation as change which comes from within an individual to one which viewed it as a change which could be enforced by external agencies was a subtle one, never explicitly described in these terms.

Confidence in the rehabilitative potential of imprisonment led to a significant increase in the number of so-called rehabilitative agents working in prison settings. Officer-teachers had been used in prisons in Scotland since the early part of the nineteenth century but they were gradually replaced by qualified teachers who introduced a wide range of academic and technical subjects, commitment to which on the part of any one prisoner was yet another measure of his 'rehabilitation'. Welfare officers, whose primary role had been to act as some form of bridge between the prisoner and the family to which he would one day return, were replaced by social workers who, along with psychologists and psychiatrists, became additional aids to prison management in its attempt to impose rehabilitation on the prisoner.

It is possible for a person to 'rehabilitate' himself in prison; that is, to make use of the experience of imprisonment to become again a full member of society. Whether it is ever possible to say that this rehabilitation is a direct result of the imprisonment is another matter. It is not possible for rehabilitation to be imposed through enforced changes of behaviour. The paternalism inherent in such an attitude, a child of its time in the early years of the twentieth century, was misplaced in practical terms since it did not achieve the desired results. It was also wrong in principle since it included an arrogance in the assumption that one human being or group of human beings could force change on another.

Confidence in this definition of rehabilitation began to wane for a variety of reasons. Those among its advocates who had mistakenly linked it with the possibility of crime reduction were eventually proved wrong and in due course their arguments were turned against themselves. The fact that the rate of recidivism among released prisoners remained so high was seen to be proof of the failure of the prison system. In reality this argument was just as ill-founded as the obverse, which expected techniques of imprisonment to affect the level of offending.

The two most important groups within the prison system, prisoners and prison staff, had always recognised that the experience of imprisonment had very little to do directly with rehabilitation. The prison officer on the gallery knew that if he reached the end of the day with the same number of prisoners as he had at its beginning (custody) and without an incident taking place (good order) he had done well. The prisoner frequently coped with the fact of imprisonment by regarding it as a period when time stood still. 'Serving his time' meant successfully divorcing the experience of imprisonment from the real world which he had left behind temporarily and to which he would return in due course. Neither of these two actors had much notion of imposing or being receptive to rehabilitation.

Such research as was carried out on different methods of treatment and training indicated that none was more effective than any other in respect of reducing rates of recidivism. Instead of concluding that perhaps the wrong proposition was being presented, those involved, first academics and then somewhat reluctantly practitioners, were drawn to the conclusion that 'nothing worked', that prison could only be a negative experience and that the best to be aimed for was that it should be as humane and as just an experience as possible in which the inherently negative effects were minimised.

These principles, encapsulated in what is generally described as the justice *model* of imprisonment, are correct in as far as they go but they do not go far enough. The vacuum left by the so-called demise of the rehabilitative *ideal* remains to be filled. It is important to recognise that the latter was an ideal rather than a model, a concept to be aimed for rather than a structure to be created. Just as it is important to pass the message to society at large and courts in particular that the sentence of imprisonment is essentially negative, so equally is it important to place before prisoners and prison staff the possibility that the experience of being in prison can be put to positive use.

The concept of rehabilitation, properly understood as change coming voluntarily from within a person, is sound. What was fundamentally flawed was the notion that this could be imposed by external agencies. This incorrect presentation of rehabilitation was a result of the paternalistic expression of the power relationship which we have already identified as being a feature of the prison system. In theory it should have been possible to reaffirm the correct understanding of the word rehabilitation and to exclude from it the erroneous accretions. In practice this additional baggage has become so much a part of the essential understanding of the word that it has proved impossible to separate the rhetoric from the reality.

Because of this it has become necessary to find a new form of words with which to restate the belief that the prisoner can make positive use of his time in prison and that it is the duty of the state, which has deprived him of his liberty, to provide him with the opportunity to do so. What is required is a set of principles which will be a modern expression of the argument presented in the early years of the nineteenth century by William Brebner that prisoners have to be given some responsibility for personal change.

Since the middle of the 1980s the Scottish Prison Service has been engaged in developing just such a set of principles, not in isolation but in the course of a series of consultation papers and discussion documents which have encouraged public debate. The beginning of the formal process can be traced to a statement made in October 1985 by the Director of the Scottish Prison Service defining the task of the service. The various elements of the task were presented in the following terms:

i. to keep in custody untried or unsentenced prisoners and to ensure that they are available to be presented to court for trial or sentence;

ii. to keep in custody, with such degree of security as is appropriate, having regard to the nature of the individual prisoner and his offence, sentenced prisoners for the duration of their sentence or for such shorter time as the Secretary of State may determine in cases where he has discretion;

iii. to provide for prisoners as full a life as is consistent with the facts of custody, in particular making available the physical necessities of life; care for physical and mental health; advice and help with personal problems; work, education, skill training, physical exercise and recreation; and opportunity to practise their religion;

iv. to promote and preserve the self-respect of prisoners;

v. to enable prisoners to retain links with family and community; and

vi. to encourage them to respond and contribute positively to society on discharge.

There were significant pointers within this statement of the principles which were being espoused. A new honesty, signalled by the use of the word 'prisoner' in preference to 'inmate', recognised the first priority of custody. The rhetoric of 'treatment and training' was discarded, to be replaced by a new set of verbs which were enabling rather than prescriptive: provide, promote, enable and encourage.

The next significant step forward came in 1988 with publication of the consultative document *Custody and Care*. The context within which this paper was published was underlined in the foreword by the Under Secretary of State.

The paper is a starting point, not an end in itself. It focuses on the job which the Scottish Prison Service is required to do and the ways in which it can be done better. As the Secretary of State has emphasised, however, imprisonment is only part of the wider context of criminal justice and penal policy. It is worth restating that the clear policy of the Government is that imprisonment should be imposed only upon those for whom there is no reasonable alternative disposal and that we have taken many steps to improve the range of alternatives available to the courts.

The first section of the discussion document described the task and responsibilities of the prison service. It recognised the need for a 'coherent corporate philosophy' to guide the service and for constant reassessment of penal policy. It emphasised that custody and care are not alternatives but complementary elements in the good management of prisons. The prison service must operate within a legal framework. Several of the domestic statutes require to be updated; the primary statute, for example, and the rules for the management of prisons were enacted in 1952. *Custody and Care* acknowledged that some priority would have to be given to these matters.

An important chapter of the document recognised that prisoners have a right to know where and in what conditions they are likely to serve their sentences. This was to be achieved by a process which was to be known as sentence planning which would set short term goals for prisoners and would take the form of quasi-contracts between individual prisoners and the system. The main adult prisons were to work towards some form of parity of regime although it was admitted that, given the significant divergences in physical standards in each prison, important differences would remain.

For the first time there was talk of a shared enterprise between the system and the prisoner:

> Getting any inmate through a period in custody demands a degree of responsible behaviour on the part of the individual and a good deal of support by the establishment. Minimum conditions or quality of life in custody can be very poor if there is a destructive attitude on the part of inmates or an unhelpful or negative approach on the part of management and staff. The aim must be to achieve the best quality of life by getting inmates to accept the necessary restrictions which custody imposes but then encouraging them to make the best use of the available opportunities.

The document went on to list and describe some key areas where this 'responsibility' and 'opportunity' overlap: privacy, the obligation to work, responsibility for personal affairs, contact with family and friends, health and other personal problems, access to information. This list seems somewhat selective but the fact that it was presented at all represented a significant step forward in thinking.

Given that the essence of imprisonment is deprivation of liberty, one of the first considerations of a prisoner is the conclusion of that punishment, that is, his release date. The way in which a prisoner passes his sentence should bear some relationship to the life which is likely to face him on release. For some short term prisoners the period in prison may be a brief intermission which can best be used to clear up domestic problems or other pressing difficulties. For long term prisoners the issues are much more complex. *Custody and Care* acknowledged the importance of making the prisoner aware of the date he is likely to be released from prison, although certainty cannot take account of possible early release on parole and is impossible for life sentence prisoners.

A sentence plan should be agreed with every prisoner, ensuring that at each stage of his sentence options and opportunities are fully reviewed and discussed. Such a plan should be a process rather than an event. It involves continuous assessment which takes account both of available facilities on the one hand and the needs and preferences of the prisoner on the other. There is to be a shared attempt on the part of the prison system and the prisoner to agree a personal plan, which will be kept under regular review, which will satisfy the needs of all concerned. The final element in this plan will be preparation for release.

Individual plans of this sort assume that each establishment has a set of regime plans which describe what facilities are available and what restrictions are imposed. *Custody and Care* indicated that each establishment would be required to formulate a clear response to the general task of the service.

> It will include a policy for security and control of inmates as well as an inventory of the regime of the establishment. This statement or regime plan will be discussed and agreed between the Governor and HQ. Thereafter it will be the joint responsibility of the establishment and HQ to pursue the agreed aims, objectives and targets within the framework of the regime plan.

These regime plans were to take account of the circumstances of each establishment and to work to the strengths of each one. As well as providing a document which could usefully be presented to both staff and prisoners as an indication of the ethos of each establishment and a commitment to what could be made available, the regime plan would have the added benefit of ensuring stability and continuity for the regime.

The document recognised that much of its content was a statement of intent and that a great deal of effort would be required to translate this into reality. Not least was the commitment necessary from staff, and the concurrent obligation on management to provide proper support and training to enable staff to carry out what was envisaged as likely to become a more complex set of tasks but which would also provide a greater degree of job satisfaction.

One of the most significant features of *Custody and Care* was that it was circulated widely both inside and outside the prison service as a consultative document on which comment and constructive criticism was invited. Following its publication, establishments embarked on the challenging task of putting flesh on the framework which it provided.

Custody and Care referred principally to proposals for the development of corporate planning in individual establishments. To be properly effective such local plans had to be placed within the context of a corporate plan for the prison service. A further step in this direction was taken with the publication in 1989 of the first business plan for the Scottish Prison Service, covering the years 1989 to 1992. The plan began with what it termed a 'mission statement'.

> The Mission of the Scottish Prison Service is to keep in custody those committed by the courts, to maintain good order in each prison, to look after inmates with humanity, and to provide them with all possible opportunities to help them to lead law abiding and useful lives after release.

Some of the terminology which had come into vogue by this time betrayed a level of imprecise definition. The prison service is a significant drain on the public purse and unquestionably has to be accountable for the resources which it uses. It also has to plan in a corporate and strategic manner. Whether one is therefore entitled to describe it as a 'business', with the implication that its core activity of involvement with individual human beings can somehow be subjected to a profit and loss balance, is doubtful. The word 'mission' is currently fashionable in some business enterprises. It is used to imply a sense of idealism in a business ethic which will otherwise have an exclusively material base. It has an evangelical overtone which does not come easily to many people.

This new enthusiasm is continued in the recently introduced notion of 'customer awareness' which seeks to discover how the prison service can best serve its various customers, be they society, the government, staff or prisoners. It is tempting to point out that a fundamental difference between a prisoner and a customer is that the latter if dissatisfied can walk out of the shop. However, it has to be recognised that despite a degree of imprecision in some terminology the principles underlying the new initiatives are central to the philosophy of punishment being presented in this book.

The business plan noted that reaction to the consultative document *Custody and Care* had been universally favourable and that there had been no criticism of the initiatives which it outlined. The purpose of the business plan was to describe how these proposals were to be developed in forthcoming years. The three year cycle related to the parallel cycle of the government's public expenditure survey. The three main assumptions contained in the plan were:

1. the estimated daily average prisoner population was 5500;
2. the number of staff would rise to 3930;
3. net annual operating costs would rise to £96.3m and gross annual capital expenditure fall to £9.7m.

The business plan went on to list a set of aims, objectives and action plans for each of the seven divisions within Prison Service Headquarters.

The latest major statement on the prison service in Scotland came in 1990 with the publication of a document entitled *Opportunity and Responsibility: Developing Approaches to the Management of the Long Term Prison System in Scotland*. The foreword to the document by the Secretary of State included an unusually direct statement:

> It is clear that the old objectives of 'treatment and training' are outmoded. A new approach is required, which will recognise the mutual responsibilities of the prisoner and the prison authorities and ensure that the long term prisoner is encouraged to address his offending behaviour and offered an appropriate range of

opportunities to use his time in prison responsibly for personal development.

This is a summary, admirable in its precision, of the new thesis which provides a positive context for imprisonment. The basic principles of rehabilitation, properly understood, are not questioned but the paternalistic rhetoric with which they have become encrusted is 'outmoded'. The key phrases of the new approach are:

mutual responsibilities;
encouraged to address offending behaviour;
offered an appropriate range of opportunities;
use his time responsibly;
personal development.

This agenda is characterised neither by strictness nor liberality, neither by oppression nor permissiveness but by honesty and consistency. It is not a set of easy options but an ideal to be aimed for, however difficult to achieve in its fullness.

In setting for itself this agenda the Scottish Prison Service has stated explicitly that its administrative goal is to be at the international forefront of best penal practice. This is a worthy ideal. The world of penology will monitor the transfer of ideal into reality with great interest.

The underpinning principle is that the offender who is admitted to prison remains a person with free will who should be allowed to retain as much responsibility as possible. The prison system should make available to the prisoner as broad a range of facilities and resources as possible. If the prisoner makes use of these they will constitute an opportunity for personal development or the resolution of personal problems. In being given the opportunity to exercise as much responsibility as possible while in prison a prisoner is more likely to equip himself to continue to do so after release.

> Whilst we believe that the primary responsibility of the
> Scottish Prison Service is to maintain secure custody and
> promote internal order, we also believe that the Service has a
> duty to provide for the prisoner a humane environment, within
> which he has an opportunity to take decisions about the progress
> of his sentence. The corollary is that the prisoner should find
> himself in a situation in which, in exercising his choice, he is
> expected to face the consequences of his decision.

The proposals for individual sentence planning which had been first described in *Custody and Care* are identified as central to the new programme. This new scheme, which will allow the prisoner to participate at each stage in the planning of his sentence, has five principal features:

1. It provides information *for* the prisoner about what is available rather than merely taking information *from* him.
2. It provides an opportunity for the prisoner to become aware of the significant elements influencing his own life.
3. It allows the prison officer to work with the prisoner to facilitate his development.
4. It involves the prisoner in the decision making process.
5. The process is subject to continuous review.

Just as the prisoner is to be encouraged to accept responsibility, so must the prison system be accountable to the prisoner. In reviewing how best this might be done the document suggests that a distinction should be made at three levels.

1. *Threshold quality of life* will include the minimum elements to which a prisoner should be entitled on admission: they include, diet, personal space, family contact, work and recreation.
2. *Appropriate Opportunities* refer to aspects of the prison regime which are likely to contribute to a prisoner's personal development, such as education, vocational training and pre-release courses.
3. Many of the aspects of regime which have hitherto been regarded as *privileges* will now fall under one of the two previous headings. Consideration will be given to allowing prisoners to enjoy additional facilities which are now taken for granted in normal life. The provision of electrical power in cells may allow prisoners access to personal items such as televisions. Facilities may also be introduced for laundry of personal clothes and arrangements for pay telephones will be extended.

One of the most important ways of reducing the harmful effects of imprisonment is by allowing the prisoner to maintain and develop links with his family. For prisoners in lower security categories there should be increased opportunity for home leaves of various kinds. The document recognises that in many other prison systems provisions are made for extended family visits within the secure perimeter for those prisoners who cannot be allowed home. This issue is to be further examined.

In discussing the balance which has to be maintained among security, good order and regime opportunities, it is intimated that prisoners should be kept in the lowest security category consistent with the need to ensure secure custody and protection of the public. The document suggests that at present too many prisoners are held in security category 'B' who could safely be reduced to security category 'C', thus making them eligible for additional activities outwith the secure perimeter of an establishment.

Opportunity and Responsibility recognises that a small number of long term prisoners will, despite all support and encouragement, be unable to settle in normal regimes. For these prisoners there is to be a limited expansion of the small unit system described in chapter six. However, there is no question that the key to general stability in the prison system is a positive and responsible expansion of the whole spectrum of opportunities in the mainstream of regimes. In a word, the emphasis now is to be on preventive rather than reactive strategies.

One of the keys to the successful implementation of this strategy, as is the case with any prison initiative, will be the extent to which staff become involved:

> We recognise that our staff are the most valuable resource of the
> Service and they will have a critical role to play in the initiatives
> outlined. We believe that the proposals in this document will
> lead to an enhanced role for staff, reinforcing their pivotal
> position in driving forward a committed, professional service.

These documents do not conceal the fact that the major principles which they present are a statement of what might and can be rather than of what is now. In other words they present an ideal rather than a model. They incorporate an attempt to relate the fairness advocated in the justice model, to the humanity which was a fundamental feature of the rehabilitative ideal. Initial response to these documents has been positive.

As is often the case in matters relating to prison which do not concern major internal unrest, the public has shown no particular interest. Academics and other external experts have generally welcomed the proposals as a genuine attempt to answer the need for a positive theoretical base for imprisonment which would go beyond negative statements about deprivation of liberty. The reaction of staff and prisoners has been similar. Following the traumatic experiences since the mid 1980s they are both keen to be convinced that there can be some form of positive expression of what goes on in prison. They have welcomed the statements of intent and will watch closely to discover whether the ideal can be matched by the reality.

In some respects the Scottish prison system has moved an immeasurable distance over the last 150 years. In others it has only now come back to the principles which were hammered out by Brebner and his colleagues in the first half of the eighteenth century. One has to recognise that imprisonment is essentially a punishment and as such is primarily a negative experience. In view of this it should only be used for those for whom there is no reasonable alternative disposal. Having accepted this, society has a duty to treat those offenders who are deprived of their liberty in a fair and just manner while they are in prison. But this in itself is not sufficient. Prisoners have to be given the opportunity to serve their sentences in a positive manner and to prepare themselves for release. To achieve this objective in a way which recognises the individuality of each prisoner without being patronising demands a new level of professionalism and commitment from prison staff. The turnkey has finally been given the opportunity to develop from a warder, to become a prison officer.

Conclusion

One of the key arguments presented in the preceding pages has been that, while the prison system in common with many other large organisations has several unique features, it is not a unique system. It is a bureaucratic structure with a typical mixture of organisational strengths and weaknesses.

Organisational weakness in the Scottish Prison Service is increased by the fact that since 1929 it has been administered in the wrong place. By becoming an arm of the mainstream administrative civil service, located specifically within the Scottish Home and Health Department, it moved from the proper position which it had previously held within the criminal justice process, and where it had maintained close links with the Scottish judicial system. There have been two main consequences of this change. The first relates to the model of imprisonment itself, the second to the influence which staff have exerted.

Failure to retain sight of the primary goal of the prison system as the penal arm of the criminal justice process has resulted in a confusion between the primary and secondary goals of imprisonment. The single primary goal of imprisonment is secure custody for the period of detention laid down by the court. This deprivation of liberty constitutes the punishment which is imprisonment. Having deprived a man or woman of liberty one can postulate several secondary goals. The most common of these are deterrence, either individual or general, and rehabilitation in one of its many guises. Properly located in their respective spheres there is no contradiction between the primary and secondary goals of imprisonment. Confusion has arisen when secondary goals have been elevated to concurrent primary status.

Matters have been further complicated by a reinterpretation of the meaning of the secondary goal of rehabilitation. In a penal context this originally referred to the restoration of an individual's civic rights and privileges at the conclusion of a period of punishment. It signified return to full membership of the community. The reinterpretation of the term was based on the concept of the prisoner, not as responsible for some breach of the law, but as in some way deficient and in need of restoration to an imposed standard of normality.

> The function of penality is to restore him to an elusive
> normality by means of training and treatment, substituting new
> values and norms for defective old ones, supplying a discipline
> previously lacking, or a physical training to counteract
> degeneracy and neglect. (Garland, 1985)

A major disadvantage of any attempt to express the secondary goal of imprisonment is that one is then tempted to measure the success or failure of imprisonment in terms of this goal. Such an attempt is doomed to failure. This was recognised many years ago by Clemmer (1958) in one of the first commentaries on the experience of imprisonment. He suggested that many men who had apparently been rehabilitated by prison were in fact people who should never have been there in the first place or who would have been 'rehabilitated' without the experience of prison. As far as so-called real criminals were concerned, he argued, the only true 'rehabilitation' was the type which kept them in prison until they were so old that they no longer had sufficient physical or mental vigour to commit crime. In a word,

> the apparent rehabilitating effect which prison life has on some
> men occurs in spite of the harmful influences of the prison
> culture.

Another unfortunate consequence of this tendency to focus on what are in reality secondary goals of imprisonment is that it ignores the fundamental question of the use of imprisonment as punishment. Some commentators suggest that this is a failure as much of the justice model as of the rehabilitative ideal. The former attempts to make the punishment as fitting as possible to the crime. It does so by concentrating on length of sentence and insisting that the deprivation of liberty is the one and only punishment. But, argue the critics, the pain caused by the conditions of imprisonment is irregular, unpredictable and inconsistent and this is an inevitable consequence of the use of prison as punishment. The question to be asked is whether prison is necessary.

> To put it even more briefly, there is no sufficiently solid
> conceptual foundation to elevate the idea of imprisonment to the

central place it holds within the structure of penal policy;
nor very much reason to think that if prisons were demolished
tomorrow anything very dreadful would happen to the world.
(Brody, 1983)

This, of course, is not a new concept. It also occurred to that often mis-
quoted penal practitioner, Alexander Paterson:

Wherever prisons are built, Courts will make use of them. If no
prison is handy, some other way of dealing with the offender
will possibly be discovered. (in Ruck, 1951)

It was indicated in the introduction that while this book was not
directly concerned with the major topical debate on the use of
punishment as a tool of social control and the place of the prison system
within this manipulation of power, there was no argument with the
major thrust of the protagonists in this debate. Indeed, the arguments
which have been advanced in this volume are not entirely unrelated to
these wider issues.

It has been shown that historically the prison system in Scotland
was clearly recognised as part of the criminal justice process. This relationship has become blurred over the last half century and requires
to be brought back into focus. The world of the prison does not exist
in a vacuum; it can only be considered within the context of the
criminal justice system as a whole. Regimes and practices in prisons
must be seen in relation to theories of criminal behaviour and, although
they might not always recognise the fact, the wider social context
affects the way in which prison staff carry out the management of
prisoners. The use of imprisonment as a penal sanction is a comparatively modern phenomenon. Its extension to a therapeutic or social
welfare model is even more recent and not native to the Scottish
tradition. Any future reassessment of the role of imprisonment will
return it to its penal model. The improper location of the prison system
in the wider social welfare rather than a criminal justice context is a
consequence of the role now played by central government in administering prisons.

There are grounds for suggesting that the current social and political
climate in Britain lends itself to such a reassessment of the use and
purpose of imprisonment.

As with many other innovations in corrections, change does not
usually come about through new insights or humanitarian

> concepts; it usually occurs as a result of economic arguments.
> (Murton, 1979)

Penal institutions are a considerable drain on the public purse. In the context of a rehabilitative model one could argue that resources for prisons were justified on the grounds that improved facilities and regimes would lead to an eventual reduction in the number of offenders. In the context of a justice model one is arguing that resources are necessary, not in the hope of rehabilitating criminals, but as a human right. In times of economic stringency this argument holds little political attraction. The academic death of the rehabilitative ideal is welcome to any government which wishes to reduce central costs. This argument has been powerfully expressed by Scull and Allen among others.

> One need not be wholly sceptical about the virtues of modern programs seeking to divert offenders from penal incarceration and releasing those already institutionalised, to recognise that these efforts have been powerfully influenced by cost concerns and that these concerns have frequently over-borne competing considerations of rehabilitation and human welfare.
> (Allen, 1981)

The second main consequence of the location of the organisation within the administrative mainstream of the civil service has been the influence which this has allowed staff to exert. The function of the senior civil servant is to serve his Minister. In day-to-day working he frequently exercises this craft in a reactive manner by interpreting various pressures. He recognises those which are transitory and which can safely be ignored. He decides how to reach an accommodation with those which are not transitory, occasionally by confrontation but more often by some form of compromise.

The most consistent pressure on the prison system has come not from any external source but from the staff who have over the last fifty years used their trade union as their voice. Internal pressure of this nature is not in itself a bad thing. An efficiently run organisation is as much in the interest of staff who have to spend a career within the system as it is of management. However, it is important that management recognises this pressure for what it is. While the interests of the service and of the staff who work within it will run parallel and overlap in the majority of instances, there will be occasions when they do not and management must recognise these. In some areas the style of management in the Scottish Prison Service comes close to being participative. The given example is the style of management used for controlling so-called difficult prisoners.

Management can use these developments for the more effective organisation of the system. The organisation of the prison system is likely to be more efficient when staff perceive management as operating in a consultative fashion and when policy places a high concern on the needs of prisoners. This is likely to occur when management is decentralised and when goal attainment is openly discussed with both staff and prisoners. This might well happen if staff are allowed to organise into local work teams and to exercise initiative and creativity in local work settings. It is not too difficult to relate this concept to that of the group officer system which has existed in varying forms in Scotland for some years. It is also a key concept within the arrangements which were introduced in 1987 under the Fresh Start banner.

This notion is also related to the traditional need for a free-flow of communication in the form of criticism, suggestions and expressions of approval as an aid to problem-solving. Such a process is democratic but does not preclude a full expression of leadership. Indeed, leadership can further the process of problem-solving by encouraging rather than impeding a full flow of communication. Such a style of leadership goes beyond that normally encountered in a bureaucratically structured organisation such as the civil service. This expression of positive leadership is a necessary and effective counter-balance to the central role played by staff in the prison service.

> [The solemn lesson] is that no prison service can implement any
> kind of policy whatever, least of all a reformative kind, unless
> the uniformed officers are consulted, involved, and convinced
> that some attention will be paid to their problems. Officers know
> this; policy-makers too must understand this. (Thomas, 1974)

This book contains a description and analysis of features of the Scottish Prison Service which have not been the subject of prior research: the influence of William Brebner, the Scottish Prison Commission and in particular its different style of administration from the English Prison Commission, the Elgin Committee of 1900 and the present system of administration. The main argument in chapter seven is that the prison system can be subjected to comparative analysis as a typical bureaucratic organisation.

The conclusion of this analysis is that many failings of the system arise not from a lack of resources but from structural weaknesses. These are principally the location in a false super-ordinate system and a consequential confusion of goals. The most important of these is a failure to recognise that the primary purpose of imprisonment is the punishment which is inflicted through loss of liberty. It has been suggested throughout that the prison officer has played a central role in the development of the prison system, particularly in Scotland, and in chapter eight it is demonstrated how this has come about as a result of both the corporate influence of the staff and the particular style of management in the Scottish Prison Service.

Having established that the *act* of imprisonment is primarily negative, one should recognise that the *experience* of imprisonment can be put to positive use. The ideal of rehabilitation is sound in principle but has fallen into disrepute as a result of imprecise definition and unsound practice. The justice model of imprisonment is appropriate in so far as it goes, which is to set a benchmark for the minimum standards which should be applied in prison administration, but it is not sufficient as a statement of what might be possible within the experience of imprisonment.

The ideal articulated within the document *Opportunity and Responsibility* (1990) is an attempt to fill this vacuum with a set of principles which underline the fact that the experience of imprisonment can be viewed as a shared enterprise. The prison system has a responsibility to create a positive environment within which the prisoner is encouraged to make use of the opportunities which are available; the prisoner in turn must accept that he has a responsibility for his actions and for any personal change of direction or attitude which he wishes to make.

Throughout the development of the prison system in Scotland both staff and prisoners have retained a healthy scepticism about the efficacy of the prison in itself as a place of reform. The circumstances facing a prisoner on release in terms of accommodation, work and family support will be more influential in deciding his future level of recidivism than any experience which he might have undergone in prison. Essentially imprisonment, the deprivation of liberty, is a negative experience. This is not a philosophy of despair but a statement of fact, which must be remembered by each judge who is charged with the responsibility of passing sentence on offenders.

Prison is a coercive institution but the coercion should not extend to obliging the prisoner to make use of the many positive resources and facilities which should be available to him during the course of his sentence. He is more likely to make use of these opportunities if he is allowed to exercise a degree of choice and is given an active part in the deliberative process. A recognition of this fact underpins the various initiatives which have begun recently within the Scottish Prison Service.

Once a criminal passes through the gates of the prison it is the responsibility of the prison system to ensure that his sentence is spent in as constructive and positive a manner as possible. This is likely to happen if there is a shared recognition of the reality of the situation which exists. All parties must be aware that the fact of imprisonment is not negotiable: the prisoner must complete the sentence which has been passed on him by the court.

The first task of the prison system is *custody*. In addition all those who live or work in prison are entitled to enjoy a safe environment; this is most likely to come about through the exercise of *good order*. If rehabilitation, understood as the imposition of a change of attitude on the prisoner, is wrong in principle and impossible to achieve in practice, there should be no argument about the obligation which the prison system has to offer as many *opportunities* as possible to the prisoner both as a means of allowing him to pass his time in prison in a positive manner and, if he so wishes, to prepare himself for release.

The conclusions reached in this book are by no means negative. The compact nature of the Scottish Prison Service, with some twenty establishments, 5000 prisoners and 4000 staff, is a singular advantage. Lines of communication are short, anonymity is not possible and accountability is an option. The degree of openness which has been signalled as being henceforth typical of the Scottish Prison Service must begin with a recognition that the major problems standing in the way of radical development of the system relate not to a shortage of resources but to organisational structure. Once this has been recognised these problems are capable of solution. If they are tackled honestly there is a distinct possibility that the Scottish Prison Service can become an acknowledged example of best practice just as happened in the days of William Brebner.

Bibliography

Statutes

1487 c. 101 *Of the Keiping of arreisted Trespassoures*
1597 c. 277 *Prison Houses suld be bigged within all Burrowes*
1823 c. 64 *Gaol Act 1823*
1829 c. 54 *Act authorising investigation into conditions in Scottish Prisons*
1835 c. 38 *Prisons Act 1835*
1839 c. 42 *An Act to Improve Prisons and Prison Discipline in Scotland*
1842 c. 67 *General Prison at Perth Act 1842*
1844 c. 34 *An Act to Amend the Law with Respect to Prisons and Prison Discipline in Scotland*
1851 c. 27 *An Act to Amend Certain Acts for the Improvement of Prisons and Prison Discipline in Scotland*
1852 c. 99 *Penal Servitude Act 1852*
1857 c. 71 *Lunacy (Scotland) Act 1857*
1860 c. 105 *The Prisons (Scotland) Administration Act 1860*
1877 c. 21 *Prisons Act 1877*
1877 c. 53 *Prisons (Scotland) Act 1877*
1887 c. 35 *The Criminal Procedure (Scotland) Act 1887*
1888 c. 49 *Peterhead Harbour of Refuge Act 1888*
1891 c. 69 *The Penal servitude Act 1891*
1898 c. 41 *Prison Act 1898*
1907 c. 17 *The Probation of Offenders Act 1907*
1908 c. 59 *Prevention of Crime Act 1908*
1909 c. 2 *The Prisons (Scotland) Act 1909*
1914 c. 58 *The Criminal Justice Act 1914*
1921 c. 50 *The Criminal Procedure (Scotland) Act 1921*
1928 c. 34 *Reorganisation of Offices (Scotland) Act 1928*
1931 c. 30 *The Probation of Offenders (Scotland) Act 1931*

1935   c.   32 *The Criminal Lunatics (Scotland) Act 1935*
1938   c.   48 *The Criminal Procedure (Scotland) Act 1938*
1939   c.   20 *Reorganisation of Offices (Scotland) Act 1939*
1948   c.   58 *The Criminal Justice Act 1948*
1949   c.   94 *Criminal Justice (Scotland) Act 1949*
1952   c.   52 *The Prisons Act 1952*
1952   c.   61 *The Prisons (Scotland) Act 1952*
1960   c.   23 *The First Offenders (Scotland) Act 1960*
1962   c.   15 *The Criminal Justice Administration Act 1962*
1963   c.   39 *The Criminal Justice (Scotland) Act 1963*
1965   c.   39 *The Criminal Procedure (Scotland) Act 1965*
1965   c.   71 *The Murder (Abolition of Death Penalty) Act 1965*
1966   c.   19 *The Law Reform (Miscellaneous Provisions)(Scotland) Act 1966*
1967   c.   80 *The Criminal Justice Act 1967*
1973   c.   65 *The Local Government (Scotland) Act 1973*
1975   c.   21 *Criminal Procedure (Scotland) Act 1975*
1980   c.   62 *The Criminal Justice (Scotland) Act 1980*
1985   c.   73 *Law Reform (Miscellaneous Provisions) (Scotland) Act 1985*
1987   c.   41 *The Criminal Justice (Scotland) Act 1987*
1988   c.   33 *The Criminal Justice Act 1988*
1989   c.   45 *Prisons (Scotland) Act 1989*

Reports

All relevant reports are listed here under 'Reports' in chronological order. Those which are more commonly known by the name of their chairmen (for example, the Mountbatten Report) are also listed alphabetically.

Report of the Select Committee of the House of Commons on Scottish Prisons (1826) HMSO, London
Report of the Departmental Committee on Prison Officers' Salaries (1979) HMSO, London
Report of a Sub-Committee Appointed to Investigate the Question of the Most Suitable Place for a Harbour of Refuge on the East Coast of Scotland (1884) HMSO, London. Cmnd 4035
Report of the Committee Appointed by the Secretary for Scotland to Consider Some Questions Which Had Been Raised by the Subordinate Staff Regarding Pay, Hours of Duty, etc (1891) Scottish Record Office HH57/44 and 188

Report from the Departmental Committee on Prisons (1895) HMSO, London. Cmnd 7702

Report from the Departmental Committee on Scottish Prisons (1900) HMSO, London. Cmnd 218

Report of the Committee Appointed to Enquire into the Conditions of Service and Superannuation of the Warder Classes in Prisons and Criminal Lunatic Asylums (1919) HMSO, London. Cmnd 313

Report of the Committee Appointed to Inquire into the Pay and Conditions of Service at the Prisons and Borstal Institutions in England and Scotland and at Broadmoor Criminal Lunatic Asylum (1923) HMSO, London. Cmnd 1959

Report of the Committee Appointed to Enquire into the Claims of the Men Dismissed from the Police and Prison Services on Account of the Strike of 1919 (1924) HMSO, London. Cmnd 2297

Report of Enquiry into the Administration and Discipline of Barlinnie Prison; and into the Existing Arrangements for the Inspection of Scottish Prisons (1935) HMSO, London. Cmnd 4860

Report by the Scottish Advisory Council on the Treatment and Rehabilitation of Offenders on the Scottish Prison System (1949) HMSO, Edinburgh

Report of the Committee on Remunerations and Conditions of Service of Certain Grades in the Prison Services (1958) HMSO, London. Cmnd 544

Report of the Inquiry into Prison Escapes and Security (1966) HMSO, London. Cmnd 3175

Report by the President's Commission on Law Enforcement and Administration of Justice (1967) US Government Printing Office, Washington

Report of the Advisory Council on the Penal System on the Regime for Long Term Prisoners in Conditions of Maximum Security (1968), HMSO, London

Report of the Canadian Commission on Corrections (1969) Queen's Printer, Ottawa

Report of the Working Party on the Treatment of Certain Male Long Term Prisoners and Potentially Violent Prisoners (1972) Scottish Home and Health Department, Edinburgh

Report of the Working Party on the Manning of Social Work Services in Penal Establishments in Scotland (1972) SHHD, Edinburgh

Report of the Committee of Inquiry on the Police (1978) HMSO, London. Cmnd 7283

Report of the Prisons Division Management Review (1978) Scottish Office, Edinburgh

Report of the Committee of Inquiry into the United Kingdom Prison Services (1979) HMSO, London. Cmnd 7673

Report of the Advisory Committee to the Solicitor General of Canada on the Management of Correctional Institutions (1984) Department of the Solicitor General, Ottawa

Report of the Control Review Committee (1984) HMSO, London

Report of the Review of Suicide Preventions at HM Detention Centre and HM Young Offenders Institution Glenochil HMSO, Edinburgh

Report on the United States Penitentiary Marion (1985) US Government Printing Office, Washington

Improving Management in Government: The Next Steps (1988) HMSO, London

Custody and Care: Policy and Plans for the Scottish Prison Service (1988) HMSO, Edinburgh

Assessment and Control: The Management of Violent Prisoners (1988) HMSO, Edinburgh

Continuity Through Cooperation: A National Framework of Policy and Practice Guidance for Social Work in Scottish Penal Establishments HMSO, Edinburgh

Opportunity and Responsibility: Developing New Approaches to the Management of the Long Term Prison System in Scotland (1990) Scottish Prison Service, Edinburgh

H M Prison Service, Review of the Organisation and Location above Establishment Level (1990) Home Office, London

Annual Reports of the Inspector of Prisons for Scotland, 1835–1859, HMSO, London

Annual Reports of the General Board of Directors of Prisons in Scotland 1840-1860 HMSO, London

Annual Reports of the Managers of the General Prison at Perth, 1862–1878 HMSO, London

Annual Reports of the Prison Commissioners for Scotland, 1879–1929 HMSO, London

Annual Reports of the Prison Department for Scotland, 1929–1938 HMSO, London

Annual Reports on Prisons in Scotland, 1939–1988 HMSO, Edinburgh

Annual Reports of the Parole Board for Scotland 1968–1988 HMSO, Edinburgh

Annual Reports of HM Chief Inspector of Prisons for Scotland 1981–1988 HMSO, Edinburgh

Hansard's Parliamentary Debates
Scottish Records Office
HH5   : Appointments, 1839–1877
HH6   : Minute Books of the General Board of Directors,1839–1860
HH7   : Letter Books of the General Board of Directors,1839–1860
HH8   : Miscellaneous Prison Papers, 1856–1894
HH12 : Miscellaneous Prison Books, 1813–1966
HH16 : Criminal Files Relating to Individuals
HH20 : Board of Management of Prisons in Scotland, Minute Book, 1861–1869
HH21 : Prison Registers, 1848–1959
HH28 : Letter Books (Scottish Office) Prisons, 1886–1889
HH35 : Minute Book of the Prison Commissioners for Scotland
HH57 : General Files, Scottish Prison and Borstal Services 1879–1972
HH60 : Scottish Prison Committees, 1899–1933

Absalom J H (1970) *The Prison Officer (England and Wales)* The Criminologist, November 1970
Allen F A (1981) *The Decline of the Rehabilitative Ideal* Yale University Press, New Haven
Argyris C (1971) *Management and Organisational Development* McGraw-Hill, New York
Argyris C (1972) *The Applicability of Organisational Sociology* Cambridge University Press, Cambridge
Babington A (1971) *The English Bastille* Macdonald, London
Baird J A (1980) *The Care of the Mentally Abnormal Offender* Journal of the Law Society of Scotland, May 1980
Baird J A (1984) *The Transfer of Scottish Prisoners: A Historical and Descriptive Study of Convicted Prisoners Transferred to Psychiatric Hospitals* unpublished MD thesis, University of Edinburgh
Baldwin J and Bottomley A K (1978) *Criminal Justice: Selected Readings* Martin Robertson, London
Bean P (1976) *Rehabilitation and Deviance* Routledge and Kegan Paul, London
Bean P (1981) *Punishment* Martin Robertson, Oxford
Black R (1982) *Stress and the Correctional Officer* Police Stress, February 1982

Blau P M (1955) *The Dynamics of Bureaucracy* in Etzioni A (1969)

Blau P M (1956) *Bureaucracy in Modern Society* Random House, New York

Blau P M and Scott W R (1966) *Formal Organisations* Routledge and Kegan Paul, London

Blauner R (1960) *Work Satisfaction and Industrial Trends* in Etzioni A (1969)

Blom-Cooper L J (1974) *Progress and Penal Reform* Oxford University Press, Oxford

Blom-Cooper L J (1978) *The Centralisation of Governmental Control of National Prison Services, with Special Reference to the Prisons Act 1877* in Freeman J (1978)

Bottomley A K (1973) *Decisions in the Penal Process* Martin Robertson, London

Bottoms A E and McClintock F H (1973) *Criminals Coming of Age* Heinemann, London

Bottoms A E and Preston R H (1980) *The Coming Penal Crisis* Scottish Academic Press, Edinburgh

Bottoms A E and Light R (1987) *Problems of Long Term Imprisonment* Gower, Aldershot

Bouza A V (1978) *Police Administration: Organization and Performance* Pergamon Press, New York

Boyle J (1977) *A Sense of Freedom* Pan Books, London

Boyle J (1984) *The Pain of Confinement: Prison Diaries* Canongate, Edinburgh

Brief A P et al (1976) *Correctional Employees' Reactions to Job Characteristics: A Data Based Argument for Job Enlargement* Journal of Criminal Justice, vol 4, 1976

Brodsky C (1982) *Work Stress in Correctional Institutions* Journal of Prison and Jail Health, vol 2, no 2, 1982

Brody S (1983) *Foundations for a Penal Policy* Home Office Research and Planning Unit, London

Brown J A C (1954) *The Social Psychology of Industry* Penguin, Middlesex

Brown W (1971) *Organisation* Heinemann, London

Buckley W (1967) *Sociology and Modern Systems Theory* Prentice Hall, Englewood Cliffs

Bullard C G (1977) *A Sociological Study of Prison Offices in New South Wales: A Stressful Occupation* University of New South Wales

Caird R (1974) *A Good and Useful Life* Hart-Davis, London

Cameron J (1983) *Prisons and Punishment in Scotland from the Middle Ages to the Present* Canongate, Edinburgh

Carlen P (1983) *Women's Imprisonment* Routledge and Kegan Paul, London

Carrell C and Laing J (1982) *The Special Unit Barlinnie Prison: Its Evolution through its Art* Third Eye Centre, Glasgow

Carson Report (1984) *Report of the Advisory Committee to the Solicitor General of Canada on the Management of Correctional Institutions* Department of the Solicitor General, Ottawa

Carter R M et al (1972) *Correctional Institutions* J B Lippincott Company, Chicago

Cartwright D (1965) *Influence, Leadership, Control* in March J G (1965)

Checkland O (1980) *Philanthropy in Victorian Scotland* John Donald, Edinburgh

Cheek F E and Miller M (1983) *The Experience of Stress for Correction Officers* Journal of Criminal Justice, vol 11, 1983

Christie N (1978) *Prisons in Society or Society as a Prison* in Freeman J (1978)

Clegg S and Dunkerley D (1980) *Organisation, Class and Control* Routledge and Kegan Paul, London

Clemmer D (1958) *The Prison Community* Holt, Rinehart and Winston, New York

Cloward R A (1960) *Social Control in the Prison* in Cloward R A et al (1960)

Cloward R A et al (1960) *Theoretical Studies in Social Organization of the Prison* Social Science Research Council, Kraus Reprint Co (1975), New York

Coggan G and Walker M (1982) *Frightened For My Life* Fontana, Glasgow

Cohen S (1983) *Social-Control Talk: Correctional Change* in Garland D and Young P (1983)

Cohen S (1985) *Visions of Social Control* Polity, London

Cohen S and Taylor L (1972) *Psychological Survival: The Experience of Long Term Imprisonment* Penguin, Middlesex

Colvin E (1978) *Prison Officers: A Sociological Portrait of the Uniformed Staff of an English Prison* unpublished PhD thesis, University of Cambridge

Conrad J (1965) *Crime and Its Correction* University of California Press, Berkeley

Cooper C L and Marshall J (1976) Occupational Sources of Stress Journal of Occupational Psychology, 49, 1976

Coyle A G (1982) *The Founding Father of the Scottish Prison Service* Journal of the Association of Scottish Prison Governors, vol 1, Summer 1982

Coyle A G (1984) *A Comparative Examination of the Prison Services in North America* Churchill Fellowship Report

Coyle A G (1986) *Prison as a Punishment* Prison Service Journal, April 1986

Coyle A G (1987) *The Scottish Experience with Small Units* in Bottoms A E and Light R (1987)

Cressey D R (1959) *Contradictory Directives in Complex Organizations: The Case of the Prison* in Hazelrigg L E (1968)

Cressey D R (1960) *Limitations on Organization of Treatment in the Modern Prison* in Cloward R A et al (1960)

Cressey D R (1961) *The Prison: Studies in Institutional Organization and Change* Holt, Rinehart and Winston, New York

Cressey D R (1965) *Prison Organizations* in March J G (1965)

Cressey D R (1972) *Sources of Resistance to Innovation in Corrections* in Carter R M et al (1972)

Cronin H (1967) *The Screw Turns* John Long, London

Cross R (1971) *Punishment, Prison and the Public* Stevens and Sons, London

Crouch B M and Alcert G P (1980) *Prison Guards' Attitudes Toward Components of the Criminal Justice System* Criminology, 18/2, 1980

Dobash R P (1979) *A Natural History of the Scottish Prison Project* unpublished final report prepared for the Social Science Research Council, Sociology and Social Administration Committee

Dobash R P (1982) *The Material, Social and Ideological Foundations of Labour in Scottish Prisons* A Paper presented at the Annual Meeting of the Society for the Study of Social Problems, San Francisco, September 1982

Dobash R P (1983) *Labour and Discipline in Scottish and English Prisons: Moral Correction and Useful Toil* Sociology, vol 17, no 1, February 1983

Downes D and Rock P (1979) *Deviant Interpretations* Martin Robertson, London

Duffee D (1974) *The Correction Officer Sub-Culture* Journal of Research in Crime and Delinquency, 11 (1974)

Duffee D (1975) *Correctional Policy and Prison Organization* Sage Publications, New York

Edmund-Davies Report (1978) *Report of the Committee of Inquiry on the Police* HMSO, London, Cmnd 7283

Elgin Report (1900) *Report from the Departmental Committee on Scottish Prisons* HMSO, London, Cmnd 218

Elgin Report (1900) *Minutes of Evidence taken by the Departmental Committee on Scottish Prisons* HMSO, London, Cmnd 219

Elliott Report (1919) *Report of the Committee Appointed to Enquire into the Conditions of Service and Superannuation of the Warder Classes in Prisons and Criminal Lunatic Asylums* HMSO, London, Cmnd 313

Emery F E (1970) *Freedom and Justice Within Walls: The Bristol Prison Experiment* Tavistock, London

Etzioni A (1964) *Modern Organizations* Prentice-Hall, New Jersey

Etzioni A (1965) *Organizational Control Structure* in March J G (1965)

Etzioni A (1969) *A Sociological Reader on Complex Organizations* Holt, Rinehart and Winston, New York

Etzioni A (1975) *A Comparative Analysis of Complex Organizations* The Free Press, New York

Evans P (1980) *Prison Crisis* Geo Allen and Unwin, London

Evans R (1982) *The Fabrication of Virtue: English Prison Architecture, 1750–1840* Cambridge University Press, Cambridge

Floud J E and Young W (1981) *Dangerousness and Criminal Justice* Heinemann, London

Fogel D (1975) '. . .We Are the Living Proof . . .' *The Justice Model for Corrections* The W H Anderson Co, Cincinnati

Fogel D (1978) *The Justice Model for Corrections* in Freeman J (1978)

Foucault M (1975) *Discipline and Punish* Peregrine, Middlesex

Fox L (1952) *The English Prison and Borstal System* Macmillan, London

Fraser D (1976) *The New Poor Law in the Nineteenth Century* Macmillan, London

Freeman J (1978) *Prisons, Past and Future* Heinemann, London

Galtung J (1961) *Prison: The Organization of Dilemma* in Cressey D R et al (1961)

Garland D W (1983) *Modern Penality: A Study of the Formation and Significance of Penal Welfare Strategies* unpublished PhD thesis, University of Edinburgh

Garland D W (1985) *Punishment and Welfare: A History of Penal Strategies* Gower, Aldershot

Garland D W (1990) *Punishment and Modern Society* Oxford University Press, Oxford

Garland D W and Young P (1983) *The Power to Punish: Contemporary Penality and Social Analysis* Heinemann, London

Geis G and Cavanagh E (1966) *Recruitment and Retention of Correctional Personnel* Crime and Delinquency, vol 3, 1966

Gladstone Report (1895) *Report from the Departmental Committee on Prisons* HMSO, London, Cmnd 7702

Glaser D (1964) *The Effectiveness of a Prison and Parole System* Bobbs-Merrill, Indianapolis

Glasgow Report (1891) *Report of the Committee Appointed by the Secretary for Scotland to Consider Some Questions Which Had Been Raised by the Subordinate Staff Regarding Pay, Hours of Duty, etc.* Scottish Record Office, HH 57/44 and 188

Goffman E (1957) *The Characteristics of Total Institutions* in Etzioni A (1969)

Goffman E (1961) *On the Characteristics of Total Institutions: Staff-Inmate Relations* in Cressey D R et al (1961)

Goffman E (1987) *Asylums* Pergerine, Middlesex

Graham H G (1899) *The Social Life of Scotland in the Eighteenth Century* (1928 edn), A and C Black Ltd, London

Grosser G H (1960) *External Setting and Internal Relations of the Prison* in Cloward R A et al (1960)

Grusky O (1959) *Role Conflict in Organization: A Study of Prison Camp Officials* in Hazelrigg L E (1968)

Grusky O and Miller G A (1970) *The Sociology of Organizations* The Free Press, New York

Hall-Williams J E (1970) *The English Penal System in Transition* Butterworth and Co, London

Hall-Williams J E (1982) *Criminology and Criminal Justice* Butterworths, London

Hart H L A (1968) *Punishment and Responsibility* Oxford University Press, Oxford

Hawkins G (1976) *The Prison: Policy and Practice* University of Chicago Press, Chicago

Hazelrigg L E (1968) *Prison Within Society: A Reader in Penology* Doubleday and Co, New York

Hepburn J R and Albonetti C (1980) *Role Conflict in Correctional Institutions* Criminology, vol 17, no 4, 1980

Hill F (1853) *Crime: Its Amount, Causes and Remedies* Murray, London

Hill F (1893) *An Autobiography of Fifty Years in Time of Reform* ed Constance Hill, Richard Bentley, London

Hobhouse F and Brockway A F (1922) *English Prisons Today* Longmans Green and Co, London

Hogarth J (1971) *Sentencing as a Human Process* University of Toronto Press, Toronto

Home Office (1983) *Management Structure in Prison Department Establishments: A Consultative Document* HMSO, London

Home Office, Scottish Office and Northern Ireland Office (1979) *Evidence Submitted to the Inquiry into the United Kingdom Prison Services (3 volumes)* HMSO, London

Ignatieff M (1978) *A Just Measure of Pain* Macmillan, London

Jacobs J B (1978) *What Prison Guards Think: A Profile of the Illinois Force* Crime and Delinquency, April 1978

Jacobs J B (1983) *New Perspectives on Prisons and Imprisonment* Cornell University Press, Ithaca

Jenkins C W and Diener J (1982) *A Survey of Stress Management Programs in State Correctional Systems in the United States* Police Stress, February 1982

Johnson R (1979) *Informal Helping Networks in Prison: The Shape of Grass-Roots Correctional Intervention* Journal of Criminal Justice, vol 7, 1979

Johnson R and Price S (1981) *The Complete Correctional Officer: Human Service and the Human Environment of the Prison* Criminal Justice and Behavior, vol 8, no 3, September 1981

Jones H and Carnes P (1977) *Open Prisons* Routledge and Kegan Paul, London

Jones J M (1980) *Organisational Aspects of Police Behaviour* Gower, Farnborough

Kahn R L et al (1964) *Organizational Stress: Studies in Role Conflict and Ambiguity* John Wiley and Sons, New York

Katz D and Kahn R L (1966) *The Social Psychology of Organizations* John Wiley, New York

Kauffman K (1981) *Prison Officers' Attitudes and Perceptions of Attitudes: A Case of Pluralistic Ignorance* Journal of Research in Crime and Delinquency, July 1981

Keats R and Urry J (1975) *Social Theory as a Science* Routledge and Kegan Paul, London

Kettle M (1979) *Prison Officers: The Inside Story* New Society, 9 August 1979

King R D and Elliott K W (1977) *Albany: Birth of a Prison - End of an Era* Routledge and Kegan Paul, London

King R D and Morgan R (1980) *The Future of the Prison System* Gower, Farnborough

Korn R R and McCorkle L W (1967) *Criminology and Penology* Holt, Rinehart and Winston, New York

Leslie J R S (1938) *Sir Evelyn Ruggles-Brise: A Memoir* John Murray, London

Likert R (1967) *The Human Organization, Its Management and Value* McGraw-Hill, New York

Lombardo L X (1981) *Guards Imprisoned: Correctional Officers at Work* Elsevier, New York

McCleery R H (1957) *Policy Change in Prison Management* in Etzioni A (1969)

McCleery R H (1961) *The Governmental Process and Informal Social Control* in Cressey D R et al (1961)

McClintock F H (1978) *The Future of Parole* in Freeman J (1978)

McClintock F H (1980) *The Future of Imprisonment in Britain* in Bottoms A E and Preston R H (1980)

McClintock F H (1983) *The Dilemma of Penal Reform Today* in Journal of the Association of Scottish Prison Governors, vol 2, 1984-85

P McConville S (1981) *A History of English Prison Administration, vol I, 1750-1877* Routledge and Kegan Paul, London

MacDonald D and Sim J (1978) *Scottish Prisons and the Special Unit* The Scottish Council for Civil Liberties, Glasgow

McGurk B J and McGurk R E (1979) *Personality Types Among Prisoners and Prison Officers* British Journal of Criminology, vol 19, no 1, January 1979

Mackenzie Report (1924), *Report of the Committee Appointed to Enquire into the Claims of the Men Dismissed from the Police and Prison Services on Account of the Strike in 1919,* HMSO, London Cmnd 2297

McLachlan N (1974) *Penal Reform and Penal History* in Blom-Cooper L (1974)

Maguire M et al (1985) *Accountability and Prisons* Tavistock, London

Manning P K (1982) *Organisational Work: Structuration of Environments* British Journal of Sociology, vol 33, no 1, March 1982

March J G (1965) *Handbook of Organizations* Rand, McNally and Co, Chicago

Marsh A et al (1985) *Staff Attitudes in the Prison Service* HMSO, London

Mathiesen T (1965) *The Defences of the Weak* Tavistock Publications, London

Mathiesen T (1971) *Across the Boundaries of Organizations: An Exploratory Study of Communication Patterns in Two Penal Institutions* The Glendessary Press, California

Mathiesen T (1979) *The Future of Control Systems: The Case of Norway* paper presented to the Conference of the European Group for the Study of Deviance and Social Control, Copenhagen, 1979

Matthews R (1989) *Privatizing Criminal Justice* Sage, London

May Report (1979) *Report of the Committee of Inquiry into the United Kingdom Prison Services* HMSO, London. Cmnd 7673

Merton R K (1957) *Social Theory and Social Structure* The Free Press of Glencoe (1963 edn), New York

Merton R K (1957) *Bureaucratic Structure and Personality* in Etzioni A (1969)

Miller A (1976) *Inside Outside: The Story of a Prison Governor* Queensgate Press, London

Milton N (1973) *John Maclean* Pluto Press, London

Mintzberg H (1979) *The Structuring of Organizations* Prentice-Hall, New Jersey

Montilla M (1979) *Prison Employee Unionism: Management Guide for Correctional Administrators* National Institute of Law Enforcement and Criminal Justice, Washington

Morris N (1974) *The Future of Imprisonment* University of Chicago Press, Chicago

Morris T (1976) *Deviance and Control: The Secular Heresy* Hutchinson, London

Morris T (1976) *The Parlous State of Prisons* in Freeman J (1978)

Morris T and Morris P (1963) *Pentonville: A Sociological Study of an English Prison* Routledge and Kegan Paul, London

Mott J (1985) *Adult Prisons and Prisoners in England and Wales 1970–1982* Home Office Research Study 84, HMSO, London

Mountbatten Report (1966) *Report of the Inquiry into Prison Escapes and Security* HMSO, London. Cmnd 3175

Murton T (1979) *Prison Management: The Past, the Present and the Possible Future* in Wolfgang M E (1979)

Norman F (1958) *Bang to Rights* Secker and Warburg, London

Ohlin L E (1956) *Sociology and the Field of Corrections* Russell Sage Foundation, New York

Ouimet Report (1969) *Report of the Canadian Commission on Corrections* Queen's Printer, Ottawa

Parsons T (1956) *Suggestions for a Sociological Approach to the Theory of Organizations* in Etzioni A (1969)

Peabody R L and Rourke F E (1965) *Public Bureaucracies* in March J G (1965)

Pellew J (1982) *The Home Office 1848–1914: From Clerks to Bureaucrats* Heinemann, London

Perrow C (1970) *Organisational Analysis* Tavistock, London

Playfair G (1971) *The Punitive Obsession* Gollancz, London

Porporino F J and Cormier R B (1982) *Consensus in Decision-Making Among Prison Case Management Officers* Canadian Journal of Criminology, 24/3, 1982

Prisgrove P (1974) *Group Structure of Prison Officers' Perceptions of Inmates* Journal of Consulting and Clinical Psychology, vol 42, no 4, 1974

Pugh D S (1971) *Organisation Theory* Penguin, Middlesex

Radzinowicz Report (1968) *Report of the Advisory Council on the Penal System on the Regime for Long Term Prisoners in Conditions of Maximum Security* HMSO, London

Reiner R (1978) *The Blue Coated Worker: A Sociological Study of Police Unionism* Cambridge University Press, Cambridge

Reynolds G W and Judge A (1968) *The Night the Police Went on Strike* Weidenfeld and Nicholson, London

Rich C E F (1932) *Recollections of a Prison Governor* Hurst and Blackett Ltd, London

Ross R R (1981) *Prison Guard/Correctional Officer: The Use and Abuse of the Human Resources of Prisons* Butterworths, Toronto

Ruck S K ed (1951) *Paterson on Prisons: Being the Collected Papers of Sir Alexander Paterson* Frederick Muller Ltd, London

Ruggles-Brise E (1921) *The English Prison System* Macmillan, London

Rusche G and Kirchheimer O (1939) *Punishment and Social Structure* Russell and Russell, New York

Ryan M and Ward T (1989) *Privatization and the Penal System* Open University Press, Milton Keynes

Salaman G and Thompson K (1973) *People and Organisations* Longman, London

Schrag C (1961) *Some Foundations for a Theory of Correction* in Cressey D R et al (1961)

Scottish Home Department (1949) *The Scottish Prison System, Report by the Scottish Advisory Council on the Treatment and Rehabilitation of Offenders* HMSO, Edinburgh

Scull A T (1977) *Decarceration, Community Treatment and the Deviant: A Radical View* Prentice-Hall, New Jersey

Selznick P (1948) *Foundations of the Theory of Organization* in Etzioni A (1969)

Shamir B and Drory A (1982) *Occupational Tedium among Prison Officers* Criminal Justice and Behaviour, vol 9, no 1, 1982

Sievwright W (1894) *Historical Sketch of the Old Depot or Prison for French Prisoners-of-War at Perth* Wright, Perth

Silverman D (1970) *The Theory of Organisations* Heinemann, London

Smith A D (1962) *Women in Prison* Stevens and Sons, London

Smith G (1979) *Social Work and the Sociology of Organisation* Routledge and Kegan Paul, London

Smith R (1984) *Prison Health Care* BMA, London

Sparks R F (1971) *Local Prisons: The Crisis in the English Penal System* Heinemann, London

Stanhope Report (1923) *Report of the Committee Appointed to Inquire into the Pay and Conditions of Service at the Prisons and Borstal Institutions in England and Scotland and at Broadmoor Criminal Lunatic Asylum* HMSO, London. Cmnd 1959

Stastny C and Tyrnauer G (1982) *Who Rules the Joint?* Lexington Books, Lexington

Stern V (1987) *Bricks of Shame* Penguin, Middlesex

Stern V (1989) *Imprisoned by our Prisons* Unwin, London

Stewart R (1963) *The Reality of Management* Heinemann, London

Stockdale E (1983) *A Short History of Prison Inspection in England* British Journal of Criminology, vol 23, no 3, July 1983

Sutherland E H and Cressey D R (1960) *Principles of Criminology* Sixth Edition, Lippincott, New York

Sykes G M (1971) *The Society of Captives* Princeton University Press, Princeton

Taggart M (1978) *The Police Federation* Police Journal, January 1978

Taylor I et al (1973) *The New Criminology: For a Social Theory of Deviance* Routledge and Kegan Paul, London

Taylor I et al (1975) *Critical Criminology* Routledge and Kegan Paul

Taylor I (1981) *Law and Order* Macmillan, London

Thomas J E (1972) *The English Prison Officer Since 1850: A Study in Conflict* Routledge and Kegan Paul, London

Thomas J E (1974) *The Prison Officer: A Conflict in Roles* Journal of Psychosomatic Research, vol 18, 1974

Thomas J E (1978) *'A Good Man For Gaoler?' – Crisis, Discontent and the Prison Staff* in Freeman J (1978)

Thomas J E (1980) *Managing the Prison Service* in King R D and Morgan R (1980)

Trasler G (1972) *The Social Relations of Persistent Offenders* in Carter R M et al (1972)

Van Groningen J (1981) *The Job Expectations of Prison Officers: A Profile of Victorian Recruits* Australian and New Zealand Journal of Criminology, 14 March 1981

Vinter R and Janowitz M (1959) *Effective Institutions for Juvenile Delinquents: A Research Statement* in Hazelrigg L E (1969)

Waddington P A J (1983) *The Training of Prison Governors* Croom-Helm, London

Walker N (1987) *Crime and Criminology* Oxford University Press, Oxford

Webb S and Webb B (1922) *English Prisons Under Local Government* Frank Cass and Co Ltd (1963), London

Weber G H (1957) *Conflicts between Professional and Non-Professional Personnel in Institutional Delinquency Treatment* in Hazelrigg L E (1968)

Weber M (1947) *The Theory of Social and Economic Organisation* Hodge, London

Weber M (1978) *Selections in Translation* Cambridge University Press, Cambridge

Webster I W et al (1983) *Reported Health, Life-Style and Occupational Stress in Prison Officers* Community Health Services, vol VII, no 3, 1983

Wilkins L (1969) *Evaluation of Penal Measures* Random House, New York

Willet T C (1983) *Prison Guards in Private* Canadian Journal of Criminology, 25/2, 1983

Williams T A (1983) *Custody and Conflict: An Organizational Study of Prison Officers' Roles and Attitudes* Australian and New Zealand Journal of Criminology, 16 March 1983

Wilson T P (1972) *Patterns of Management and Adaptations to Organizational Roles: A Study of Prison Inmates* in Carter R M et al (1972)

Wolff M (1967) *Prison* Eyre and Spottiswoode, London

Wolfgang M E (1979) *Prisons: Present and Possible* Lexington Books, Lexington

Wolin S S (1960) *A Critique of Organizational Theories* in Etzioni A (1969)

Wootton B (1978) *Crime and Penal Policy* Allen and Unwin, London

Wynne J M (1978) *Prison Employee Unionism: The Impact of Correctional Administration and Programs* US National Institute of Law Enforcement and Criminal Justice, Washington

Wynn Parry Report (1958) *Report of the Committee on Remunerations and Conditions of Service of Certain Grades in the Prison Services* HMSO, London. Cmnd 544

Zald M N (1960) *The Correctional Institution for Juvenile Offenders: An Analysis of Organizational Character* in Hazelrigg L E (1968)

'Zeno' (1968) *Life* Macmillan, London

Index